Tales by George Crabbe

George Crabbe was born on December 24th, 1754 in Aldeburgh, Suffolk. He was sent to school at a very young age and soon developed an avid and precocious interest in books.

Crabbe was sent first to a boarding-school at Bungay, and a few years later to a school at Stowmarket, where he learnt mathematics and Latin. His early reading included William Shakespeare, Alexander Pope, Abraham Cowley, Sir Walter Raleigh and Edmund Spenser.

Medicine had now been settled on as his future career and, after three years at Stowmarket, in 1768, he was apprenticed to a local doctor at Wickhambrook, near Bury St Edmunds.

In 1772, a lady's magazine offered a prize for the best poem on 'hope'. Crabbe entered and won. The magazine then printed other short pieces of his during the year.

His first major work, Inebriety, was self-published in 1775. By this time he had completed his medical training and returned to Aldeburgh. Low finances meant his intention to go to London to study at a hospital was abandoned and instead he worked as a warehouseman.

The following year, 1777, he did travel to London to practice medicine, but returned home with financial woes. Crabbe continued to practice as a surgeon but with limited surgical skills, he received only the poorest of patients, together with small and undependable fees.

He moved to London again in April 1780, to see if he could make it as a poet, or, if that failed, as a doctor. By the end of May he had been forced to pawn his surgical instruments.

With the publication in May 1783 of his poem The Village, Crabbe achieved popularity with both the public and critics. Samuel Johnson said of it in a letter to Reynolds "I have sent you back Mr. Crabbe's poem, which I read with great delight. It is original, vigorous, and elegant."

In 1796 their third son, Edmund, died at the age of six. The death shredded Sarah's mental health and she never recovered. Crabbe, a devoted husband, tended her until her death many years later.

In September 1807, Crabbe published a new volume of poems which included The Library, The Newspaper, The Village and The Parish Register, to which were added Sir Eustace Grey and The Hall of Justice. It had been decades since his last publication but now he was seen as an important poet.

Crabbe's next volume of poetry, Tales, was published in 1812. It received a warm welcome from the poet's admirers, and critics. It is now considered Crabbe's masterpiece.

In the summer of 1813, Sarah felt well enough to visit London again. George, Sarah and their two sons spent nearly three months there. The family returned to Muston in September, and at October's end Sarah died at age 63.

In June 1819, Crabbe published his collection Tales of the Hall.

Around 1820 Crabbe began suffering from frequent severe attacks of neuralgia, and this, together with his age, made him less able to travel to London.

In November 1822 he went to see his son George. He was able to preach twice for his son, who congratulated him on the power of his voice. "I will venture a good sum, sir," he said, "that you will be assisting me ten years hence." "Ten weeks" was Crabbe's answer. The prediction proved eerily accurate.

George Crabbe died on February 3rd, 1832, aged 77 at Trowbridge, Wiltshire with his two sons by his side.

Index of Contents

TALE I

THE DUMB ORATORS; OR THE BENEFIT OF SOCIETY

With fair round belly, with good capon lined,
With eyes severe—
Full of wise saws and modern instances.
SHAKESPEARE, As You Like It.

Deep shame hath struck me dumb.
King John.

He gives the bastinado with his tongue;
Our ears are cudgell'd.
King John.

. . . . Let's kill all the lawyers;
Now show yourselves men; 'tis for liberty:
We will not leave one lord or gentleman.
Henry VI. Pt II.

And thus the whirligig of time brings in his revenges.
Twelfth Night.

That all men would be cowards if they dare,
Some men we know have courage to declare;
And this the life of many a hero shows,
That, like the tide, man's courage ebbs and flows:
With friends and gay companions round them, then
Men boldly speak and have the hearts of men;
Who, with opponents seated miss the aid
Of kind applauding looks, and grow afraid;
Like timid travelers in the night, they fear
Th' assault of foes, when not a friend is near.
In contest mighty, and of conquest proud,
Was Justice Bolt, impetuous, warm, and loud;
His fame, his prowess all the country knew,
And disputants, with one so fierce, were few:
He was a younger son, for law design'd,
With dauntless look and persevering mind;
While yet a clerk, for disputation famed,
No efforts tired him, and no conflicts tamed.
Scarcely he bade his master's desk adieu,
When both his brothers from the world withdrew.
An ample fortune he from them possessed,
And was with saving care and prudence bless'd.
Now would he go and to the country give
Example how an English 'squire should live;
How bounteous, yet how frugal man may be,
By well-order'd hospitality;
He would the rights of all so well maintain.
That none should idle be, and none complain.
All this and more he purposed—and what man
Could do, he did to realise his plan;
But time convinced him that we cannot keep

A breed of reasoners like a flock of sheep;
For they, so far from following as we lead,
Make that a cause why they will not proceed.
Man will not follow where a rule is shown,
But loves to take a method of his own:
Explain the way with all your care and skill,
This will he quit, if but to prove he will.—
Yet had our Justice honour—and the crowd,
Awed by his presence, their respect avow'd.
In later years he found his heart incline,
More than in youth, to gen'rous food and wine;
But no indulgence check'd the powerful love
He felt to teach, to argue, and reprove.
Meetings, or public calls, he never miss'd—
To dictate often, always to assist.
Oft he the clergy join'd, and not a cause
Pertain'd to them but he could quote the laws;
He upon tithes and residence display'd
A fund of knowledge for the hearer's aid;
And could on glebe and farming, wool and grains
A long discourse, without a pause, maintain.
To his experience and his native sense
He join'd a bold imperious eloquence;
The grave, stern look of men inform'd and wise,
A full command of feature, heart, and eyes,
An awe-compelling frown, and fear-inspiring size.
When at the table, not a guest was seen
With appetite so lingering, or so keen;
But when the outer man no more required,
The inner waked, and he was man inspired.
His subjects then were those, a subject true
Presents in fairest form to public view;
Of church and state, of law, with mighty strength
Of words he spoke, in speech of mighty length:
And now, into the vale of years declined,
He hides too little of the monarch-mind:
He kindles anger by untimely jokes,
And opposition by contempt provokes;
Mirth he suppresses by his awful frown,
And humble spirits, by disdain, keeps down;
Blamed by the mild, approved by the severe,
The prudent fly him, and the valiant fear.
For overbearing is his proud discourse,
And overwhelming of his voice the force;
And overpowering is he when he shows
What floats upon a mind that always overflows.
This ready man at every meeting rose,
Something to hint, determine, or propose;

And grew so fond of teaching, that he taught
Those who instruction needed not or sought:
Happy our hero, when he could excite
Some thoughtless talker to the wordy fight:
Let him a subject at his pleasure choose,
Physic or law, religion or the muse;
On all such themes he was prepared to shine,—
Physician, poet, lawyer, and divine.
Hemm'd in by some tough argument, borne down
By press of language and the awful frown,
In vain for mercy shall the culprit plead;
His crime is past, and sentence must proceed:
Ah! suffering man, have patience, bear thy woes—
For lo! the clock—at ten the Justice goes.
This powerful man, on business, or to please
A curious taste, or weary grown of ease,
On a long journey travelled many a mile
Westward, and halted midway in our isle;
Content to view a city large and fair,
Though none had notice—what a man was there!
Silent two days, he then began to long
Again to try a voice so loud and strong;
To give his favourite topics some new grace,
And gain some glory in such distant place;
To reap some present pleasure, and to sow
Seeds of fair fame, in after-time to grow:
Here will men say, "We heard, at such an hour,
The best of speakers—wonderful his power."
Inquiry made, he found that day would meet
A learned club, and in the very street:
Knowledge to gain and give, was the design;
To speak, to hearken, to debate, and dine:
This pleased our traveller, for he felt his force
In either way, to eat or to discourse.
Nothing more easy than to gain access
To men like these, with his polite address:
So he succeeded, and first look'd around,
To view his objects and to take his ground;
And therefore silent chose awhile to sit,
Then enter boldly by some lucky hit;
Some observation keen or stroke severe,
To cause some wonder or excite some fear.
Now, dinner past, no longer he supprest
His strong dislike to be a silent guest;
Subjects and words were now at his command—
When disappointment frown'd on all he plann'd;
For, hark!—he heard amazed, on every side,
His church insulted and her priests belied;

The laws reviled, the ruling power abused,
The land derided, and its foes excused:—
He heard and ponder'd—What, to men so vile,
Should be his language?—For his threat'ning style
They were too many;—if his speech were meek,
They would despise such poor attempts to speak:
At other times with every word at will,
He now sat lost, perplex'd, astonish'd, still.
Here were Socinians, Deists, and indeed
All who, as foes to England's Church, agreed;
But still with creeds unlike, and some without a creed:
Here, too, fierce friends of liberty he saw,
Who own'd no prince and who obey no law;
There were reformers of each different sort,
Foes to the laws, the priesthood, and the court;
Some on their favourite plans alone intent,
Some purely angry and malevolent:
The rash were proud to blame their country's laws;
The vain, to seem supporters of a cause;
One call'd for change, that he would dread to see;
Another sigh'd for Gallic liberty!
And numbers joining with the forward crew,
For no one reason—but that numbers do.
"How," said the Justice, "can this trouble rise,
This shame and pain, from creatures I despise?"
And Conscience answer'd—"The prevailing cause
Is thy delight in listening to applause;
Here, thou art seated with a tribe, who spurn
Thy favourite themes, and into laughter turn
Thy fears and wishes: silent and obscure,
Thyself, shalt thou the long harangue endure;
And learn, by feeling, what it is to force
On thy unwilling friends the long discourse:
What though thy thoughts be just, and these, it seems,
Are traitors' projects, idiots' empty schemes;
Yet minds, like bodies, cramm'd, reject their food,
Nor will be forced and tortured for their good!"
At length, a sharp, shrewd, sallow man arose,
And begg'd he briefly might his mind disclose;
"It was his duty, in these worst of times,
T'inform the govern'd of their rulers' crimes:"
This pleasant subject to attend, they each
Prepare to listen, and forbore to teach.
Then voluble and fierce the wordy man
Through a long chain of favourite horrors ran:—
First of the Church, from whose enslaving power
He was deliver'd, and he bless'd the hour;
"Bishops and deans, and prebendaries all,"

He said, "were cattle fatt'ning in the stall;
Slothful and pursy, insolent and mean,
Were every bishop, prebendary, dean,
And wealthy rector: curates, poorly paid,
Were only dull;—he would not them upbraid."
From priests he turn'd to canons, creeds, and prayers,
Rubrics and rules, and all our Church affairs;
Churches themselves, desk, pulpit, altar, all
The Justice reverenced—and pronounced their fall.
Then from religion Hammond turn'd his view
To give our Rulers the correction due;
Not one wise action had these triflers plann'd;
There was, it seem'd, no wisdom in the land,
Save in this patriot tribe, who meet at times
To show the statesman's errors and his crimes.
Now here was Justice Bolt compell'd to sit,
To hear the deist's scorn, the rebel's wit;
The fact mis-stated, the envenom'd lie,
And, staring spell-bound, made not one reply.
Then were our Laws abused—and with the laws,
All who prepare, defend, or judge a cause:
"We have no lawyer whom a man can trust,"
Proceeded Hammond—"if the laws were just;
But they are evil; 'tis the savage state
Is only good, and ours sophisticate!
See! the free creatures in their woods and plains,
Where without laws each happy monarch reigns,
King of himself—while we a number dread,
By slaves commanded and by dunces led:
Oh, let the name with either state agree—
Savage our own we'll name, and civil theirs shall be."
The silent Justice still astonish'd sat,
And wonder'd much whom he was gazing at;
Twice he essay'd to speak—but in a cough,
The faint, indignant, dying speech went off:
"But who is this?" thought he—"a demon vile,
With wicked meaning and a vulgar style:
Hammond they call him: they can give the name
Of man to devils.—Why am I so tame?
Why crush I not the viper?"—Fear replied,
Watch him awhile, and let his strength be tried:
He will be foil'd, if man; but if his aid
Be from beneath, 'tis well to be afraid."
"We are call'd free!" said Hammond—"doleful times,
When rulers add their insult to their crimes;
For should our scorn expose each powerful vice,
It would be libel, and we pay the price."
Thus with licentious words the man went on,

Proving that liberty of speech was gone;
That all were slaves—nor had we better chance
For better times, than as allies to France.
Loud groan'd the Stranger—Why, he must relate,
And own'd, "In sorrow for his country's fate;"
"Nay, she were safe," the ready man replied,
"Might patriots rule her, and could reasoners guide;
When all to vote, to speak, to teach, are free,
Whate'er their creeds or their opinions be;
When books of statutes are consumed in flames,
And courts and copyholds are empty names:
Then will be times of joy—but ere they come,
Havock, and war, and blood must be our doom."
The man here paused—then loudly for Reform
He call'd, and hail'd the prospect of the storm:
The wholesome blast, the fertilizing flood—
Peace gain'd by tumult, plenty bought with blood:
Sharp means, he own'd; but when the land's disease
Asks cure complete, no med'cines are like these.
Our Justice now, more led by fear than rage,
Saw it in vain with madness to engage;
With imps of darkness no man seeks to fight,
Knaves to instruct, or set deceivers right:
Then as the daring speech denounced these woes,
Sick at the soul, the grieving Guest arose;
Quick on the board his ready cash he threw,
And from the demons to his closet flew:
There when secured, he pray'd with earnest seal,
That all they wish'd these patriot-souls might feel;
"Let them to France, their darling country, haste,
And all the comforts of a Frenchman taste;
Let them his safety, freedom, pleasure know,
Feel all their rulers on the land bestow;
And be at length dismiss'd by one unerring blow,—
Not hack'd and hew'd by one afraid to strike,
But shorn by that which shears all men alike;
Nor, as in Britain, let them curse delay
Of law, but borne without a form away—
Suspected, tried, condemn'd, and carted in a day;
Oh! let them taste what they so much approve,
These strong fierce freedoms of the land they love." [2]
Home came our hero, to forget no more
The fear he felt and ever must deplore:
For though he quickly join'd his friends again,
And could with decent force his themes maintain,
Still it occurr'd that, in a luckless time,
He fail'd to fight with heresy and crime;
It was observed his words were not so strong,

His tones so powerful, his harangues so long,
As in old times—for he would often drop
The lofty look, and of a sudden stop;
When conscience whisper'd, that he once was still,
And let the wicked triumph at their will;
And therefore now, when not a foe was near,
He had no right so valiant to appear.
Some years had pass'd, and he perceived his fears
Yield to the spirit of his earlier years—
When at a meeting, with his friends beside,
He saw an object that awaked his pride;
His shame, wrath, vengeance, indignation—all
Man's harsher feelings did that sight recall.
For, lo! beneath him fix'd, our Man of Law
That lawless man the Foe of Order saw;
Once fear'd, now scorn'd; once dreaded, now abhorrd:
A wordy man, and evil every word:
Again he gazed—"It is," said he "the same
Caught and secure: his master owes him shame;"
So thought our hero, who each instant found
His courage rising, from the numbers round.
As when a felon has escaped and fled,
So long, that law conceives the culprit dead;
And back recall'd her myrmidons, intent
On some new game, and with a stronger scent;
Till she beholds him in a place, where none
Could have conceived the culprit would have gone;
There he sits upright in his seat, secure,
As one whose conscience is correct and pure;
This rouses anger for the old offence,
And scorn for all such seeming and pretence:
So on this Hammond look'd our hero bold,
Rememb'ring well that vile offence of old;
And now he saw the rebel dar'd t'intrude
Among the pure, the loyal, and the good;
The crime provok'd his wrath, the folly stirr'd his blood:
Nor wonder was it, if so strange a sight
Caused joy with vengeance, terror with delight;
Terror like this a tiger might create,
A joy like that to see his captive state,
At once to know his force and then decree his fate.
Hammond, much praised by numerous friends, was come
To read his lectures, so admired at home;
Historic lectures, where he loved to mix
His free plain hints on modern politics:
Here, he had heard, that numbers had design,
Their business finish'd, to sit down and dine;
This gave him pleasure, for he judged it right

To show by day that he could speak at night.
Rash the design—for he perceived, too late,
Not one approving friend beside him sate;
The greater number, whom he traced around,
Were men in black, and he conceived they frown'd.
"I will not speak," he thought; "no pearls of mine
Shall be presented to this herd of swine;"
Not this avail'd him, when he cast his eye
On Justice Bolt; he could not fight, nor fly:
He saw a man to whom he gave the pain,
Which now he felt must be return'd again;
His conscience told him with what keen delight
He, at that time, enjoy'd a stranger's fright;
That stranger now befriended—he alone,
For all his insult, friendless, to atone;
Now he could feel it cruel that a heart
Should be distress'd, and none to take its part;
"Though one by one," said Pride, "I would defy
Much greater men, yet meeting every eye,
I do confess a fear—but he will pass me by."
Vain hope! the Justice saw the foe's distress,
With exultation he could not suppress;
He felt the fish was hook'd—and so forbore,
In playful spite to draw it to the shore.
Hammond look'd round again; but none were near,
With friendly smile to still his growing fear;
But all above him seem'd a solemn row
Of priests and deacons, so they seem'd below;
He wonder'd who his right-hand man might be—
Vicar of Holt cum Uppingham was he;
And who the man of that dark frown possess'd—
Rector of Bradley and of Barton-west;
"A pluralist," he growl'd—but check'd the word,
That warfare might not, by his zeal, be stirr'd.
But now began the man above to show
Fierce looks and threat'nings to the man below;
Who had some thoughts his peace by flight to seek—
But how then lecture, if he dar'd not speak!—
Now as the Justice for the war prepared,
He seem'd just then to question if he dared:
"He may resist, although his power be small,
And growing desperate may defy us all;
One dog attack, and he prepares for flight—
Resist another, and he strives to bite;
Nor can I say, if this rebellious cur
Will fly for safety, or will scorn to stir."
Alarm'd by this, he lash'd his soul to rage,
Burn'd with strong shame, and hurried to engage.

As a male turkey straggling on the green,
When by fierce harriers, terriers, mongrels seen,
He feels the insult of the noisy train
And skulks aside, though moved by much disdain;
But when that turkey, at his own barn-door,
Sees one poor straying puppy and no more,
(A foolish puppy who had left the pack,
Thoughtless what foe was threat'ning at his back)
He moves about, as ship prepared to sail,
He hoists his proud rotundity of tail,
The half-seal'd eyes and changeful neck he shows,
Where, in its quick'ning colours, vengeance glows;
From red to blue the pendent wattles turn,
Blue mix'd with red, as matches when they burn;
And thus th' intruding snarler to oppose,
Urged by enkindling wrath, he gobbling goes.
So look'd our hero in his wrath, his cheeks
Flush'd with fresh fires and glow'd in tingling streaks,
His breath by passion's force awhile restrain'd,
Like a stopp'd current greater force regain'd;
So spoke, so look'd he, every eye and ear
Were fix'd to view him, or were turn'd to hear.
"My friends, you know me, you can witness all,
How, urged by passion, I restrain my gall;
And every motive to revenge withstand—
Save when I hear abused my native land.
"Is it not known, agreed, confirm'd, confess'd,
That, of all people, we are govern'd best?
We have the force of monarchies; are free,
As the most proud republicans can be;
And have those prudent counsels that arise
In grave and cautious aristocracies;
And live there those, in such all-glorious state.
Traitors protected in the land they hate?
Rebels, still warring with the laws that give
To them subsistence?—Yes, such wretches live.
"Ours is a Church reformed, and now no more
Is aught for man to mend or to restore;
'Tis pure in doctrines, 'tis correct in creeds,
Has nought redundant, and it nothing needs;
No evil is therein—no wrinkle, spot,
Stain, blame, or blemish:—I affirm there's not.
"All this you know—now mark what once befell,
With grief I bore it, and with shame I tell:
I was entrapp'd—yes, so it came to pass,
'Mid heathen rebels, a tumultuous class;
Each to his country bore a hellish mind,
Each like his neighbour was of cursed kind;

The land that nursed them, they blasphemed; the laws,
Their sovereign's glory, and their country's cause:
And who their mouth, their master-fiend, and who
Rebellion's oracle?—You, catiff, you!"
He spoke, and standing stretch'd his mighty arm,
And fix'd the Man of Words, as by a charm.
"How raved that railer! Sure some hellish power
Restrain'd my tongue in that delirious hour,
Or I had hurl'd the shame and vengeance due
On him, the guide of that infuriate crew;
But to mine eyes, such dreadful looks appear'd,
Such mingled yell of lying words I heard,
That I conceived around were demons all,
And till I fled the house, I fear'd its fall.
"Oh! could our country from our coasts expel
Such foes! to nourish those who wish her well:
This her mild laws forbid, but we may still
From us eject them by our sovereign will;
This let us do."—He said, and then began
A gentler feeling for the silent man;
E'en in our hero's mighty soul arose
A touch of pity for experienced woes;
But this was transient, and with angry eye
He sternly look'd, and paused for a reply.
'Twas then the Man of many Words would speak—
But, in his trial, had them all to seek:
To find a friend he look'd the circle round,
But joy or scorn in every feature found;
He sipp'd his wine, but in those times of dread
Wine only adds confusion to the head;
In doubt he reason'd with himself—"And how
Harangue at night, if I be silent now?"
From pride and praise received, he sought to draw
Courage to speak, but still remain'd the awe;
One moment rose he with a forced disdain,
And then, abash'd, sunk sadly down again;
While in our hero's glance he seem'd to read,
"Slave and insurgent! what hast thou to plead?"
By desperation urged, he now began:
"I seek no favour—I—the rights of man!
Claim; and I—nay!—but give me leave—and I
Insist—a man—that is—and in reply,
I speak,"—Alas! each new attempt was vain:
Confused he stood, he sate, he rose again;
At length he growl'd defiance, sought the door,
Cursed the whole synod, and was seen no more.
"Laud we," said Justice Bolt, "the Powers above:
Thus could our speech the sturdiest foe remove."

Exulting now, he gain'd new strength of fame,
And lost all feelings of defeat and shame.
"He dared not strive, you witness'd—dared not lift
His voice, nor drive at his accursed drift:
So all shall tremble, wretches who oppose
Our Church or State—thus be it to our foes."
He spoke, and, seated with his former air,
Look'd his full self, and fill'd his ample chair;
Took one full bumper to each favourite cause,
And dwelt all night on politics and laws,
With high applauding voice, that gain'd him high applause.

TALE II

THE PARTING HOUR

.... I did not take my leave of him, but had
Most pretty things to say: ere I could tell him
How I would think of him, at certain hours
Such thoughts and such;—or ere I could
Give him that parting kiss, which I had set
Betwixt two charming words—comes in my father.
SHAKESPEARE, Cymbeline.

Grief hath changed me since you saw me last,
And careful hours with Time's deformed hand
Have written strange defeatures o'er my face.
Comedy of Errors.

Oh! if thou be the same Egean, speak,
And speak unto the same Emilia.
Comedy of Errors.

I ran it through, ev'n from my boyish days
To the very moment that she bade me tell it,
Wherein I spake of most disastrous chances,
Of moving accidents by flood and field
Of being taken by the insolent foe,
And sold to slavery.
Othello.

An old man, broken with the storms of fate,
Is come to lay his weary bones among you:
Give him a little earth for charity.
Henry VIII.

Minutely trace man's life; year after year,
Through all his days let all his deeds appear,
And then though some may in that life be strange,
Yet there appears no vast nor sudden change:
The links that bind those various deeds are seen,
And no mysterious void is left between.
But let these binding links be all destroyed,
All that through years he suffer'd or enjoy'd,
Let that vast gap be made, and then behold—
This was the youth, and he is thus when old;
Then we at once the work of time survey,
And in an instant see a life's decay;
Pain mix'd with pity in our bosoms rise,
And sorrow takes new sadness from surprise.
Beneath yon tree, observe an ancient pair—
A sleeping man; a woman in her chair,
Watching his looks with kind and pensive air;
Nor wife, nor sister she, nor is the name
Nor kindred of this friendly pair the same;
Yet so allied are they, that few can feel
Her constant, warm, unwearied, anxious zeal;
Their years and woes, although they long have loved,
Keep their good name and conduct unreproved:
Thus life's small comforts they together share,
And while life lingers for the grave prepare.
No other subjects on their spirits press,
Nor gain such int'rest as the past distress:
Grievous events, that from the mem'ry drive
Life's common cares, and those alone survive,
Mix with each thought, in every action share,
Darken each dream, and blend with every prayer.
To David Booth, his fourth and last-born boy,
Allen his name, was more than common joy;
And as the child grew up, there seem'd in him
A more than common life in every limb;
A strong and handsome stripling he became,
And the gay spirit answer'd to the frame;
A lighter, happier lad was never seen,
For ever easy, cheerful, or serene;
His early love he fix'd upon a fair
And gentle maid—they were a handsome pair.
They at an infant-school together play'd,
Where the foundation of their love was laid:
The boyish champion would his choice attend
In every sport, in every fray defend.
As prospects open'd, and as life advanced,
They walk'd together, they together danced;

On all occasions, from their early years,
They mix'd their joys and sorrows, hopes and fears;
Each heart was anxious, till it could impart
Its daily feelings to its kindred heart;
As years increased, unnumber'd petty wars
Broke out between them; jealousies and jars;
Causeless indeed, and follow'd by a peace,
That gave to love—growth, vigour, and increase.
Whilst yet a boy, when other minds are void,
Domestic thoughts young Allen's hours employ'd.
Judith in gaining hearts had no concern,
Rather intent the matron's part to learn;
Thus early prudent and sedate they grew,
While lovers, thoughtful—and though children, true.
To either parents not a day appeard,
When with this love they might have interfered.
Childish at first, they cared not to restrain;
And strong at last, they saw restriction vain;
Nor knew they when that passion to reprove,
Now idle fondness, now resistless love.
So while the waters rise, the children tread
On the broad estuary's sandy bed;
But soon the channel fills, from side to side
Comes danger rolling with the deep'ning tide;
Yet none who saw the rapid current flow
Could the first instant of that danger know.
The lovers waited till the time should come
When they together could possess a home:
In either house were men and maids unwed,
Hopes to be soothed, and tempers to be led.
Then Allen's mother of his favourite maid
Spoke from the feelings of a mind afraid:
"Dress and amusements were her sole employ,"
She said—"entangling her deluded boy;"
And yet, in truth, a mother's jealous love
Had much imagined and could little prove;
Judith had beauty—and if vain, was kind,
Discreet and mild, and had a serious mind.
Dull was their prospect.—When the lovers met,
They said, "We must not—dare not venture yet."
"Oh! could I labour for thee," Allen cried,
"Why should our friends be thus dissatisfied;
On my own arm I could depend, but they
Still urge obedience—must I yet obey?"
Poor Judith felt the grief, but grieving begg'd delay.
At length a prospect came that seem'd to smile,
And faintly woo them, from a Western Isle;
A kinsman there a widow's hand had gain'd,

"Was old, was rich, and childless yet remain'd;
Would some young Booth to his affairs attend,
And wait awhile, he might expect a friend."
The elder brothers, who were not in love,
Fear'd the false seas, unwilling to remove;
But the young Allen, an enamour'd boy,
Eager an independence to enjoy,
Would through all perils seek it,—by the sea,—
Through labour, danger, pain, or slavery.
The faithful Judith his design approved,
For both were sanguine, they were young, and loved.
The mother's slow consent was then obtain'd;
The time arrived, to part alone remain'd:
All things prepared, on the expected day
Was seen the vessel anchor'd in the bay.
From her would seamen in the evening come,
To take th' adventurous Allen from his home;
With his own friends the final day he pass'd,
And every painful hour, except the last.
The grieving father urged the cheerful glass,
To make the moments with less sorrow pass;
Intent the mother look'd upon her son,
And wish'd th' assent withdrawn, the deed undone;
The younger sister, as he took his way,
Hung on his coat, and begg'd for more delay:
But his own Judith call'd him to the shore,
Whom he must meet, for they might meet no more;—
And there he found her—faithful, mournful, true,
Weeping, and waiting for a last adieu!
The ebbing tide had left the sand, and there
Moved with slow steps the melancholy pair:
Sweet were the painful moments—but, how sweet,
And without pain, when they again should meet!
Now either spoke as hope and fear impress'd
Each their alternate triumph in the breast.
Distance alarm'd the maid—she cried, "'Tis far!"
And danger too—"it is a time of war:
Then in those countries are diseases strange,
And women gay, and men are prone to change:
What then may happen in a year, when things
Of vast importance every moment brings!
But hark! an oar!" she cried, yet none appear'd—
'Twas love's mistake, who fancied what it fear'd;
And she continued—"Do, my Allen, keep
Thy heart from evil, let thy passions sleep;
Believe it good, nay glorious, to prevail,
And stand in safety where so many fail;
And do not, Allen, or for shame, or pride,

Thy faith abjure, or thy profession hide;
Can I believe his love will lasting prove,
Who has no rev'rence for the God I love?
I know thee well! how good thou art and kind;
But strong the passions that invade thy mind—
Now, what to me hath Allen, to commend?"
"Upon my mother," said the youth," attend;
Forget her spleen, and, in my place appear,
Her love to me will make my Judith dear,
Oft I shall think (such comforts lovers seek),
Who speaks of me, and fancy what they speak;
Then write on all occasions, always dwell
On hope's fair prospects, and be kind and well,
And ever choose the fondest, tenderest style."
She answer'd, "No," but answer'd with a smile.
"And now, my Judith, at so sad a time,
Forgive my fear, and call it not my crime;
When with our youthful neighbours 'tis thy chance
To meet in walks, the visit, or the dance,
When every lad would on my lass attend,
Choose not a smooth designer for a friend:
That fawning Philip!—nay, be not severe,
A rival's hope must cause a lover's fear."
Displeased she felt, and might in her reply
Have mix'd some anger, but the boat was nigh,
Now truly heard!—it soon was full in sight;—
Now the sad farewell, and the long good-night;
For see!—his friends come hast'ning to the beach,
And now the gunwale is within the reach:
"Adieu!—farewell!—remember!"—and what more
Affection taught, was utter'd from the shore.
But Judith left them with a heavy heart,
Took a last view, and went to weep apart.
And now his friends went slowly from the place,
Where she stood still, the dashing oar to trace,
Till all were silent!—for the youth she pray'd,
And softly then return'd the weeping maid.
They parted, thus by hope and fortune led,
And Judith's hours in pensive pleasure fled;
But when return'd the youth?—the youth no more
Return'd exulting to his native shore;
But forty years were past, and then there came
A worn-out man with wither'd limbs and lame,
His mind oppress'd with woes, and bent with age his frame.
Yes! old and grieved, and trembling with decay,
Was Allen landing in his native bay,
Willing his breathless form should blend with kindred clay.
In an autumnal eve he left the beach,

In such an eve he chanced the port to reach:
He was alone; he press'd the very place
Of the sad parting, of the last embrace:
There stood his parents, there retired the maid,
So fond, so tender, and so much afraid;
And on that spot, through many years, his mind
Turn'd mournful back, half sinking, half resign'd.
No one was present; of its crew bereft,
A single boat was in the billows left;
Sent from some anchor'd vessel in the bay,
At the returning tide to sail away.
O'er the black stern the moonlight softly play'd,
The loosen'd foresail flapping in the shade;
All silent else on shore; but from the town
A drowsy peal of distant bells came down:
From the tall houses here and there, a light
Served some confused remembrance to excite:
"There," he observed, and new emotions felt,
"Was my first home—and yonder Judith dwelt;
Dead! dead are all! I long—I fear to know,"
He said, and walk'd impatient, and yet slow.
Sudden there broke upon his grief a noise
Of merry tumult and of vulgar joys:
Seamen returning to their ship, were come,
With idle numbers straying from their home;
Allen among them mix'd, and in the old
Strove some familiar features to behold;
While fancy aided memory:—"Man! what cheer?"
A sailor cried; "Art thou at anchor here?"
Faintly he answer'd, and then tried to trace
Some youthful features in some aged face:
A swarthy matron he beheld, and thought
She might unfold the very truths he sought:
Confused and trembling, he the dame address'd:
"The Booths! yet live they?" pausing and oppress'd;
Then spake again:—"Is there no ancient man,
David his name?—assist me, if you can.—
Flemings there were—and Judith, doth she live?"
The woman gazed, nor could an answer give,'
Yet wond'ring stood, and all were silent by,
Feeling a strange and solemn sympathy.
The woman musing said—"She knew full well
Where the old people came at last to dwell;
They had a married daughter, and a son,
But they were dead, and now remain'd not one."
"Yes," said an elder, who had paused intent
On days long past, "there was a sad event;—
One of these Booths—it was my mother's tale—

Here left his lass, I know not where to sail:
She saw their parting, and observed the pain;
But never came th' unhappy man again:"
"The ship was captured"—Allen meekly said,
"And what became of the forsaken maid?"
The woman answer'd: "I remember now,
She used to tell the lasses of her vow,
And of her lover's loss, and I have seen
The gayest hearts grow sad where she bas been;
Yet in her grief she married, and was made
Slave to a wretch, whom meekly she obey'd,
And early buried—but I know no more:
And hark! our friends are hast'ning to the shore."
Allen soon found a lodging in the town,
And walk'd a man unnoticed up and down,
This house, and this, he knew, and thought a face
He sometimes could among a number trace:
Of names remember'd there remain'd a few,
But of no favourites, and the rest were new:
A merchant's wealth, when Allen went to sea,
Was reckon'd boundless.—Could he living be?
Or lived his son? for one he had, the heir
To a vast business, and a fortune fair.
No! but that heir's poor widow, from her shed,
With crutches went to take her dole of bread:
There was a friend whom he had left a boy,
With hope to sail the master of a hoy;
Him, after many a stormy day, he found
With his great wish, his life's whole purpose, crown'd.
This hoy's proud captain look'd in Allen's face,—
"Yours is, my friend," said he, "a woeful case;
We cannot all succeed: I now command
The Betsy sloop, and am not much at land:
But when we meet, you shall your story tell
Of foreign parts—I bid you now farewell!"
Allen so long had left his native shore,
He saw but few whom he had seen before;
The older people, as they met him, cast
A pitying look, oft speaking as they pass'd—
"The man is Allen Booth, and it appears
He dwelt among us in his early years:
We see the name engraved upon the stones,
Where this poor wanderer means to lay his bones,"
Thus where he lived and loved—unhappy change!—
He seems a stranger, and finds all are strange.
But now a widow, in a village near,
Chanced of the melancholy man to hear;
Old as she was, to Judith's bosom came

Some strong emotions at the well-known name;
He was her much-loved Allen, she had stay'd
Ten troubled years, a sad afflicted maid;
Then was she wedded, of his death assured.
And much of mis'ry in her lot endured;
Her husband died; her children sought their bread
In various places, and to her were dead.
The once fond lovers met; not grief nor age,
Sickness nor pain, their hearts could disengage:
Each had immediate confidence; a friend
Both now beheld, on whom they might depend:
"Now is there one to whom I can express
My nature's weakness, and my soul's distress."
Allen look'd up, and with impatient heart—
"Let me not lose thee—never let us part:
So heaven this comfort to my sufferings give,
It is not all distress to think and live."
Thus Allen spoke—for time had not removed
The charms attach'd to one so fondly loved;
Who with more health, the mistress of their cot,
Labours to soothe the evils of his lot.
To her, to her alone, his various fate,
At various times, 'tis comfort to relate;
And yet his sorrow—she too loves to hear
What wrings her bosom, and compels the tear.
First he related how he left the shore,
Alarm'd with fears that they should meet no more.
Then, ere the ship had reach'd her purposed course,
They met and yielded to the Spanish force;
Then 'cross th' Atlantic seas they bore their prey,
Who grieving landed from their sultry bay:
And marching many a burning league, he found
Himself a slave upon a miner's ground:
There a good priest his native language spoke,
And gave some ease to his tormenting yoke;
Kindly advanced him in his master's grace,
And he was station'd in an easier place;
There, hopeless ever to escape the land,
He to a Spanish maiden gave his hand;
In cottage shelter'd from the blaze of day,
He saw his happy infants round him play;
Where summer shadows, made by lofty trees,
Waved o'er his seat, and soothed his reveries;
E'en then he thought of England, nor could sigh,
But his fond Isabel demanded, "Why?"
Grieved by the story, she the sigh repaid,
And wept in pity for the English maid:
Thus twenty years were pass d, and pass'd his views

Of further bliss, for he had wealth to lose:
His friend now dead, some foe had dared to paint
"His faith as tainted: he his spouse would taint;
Make all his children infidels, and found
An English heresy on Christian ground."
"Whilst I was poor," said Allen, "none would care
What my poor notions of religion were;
None ask'd me whom I worshipp'd, how I pray'd,
If due obedience to the laws were paid:
My good adviser taught me to be still,
Nor to make converts had I power or will.
I preach'd no foreign doctrine to my wife,
And never mention'd Luther in my life;
I, all they said, say what they would, allow'd,
And when the fathers bade me bow, I bow'd;
Their forms I follow'd, whether well or sick,
And was a most obedient Catholic.
But I had money, and these pastors found
My notions vague, heretical, unsound:
A wicked book they seized; the very Turk
Could not have read a more pernicious work;
To me pernicious, who if it were good
Or evil question'd not, nor understood:
Oh! had I little but the book possess'd,
I might have read it, and enjoy'd my rest."
Alas! poor Allen—through his wealth was seen
Crimes that by poverty conceal'd had been:
Faults that in dusty pictures rest unknown,
Are in an instant through the varnish shown.
He told their cruel mercy; how at last,
In Christian kindness for the merits past,
They spared his forfeit life, but bade him fly,
Or for his crime and contumacy die;
Fly from all scenes, all objects of delight:
His wife, his children, weeping in his sight,
All urging him to flee, he fled, and cursed his flight.
He next related how he found a way,
Guideless and grieving, to Campeachy-Bay:
There in the woods he wrought, and there, among
Some lab'ring seamen, heard his native tongue:
The sound, one moment, broke upon his pain
With joyful force; he long'd to hear again:
Again he heard; he seized an offer'd hand,
"And when beheld you last our native land!"
He cried, "and in what country? quickly say."
The seamen answer'd—strangers all were they;
Only one at his native port had been;
He, landing once, the quay and church had seen,

For that esteem'd; but nothing more he knew.
Still more to know, would Allen join the crew,
Sail where they sail'd, and, many a peril past,
They at his kinsman's isle their anchor cast;
But him they found not, nor could one relate
Aught of his will, his wish, or his estate.
This grieved not Allen; then again he sail'd
For England's coast, again his fate prevailed:
War raged, and he, an active man and strong,
Was soon impress'd, and served his country long.
By various shores he pass'd, on various seas,
Never so happy as when void of ease.—
And then he told how in a calm distress'd,
Day after day his soul was sick of rest;
When, as a log upon the deep they stood,
Then roved his spirit to the inland wood;
Till, while awake, he dream'd, that on the seas
Were his loved home, the hill, the stream, the trees:
He gazed, he pointed to the scenes:—"There stand
My wife, my children, 'tis my lovely land.
See! there my dwelling—oh! delicious scene
Of my best life:—unhand me—are ye men?"
And thus the frenzy ruled him, till the wind
Brush'd the fond pictures from the stagnant mind.
He told of bloody fights, and how at length
The rage of battle gave his spirits strength:
'Twas in the Indian seas his limb he lost,
And he was left half-dead upon the coast;
But living gain'd, 'mid rich aspiring men,
A fair subsistence by his ready pen.
"Thus," he continued, "pass'd unvaried years,
Without events producing hopes or fears."
Augmented pay procured him decent wealth,
But years advancing undermined his health;
Then oft-times in delightful dream he flew
To England's shore, and scenes his childhood knew:
He saw his parents, saw his fav'rite maid,
No feature wrinkled, not a charm decay'd;
And thus excited, in his bosom rose
A wish so strong, it baffled his repose:
Anxious he felt on English earth to lie;
To view his native soil, and there to die.
He then described the gloom, the dread he found,
When first he landed on the chosen ground,
Where undefined was all he hoped and fear'd,
And how confused and troubled all appear'd;
His thoughts in past and present scenes employ'd,
All views in future blighted and destroy'd:

His were a medley of be wild'ring themes,
Sad as realities, and wild as dreams.
Here his relation closes, but his mind
Flies back again some resting-place to find;
Thus silent, musing through the day, he sees
His children sporting by those lofty trees,
Their mother singing in the shady scene,
Where the fresh springs burst o'er the lively green;—
So strong his eager fancy, he affrights
The faithful widow by its powerful flights;
For what disturbs him he aloud will tell,
And cry—"'Tis she, my wife! my Isabel!
Where are my children?"—Judith grieves to hear
How the soul works in sorrows so severe;
Assiduous all his wishes to attend,
Deprived of much, he yet may boast a friend;
Watch'd by her care, in sleep, his spirit takes
Its flight, and watchful finds her when he wakes.
'Tis now her office; her attention see!
While her friend sleeps beneath that shading tree,
Careful, she guards him from the glowing heat,
And pensive muses at her Allen's feet.
And where is he? Ah! doubtless in those scenes
Of his best days, amid the vivid greens.
Fresh with unnumber'd rills, where ev'ry gale
Breathes the rich fragrance of the neighb'ring vale.
Smiles not his wife, and listens as there comes
The night-bird's music from the thick'ning glooms?
And as he sits with all these treasures nigh,
Blaze not with fairy-light the phosphor-fly,
When like a sparkling gem it wheels illumined by?
This is the joy that now so plainly speaks
In the warm transient flushing of his cheeks;
For he is list'ning to the fancied noise
Of his own children, eager in their joys:
All this he feels, a dream's delusive bliss
Gives the expression, and the glow like this.
And now his Judith lays her knitting by,
These strong emotions in her friend to spy
For she can fully of their nature deem—
But see! he breaks the long protracted theme,
And wakes, and cries—"My God! 'twas but a dream."

TALE III

THE GENTLEMAN FARMER

Pause then,
And weigh thy value with an even hand;
If thou beest rated by thy estimation,
Thou dost deserve enough.
SHAKESPEARE, Merchant of Venice.

Because I will not do them wrong to mistrust any,
I will do myself the right to trust none: and the
fine is (for which I may go the finer), I will live a bachelor.
Much Ado about Nothing.

Throw physic to the dogs, I'll none of it.
Macbeth.

His promises are, as he then was, mighty;
And his performance, as he now is, nothing.
Henry VIII.

Gwyn was a farmer, whom the farmers all,
Who dwelt around, "the Gentleman" would call;
Whether in pure humility or pride,
They only knew, and they would not decide.
Far different he from that dull plodding tribe
Whom it was his amusement to describe;
Creatures no more enliven'd than a clod,
But treading still as their dull fathers trod;
Who lived in times when not a man had seen
Corn sown by drill, or thresh'd by a machine!
He was of those whose skill assigns the prize
For creatures fed in pens, and stalls, and sties;
And who, in places where improvers meet,
To fill the land with fatness, had a seat;
Who in large mansions live like petty kings,
And speak of farms but as amusing things;
Who plans encourage, and who journals keep,
And talk with lords about a breed of sheep.
Two are the species in this genus known;
One, who is rich in his profession grown,
Who yearly finds his ample stores increase,
From fortune's favours and a favouring lease;
Who rides his hunter, who his house adorns;
Who drinks his wine, and his disbursements scorns;
Who freely lives, and loves to show he can,—
This is the Farmer made the Gentleman.
The second species from the world is sent,
Tired with its strife, or with his wealth content;

In books and men beyond the former read
To farming solely by a passion led,
Or by a fashion; curious in his land;
Now planning much, now changing what he plann'd;
Pleased by each trial, not by failures vex'd,
And ever certain to succeed the next;
Quick to resolve, and easy to persuade,—
This is the Gentleman, a farmer made.
Gwyn was of these; he from the world withdrew
Early in life, his reasons known to few;
Some disappointments said, some pure good sense,
The love of land, the press of indolence;
His fortune known, and coming to retire,
If not a Farmer, men had call'd him 'Squire.
Forty and five his years, no child or wife
Cross'd the still tenour of his chosen life;
Much land he purchased, planted far around,
And let some portions of superfluous ground
To farmers near him, not displeased to say
"My tenants," nor "our worthy landlord," they.
Fix'd in his farm, he soon display'd his skill
In small-boned lambs, the horse-hoe, and the drill;
From these he rose to themes of nobler kind,
And show'd the riches of a fertile mind;
To all around their visits he repaid
And thus his mansion and himself display'd.
His rooms were stately, rather fine than neat,
And guests politely call'd his house a Seat;
At much expense was each apartment graced,
His taste was gorgeous, but it still was taste;
In full festoons the crimson curtains fell,
The sofas rose in bold elastic swell;
Mirrors in gilded frames display'd the tints
Of glowing carpets and of colour'd prints:
The weary eye saw every object shine,
And all was costly, fanciful, and fine.
As with his friends he pass'd the social hours,
His generous spirit scorn'd to hide its powers;
Powers unexpected, for his eye and air
Gave no sure signs that eloquence was there;
Oft he began with sudden fire and force,
As loth to lose occasion for discourse;
Some, 'tis observed, who feel a wish to speak,
Will a due place for introduction seek;
On to their purpose step by step they steal,
And all their way, by certain signals, feel;
Others plunge in at once, and never heed
Whose turn they take, whose purpose they impede;

Resolved to shine, they hasten to begin,
Of ending thoughtless—and of these was Gwyn.
And thus he spake:—
"It grieves me to the soul,
To see how man submits to man's control;
How overpower'd and shackled minds are led
In vulgar tracks, and to submission bred;
The coward never on himself relies,
But to an equal for assistance flies;
Man yields to custom, as he bows to fate,
In all things ruled—mind, body, and estate;
In pain, in sickness, we for cure apply
To them we know not, and we know not why;
But that the creature has some jargon read,
And got some Scotchman's system in his head;
Some grave impostor, who will health ensure,
Long as your patience or your wealth endure,
But mark them well, the pale and sickly crew,
They have not health, and can they give it you?
These solemn cheats their various methods choose,
A system fires them, as a bard his muse:
Hence wordy wars arise; the learn'd divide,
And groaning patients curse each erring guide.
"Next, our affairs are govern'd, buy or sell,
Upon the deed the law must fix its spell;
Whether we hire or let, we must have still
The dubious aid of an attorney's skill;
They take a part in every man's affairs,
And in all business some concern is theirs;
Because mankind in ways prescribed are found
Like flocks that follow on a beaten ground.
Each abject nature in the way proceeds,
That now to shearing, now to slaughter leads.
Should you offend, though meaning no offence,
You have no safety in your innocence;
The statute broken then is placed in view,
And men must pay for crimes they never knew;
Who would by law regain his plunder'd store,
Would pick up fallen merc'ry from the floor;
If he pursue it, here and there it slides,
He would collect it, but it more divides;
This part and this he stops, but still in vain,
It slips aside, and breaks in parts again;
Till, after time and pains, and care and cost,
He finds his labour and his object lost.
But most it grieves me (friends alone are round),
To see a man in priestly fetters bound;
Guides to the soul, these friends of Heaven contrive,

Long as man lives, to keep his fears alive:
Soon as an infant breathes, their rites begin;
Who knows not sinning, must be freed from sin;
Who needs no bond, must yet engage in vows;
Who has no judgment, must a creed espouse:
Advanced in life, our boys are bound by rules,
Are catechised in churches, cloisters, schools,
And train'd in thraldom to be fit for tools:
The youth grown up, he now a partner needs,
And lo! a priest, as soon as he succeeds.
What man of sense can marriage-rites approve?
What man of spirit can be bound to love?
Forced to be kind! compell'd to be sincere!
Do chains and fetters make companions dear?
Pris'ners indeed we bind; but though the bond
May keep them safe, it does not make them fond:
The ring, the vow, the witness, licence, prayers,
All parties known! made public all affairs!
Such forms men suffer, and from these they date
A deed of love begun with all they hate:
Absurd! that none the beaten road should shun,
But love to do what other dupes have done.
"Well, now your priest has made you one of twain,
Look you for rest? Alas! you look in vain.
If sick, he comes; you cannot die in peace,
Till he attends to witness your release;
To vex your soul, and urge you to confess
The sins you feel, remember, or can guess;
Nay, when departed, to your grave he goes—
But there indeed he hurts not your repose.
"Such are our burthens; part we must sustain,
But need not link new grievance to the chain:
Yet men like idiots will their frames surround
With these vile shackles, nor confess they're bound;
In all that most confines them they confide,
Their slavery boast, and make their bonds their pride;
E'en as the pressure galls them, they declare
(Good souls!) how happy and how free they are!
As madmen, pointing round their wretched cells,
Cry, 'Lo! the palace where our honour dwells.'
"Such is our state: but I resolve to live
By rules my reason and my feelings give;
No legal guards shall keep enthrall'd my mind,
No Slaves command me, and no teachers blind.
Tempted by sins, let me their strength defy,
But have no second in a surplice by;
No bottle-holder, with officious aid,
To comfort conscience, weaken'd and afraid:

Then if I yield, my frailty is not known;
And, if I stand, the glory is my own.
"When Truth and Reason are our friends, we seem
Alive! awake!—the superstitious dream.
Oh! then, fair truth, for thee alone I seek,
Friend to the wise, supporter of the weak;
From thee we learn whate'er is right and just:
Forms to despise, professions to distrust;
Creeds to reject, pretensions to deride,
And, following thee, to follow none beside."
Such was the speech: it struck upon the ear
Like sudden thunder none expect to hear.
He saw men's wonder with a manly pride,
And gravely smiled at guest electrified.
"A farmer this!" they said, "Oh! let him seek
That place where he may for his country speak;
On some great question to harangue for hours,
While speakers, hearing, envy nobler powers!"
Wisdom like this, as all things rich and rare,
Must be acquired with pains, and kept with care;
In books he sought it, which his friends might view,
When their kind host the guarding curtain drew.
There were historic works for graver hours,
And lighter verse to spur the languid powers;
There metaphysics, logic there had place;
But of devotion not a single trace—
Save what is taught in Gibbon's florid page,
And other guides of this inquiring age.
There Hume appear'd, and near a splendid book
Composed by Gay's "good lord of Bolingbroke:"
With these were mix'd the light, the free, the vain,
And from a corner peep'd the sage Tom Paine;
Here four neat volumes Chesterfield were named,
For manners much and easy morals famed;
With chaste Memoirs of females, to be read
When deeper studies had confused the head.
Such his resources, treasures where he sought
For daily knowledge till his mind was fraught:
Then, when his friends were present, for their use
He would the riches he had stored produce;
He found his lamp burn clearer when each day
He drew for all he purposed to display;
For these occasions forth his knowledge sprung,
As mustard quickens on a bed of dung:
All was prepared, and guests allow'd the praise
For what they saw he could so quickly raise.
Such this new friend; and when the year came round,
The same impressive, reasoning sage was found:

Then, too, was seen the pleasant mansion graced
With a fair damsel—his no vulgar taste;
The neat Rebecca—sly, observant, still,
Watching his eye, and waiting on his will;
Simple yet smart her dress, her manners meek,
Her smiles spoke for her, she would seldom speak:
But watch'd each look, each meaning to detect,
And (pleased with notice) felt for all neglect.
With her lived Gwyn a sweet harmonious life,
Who, forms excepted, was a charming wife:
The wives indeed, so made by vulgar law,
Affected scorn, and censured what they saw,
And what they saw not, fancied; said 'twas sin,
And took no notice of the wife of Gwyn:
But he despised their rudeness, and would prove
Theirs was compulsion and distrust, not love;
"Fools as they were! could they conceive that rings
And parsons' blessings were substantial things?"
They answer'd "Yes;" while he contemptuous spoke
Of the low notions held by simple folk;
Yet, strange that anger in a man so wise
Should from the notions of these fools arise;
Can they so vex us, whom we so despise?
Brave as he was, our hero felt a dread
Lest those who saw him kind should think him led;
If to his bosom fear a visit paid,
It was, lest he should be supposed afraid:
Hence sprang his orders; not that he desired
The things when done: obedience he required;
And thus, to prove his absolute command,
Ruled every heart, and moved each subject hand;
Assent he ask'd for every word and whim,
To prove that he alone was king of him.
The still Rebecca, who her station knew,
With ease resign'd the honours not her due:
Well pleased she saw that men her board would grace,
And wish'd not there to see a female face;
When by her lover she his spouse was styled,
Polite she thought it, and demurely smiled;
But when he wanted wives and maidens round
So to regard her, she grew grave and frown'd;
And sometimes whisper'd—"Why should you respect
These people's notions, yet their forms reject?"
Gwyn, though from marriage bond and fetter free,
Still felt abridgment in his liberty;
Something of hesitation he betray'd,
And in her presence thought of what he said.
Thus fair Rebecca, though she walk'd astray,

His creed rejecting, judged it right to pray,
To be at church, to sit with serious looks,
To read her Bible and her Sunday-books:
She hated all those new and daring themes,
And call'd his free conjectures "devil's dreams:"
She honour'd still the priesthood in her fall,
And claim'd respect and reverence for them all;
Call'd them "of sin's destructive power the foes,
And not such blockheads as he might suppose."
Gwyn to his friends would smile, and sometimes say,
"'Tis a kind fool; why vex her in her way?"
Her way she took, and still had more in view,
For she contrived that he should take it too.
The daring freedom of his soul, 'twas plain,
In part was lost in a divided reign;
A king and queen, who yet in prudence sway'd
Their peaceful state, and were in turn obey'd.
Yet such our fate, that when we plan the best,
Something arises to disturb our rest:
For though in spirits high, in body strong,
Gwyn something felt—he knew not what—was wrong,
He wish'd to know, for he believed the thing,
If unremoved, would other evil bring:
"She must perceive, of late he could not eat,
And when he walk'd he trembled on his feet:
He had forebodings, and he seem'd as one
Stopp'd on the road, or threaten'd by a dun;
He could not live, and yet, should he apply
To those physicians—he must sooner die."
The mild Rebecca heard with some disdain,
And some distress, her friend and lord complain:
His death she fear'd not, but had painful doubt
What his distemper'd nerves might bring about;
With power like hers she dreaded an ally,
And yet there was a person in her eye;—
She thought, debated, fix'd—"Alas!" she said,
"A case like yours must be no more delay'd;
You hate these doctors; well! but were a friend
And doctor one, your fears would have an end:
My cousin Mollet—Scotland holds him now—
Is above all men skilful, all allow;
Of late a Doctor, and within a while
He means to settle in this favoured isle:
Should he attend you, with his skill profound,
You must be safe, and shortly would be sound."
When men in health against Physicians rail,
They should consider that their nerves may fail;
Who calls a Lawyer rogue, may find, too late,

On one of these depends his whole estate;
Nay, when the world can nothing more produce,
The Priest, th' insulted priest, may have his use;
Ease, health, and comfort lift a man so high,
These powers are dwarfs that he can scarcely spy;
Pain, sickness, langour, keep a man so low,
That these neglected dwarfs to giants grow:
Happy is he who through the medium sees
Of clear good sense—but Gwyn was not of these.
He heard and he rejoiced: "Ah! let him come,
And till he fixes, make my house his home."
Home came the Doctor—he was much admired;
He told the patient what his case required;
His hours for sleep, his time to eat and drink,
When he should ride, read, rest, compose, or think.
Thus join'd peculiar skill and art profound,
To make the fancy-sick no more than fancy-sound.
With such attention, who could long be ill?
Returning health proclaim'd the Doctor's skill.
Presents and praises from a grateful heart
Were freely offer'd on the patient's part;
In high repute the Doctor seem'd to stand,
But still had got no footing in the land;
And, as he saw the seat was rich and fair,
He felt disposed to fix his station there:
To gain his purpose he perform'd the part
Of a good actor, and prepared to start;
Not like a traveller in a day serene,
When the sun shone and when the roads were clean;
Not like the pilgrim, when the morning gray,
The ruddy eve succeeding, sends his way;
But in a season when the sharp east wind
Had all its influence on a nervous mind;
When past the parlour's front it fiercely blew,
And Gwyn sat pitying every bird that flew,
This strange physician said—"Adieu! Adieu!
Farewell!—Heaven bless you!—if you should—but no,
You need not fear—farewell! 'tis time to go."
The Doctor spoke; and as the patient heard,
His old disorders (dreadful train!) appear'd;
"He felt the tingling tremor, and the stress
Upon his nerves that he could not express;
Should his good friend forsake him, he perhaps
Might meet his death, and surely a relapse."
So, as the Doctor seem'd intent to part,
He cried in terror—"Oh! be where thou art:
Come, thou art young, and unengaged; oh! come,
Make me thy friend, give comfort to mine home;

I have now symptoms that require thine aid,
Do, Doctor, stay:"—th' obliging Doctor stay'd.
Thus Gwyn was happy; he had now a friend,
And a meek spouse on whom he could depend:
But now possess'd of male and female guide,
Divided power he thus must subdivide:
In earlier days he rode, or sat at ease
Reclined, and having but himself to please;
Now if he would a fav'rite nag bestride,
He sought permission—"Doctor, may I ride?"
(Rebecca's eye her sovereign pleasure told)—
"I think you may, but guarded from the cold,
Ride forty minutes."—Free and happy soul,
He scorn'd submission, and a man's control;
But where such friends in every care unite
All for his good, obedience is delight.
Now Gwyn a sultan bade affairs adieu,
Led and assisted by the faithful two;
The favourite fair, Rebecca, near him sat,
And whisper'd whom to love, assist, or hate;
While the chief vizier eased his lord of cares,
And bore himself the burden of affairs:
No dangers could from such alliance flow,
But from that law that changes all below.
When wintry winds with leaves bestrew'd the ground,
And men were coughing all the village round;
When public papers of invasion told,
Diseases, famines, perils new and old;
When philosophic writers fail'd to clear
The mind of gloom, and lighter works to cheer;
Then came fresh terrors on our hero's mind—
Fears unforeseen, and feelings undefined.
"In outward ills," he cried, "I rest assured
Of my friend's aid; they will in time be cured;
But can his art subdue, resist, control
These inward griefs and troubles of the soul?
Oh! my Rebecca! my disorder'd mind
No help in study, none in thought can find;
What must I do, Rebecca?" She proposed
The Parish-guide; but what could be disclosed
To a proud priest?—"No! him have I defied,
Insulted, slighted—shall he be my guide?
But one there is, and if report be just,
A wise good man, whom I may safely trust;
Who goes from house to house, from ear to ear,
To make his truths, his Gospel-truths, appear;
True if indeed they be, 'tis time that I should hear:
Send for that man; and if report be just,

I, like Cornelius, will the teacher trust;
But if deceiver, I the vile deceit
Shall soon discover, and discharge the cheat."
To Doctor Mollet was the grief confess"d,
While Gwyn the freedom of his mind expressed;
Yet own'd it was to ills and errors prone,
And he for guilt and frailty must atone.
"My books, perhaps," the wav'ring mortal cried,
"Like men deceive; I would be satisfied;—
And to my soul the pious man may bring
Comfort and light:—do let me try the thing."
The cousins met, what pass'd with Gwyn was told:
"Alas!" the Doctor said, "how hard to hold
These easy minds, where all impressions made
At first sink deeply, and then quickly fade;
For while so strong these new-born fancies reign,
We must divert them, to oppose is vain:
You see him valiant now, he scorns to heed
The bigot's threat'nings or the zealot's creed;
Shook by a dream, he next for truth receives
What frenzy teaches, and what fear believes;
And this will place him in the power of one
Whom we must seek, because we cannot shun."
Wisp had been ostler at a busy inn,
Where he beheld and grew in dread of sin;
Then to a Baptists' meeting found his way,
Became a convert, and was taught to pray;
Then preach'd; and, being earnest and sincere,
Brought other sinners to religious fear:
Together grew his influence and his fame,
Till our dejected hero heard his name:
His little failings were a grain of pride,
Raised by the numbers he presumed to guide;
A love of presents, and of lofty praise
For his meek spirit and his humble ways;
But though this spirit would on flattery feed,
No praise could blind him and no arts mislead:—
To him the Doctor made the wishes known
Of his good patron, but conceal'd his own;
He of all teachers had distrust and doubt,
And was reserved in what he came about;
Though on a plain and simple message sent,
He had a secret and a bold intent:
Their minds at first were deeply veil'd; disguise
Form'd the slow speech, and oped the eager eyes;
Till by degrees sufficient light was thrown
On every view, and all the business shown.
Wisp, as a skilful guide who led the blind,

Had powers to rule and awe the vapourish mind;
But not the changeful will, the wavering fear to bind:
And should his conscience give him leave to dwell
With Gwyn, and every rival power expel
(A dubious point), yet he, with every care,
Might soon the lot of the rejected share;
And other Wisps he found like him to reign,
And then be thrown upon the world again:
He thought it prudent then, and felt it just,
The present guides of his new friend to trust:
True, he conceived, to touch the harder heart
Of the cool Doctor, was beyond his art;
But mild Rebecca he could surely sway,
While Gwyn would follow where she led the way:
So to do good, (and why a duty shun,
Because rewarded for the good when done?)
He with his friends would join in all they plann'd,
Save when his faith or feelings should withstand;
There he must rest sole judge of his affairs,
While they might rule exclusively in theirs.
When Gwyn his message to the teacher sent,
He fear'd his friends would show their discontent;
And prudent seem'd it to th' attendant pair,
Not all at once to show an aspect fair:
On Wisp they seem'd to look with jealous eye,
And fair Rebecca was demure and shy;
But by degrees the teacher's worth they knew,
And were so kind, they seem'd converted too.
Wisp took occasion to the nymph to say,
"You must be married: will you name the day?"
She smiled,—"'Tis well: but should he not comply,
Is it quite safe th' experiment to try?"—
"My child," the teacher said, "who feels remorse,
(And feels not he?) must wish relief of course:
And can he find it, while he fears the crime!—
You must be married; will you name the time?"
Glad was the patron as a man could be,
Yet marvell'd too, to find his guides agree;
"But what the cause?" he cried; "'tis genuine love for me."
Each found his part, and let one act describe
The powers and honours of th' accordant tribe:—
A man for favour to the mansion speeds,
And cons his threefold task as he proceeds;
To teacher Wisp he bows with humble air,
And begs his interest for a barn's repair:
Then for the Doctor he inquires, who loves
To hear applause for what his skill improves,
And gives for praise, assent—and to the Fair

He brings of pullets a delicious pair;
Thus sees a peasant, with discernment nice,
A love of power, conceit, and avarice.
Lo! now the change complete: the convert Gwyn
Has sold his books, and has renounced his sin;
Mollet his body orders, Wisp his soul,
And o'er his purse the Lady takes control;
No friends beside he needs, and none attend—
Soul, body, and estate, has each a friend;
And fair Rebecca leads a virtuous life—
She rules a mistress, and she reigns a wife.

TALE IV

PROCRASTINATION

Heaven witness
I have been to you ever true and humble.
SHAKESPEARE, Henry VIII.

Gentle lady,
When I did first impart my love to you,
I freely told you all the wealth I had.
Merchant of Venice.

The fatal time
Cuts off all ceremonies and vows of love,
And ample interchange of sweet discourse,
Which so long sunder'd friends should dwell upon.
Richard III.

I know thee not, old man; fall to thy prayers.
Henry IV.

Farewell,
Thou pure impiety, thou impious purity,
For thee I'll lock up all the gates of love.
Much Ado about Nothing.

Love will expire—the gay, the happy dream
Will turn to scorn, indiff'rence, or esteem:
Some favour'd pairs, in this exchange, are blest,
Nor sigh for raptures in a state of rest;
Others, ill match'd, with minds unpair'd, repent
At once the deed, and know no more content;

From joy to anguish they, in haste, decline,
And, with their fondness, their esteem resign;
More luckless still their fate, who are the prey
Of long-protracted hope and dull delay:
'Mid plans of bliss the heavy hours pass on,
Till love is withered, and till joy is gone.
This gentle flame two youthful hearts possess'd,
The sweet disturber of unenvied rest;
The prudent Dinah was the maid beloved,
And the kind Rupert was the swain approved:
A wealthy Aunt her gentle niece sustain'd,
He, with a father, at his desk remain'd;
The youthful couple, to their vows sincere,
Thus loved expectant; year succeeding year,
With pleasant views and hopes, but not a prospect near.
Rupert some comfort in his station saw,
But the poor virgin lived in dread and awe;
Upon her anxious looks the widow smiled,
And bade her wait, "for she was yet a child."
She for her neighbour had a due respect,
Nor would his son encourage or reject;
And thus the pair, with expectation vain,
Beheld the seasons change and change again;
Meantime the nymph her tender tales perused,
Where cruel aunts impatient girls refused:
While hers, though teasing, boasted to be kind,
And she, resenting, to be all resign'd.
The dame was sick, and when the youth applied
For her consent, she groan'd, and cough'd, and cried,
Talk'd of departing, and again her breath
Drew hard, and cough'd, and talk'd again of death:
"Here may you live, my Dinah! here the boy
And you together my estate enjoy:"
Thus to the lovers was her mind expressed,
Till they forbore to urge the fond request.
Servant, and nurse, and comforter, and friend,
Dinah had still some duty to attend;
But yet their walk, when Rupert's evening call
Obtain'd an hour, made sweet amends for all;
So long they now each other's thoughts had known,
That nothing seem'd exclusively their own:
But with the common wish, the mutual fear,
They now had travelled to their thirtieth year.
At length a prospect open'd—but alas!
Long time must yet, before the union, pass.
Rupert was call'd, in other clime, t'increase
Another's wealth, and toil for future peace.
Loth were the lovers; but the aunt declared

'Twas fortune's call, and they must be prepar'd:
"You now are young, and for this brief delay,
And Dinah's care, what I bequeath will pay;
All will be yours; nay, love, suppress that sigh;
The kind must suffer, and the best must die:"
Then came the cough, and strong the signs it gave
Of holding long contention with the grave.
The lovers parted with a gloomy view,
And little comfort, but that both were true;
He for uncertain duties doom'd to steer,
While hers remain'd too certain and severe.
Letters arrived, and Rupert fairly told
"His cares were many, and his hopes were cold:
The view more clouded, that was never fair,
And love alone preserved him from despair;"
In other letters brighter hopes he drew,
"His friends were kind, and he believed them true."
When the sage widow Dinah's grief descried,
She wonder'd much why one so happy sigh'd:
Then bade her see how her poor aunt sustain'd
The ills of life, nor murmur'd nor complain'd.
To vary pleasures, from the lady's chest
Were drawn the pearly string and tabby vest;
Beads, jewels, laces, all their value shown,
With the kind notice—"They will be your own."
This hope, these comforts, cherish'd day by day,
To Dinah's bosom made a gradual way;
Till love of treasure had as large a part,
As love of Rupert, in the virgin's heart.
Whether it be that tender passions fail,
From their own nature, while the strong prevail;
Or whether av'rice, like the poison-tree,
Kills all beside it, and alone will be;
Whatever cause prevail'd, the pleasure grew
In Dinah's soul,—she loved the hoards to view;
With lively joy those comforts she survey'd,
And love grew languid in the careful maid.
Now the grave niece partook the widow's cares,
Look'd to the great, and ruled the small affairs;
Saw clean'd the plate, arranged the china-show,
And felt her passion for a shilling grow:
Th' indulgent aunt increased the maid's delight,
By placing tokens of her wealth in sight;
She loved the value of her bonds to tell,
And spake of stocks, and how they rose and fell.
This passion grew, and gain'd at length such sway,
That other passions shrank to make it way;
Romantic notions now the heart forsook,

She read but seldom, and she changed her book;
And for the verses she was wont to send,
Short was her prose, and she was Rupert's friend.
Seldom she wrote, and then the widow's cough,
And constant call, excused her breaking off;
Who now oppressed, no longer took the air,
But sat and dozed upon an easy chair.
The cautious doctor saw the case was clear,
But judged it best to have companions near;
They came, they reason'd, they prescribed,—at last,
Like honest men, they said their hopes were past;
Then came a priest—'tis comfort to reflect
When all is over, there was no neglect:
And all was over.—By her husband's bones,
The widow rests beneath the sculptured stones,
That yet record their fondness and their fame,
While all they left the virgin's care became;
Stock, bonds, and buildings; it disturb'd her rest,
To think what load of troubles she possessed:
Yet, if a trouble, she resolved to take
Th' important duty for the donor's sake;
She too was heiress to the widow's taste,
Her love of hoarding, and her dread of waste.
Sometimes the past would on her mind intrude,
And then a conflict full of care ensued;
The thoughts of Rupert on her mind would press,
His worth she knew, but doubted his success:
Of old she saw him heedless; what the boy
Forebore to save, the man would not enjoy;
Oft had he lost the chance that care would seize,
Willing to live, but more to live at ease:
Yet could she not a broken vow defend,
And Heav'n, perhaps, might yet enrich her friend.
Month after month was pass'd, and all were spent
In quiet comfort, and in rich content;
Miseries there were, and woes the world around,
But these had not her pleasant dwelling found;
She knew that mothers grieved, and widows wept,
And she was sorry, said her prayers, and slept:
Thus passed the seasons, and to Dinah's board
Gave what the seasons to the rich afford;
For she indulged, nor was her heart so small,
That one strong passion should engross it all.
A love of splendour now with av'rice strove,
And oft appeared to be the stronger love:
A secret pleasure fill'd the Widow's breast,
When she reflected on the hoards possess'd;
But livelier joy inspired th' ambitious Maid,

When she the purchase of those hoards display'd:
In small but splendid room she loved to see
That all was placed in view and harmony.
There, as with eager glance she look'd around,
She much delight in every object found.
While books devout were near her—to destroy,
Should it arise, an overflow of joy.
Within that fair apartment guests might see
The comforts cull'd for wealth by vanity:
Around the room an Indian paper blazed,
With lively tint and figures boldly raised;
Silky and soft upon the floor below,
Th' elastic carpet rose with crimson glow;
All things around implied both cost and care,
What met the eye was elegant or rare:
Some curious trifles round the room were laid,
By hope presented to the wealthy Maid;
Within a costly case of varnish'd wood,
In level rows, her polish'd volumes stood;
Shown as a favour to a chosen few,
To prove what beauty for a book could do:
A silver urn with curious work was fraught;
A silver lamp from Grecian pattern wrought:
Above her head, all gorgeous to behold,
A time-piece stood on feet of burnish'd gold;
A stag's-head crest adorn'd the pictured case,
Through the pure crystal shone the enamel'd face;
And while on brilliants moved the hands of steel,
It click'd from pray'r to pray'r, from meal to meal.
Here as the lady sat, a friendly pair
Stept in t'admire the view, and took their chair:
They then related how the young and gay
Were thoughtless wandering in the broad highway:
How tender damsels sail'd in tilted boats,
And laugh'd with wicked men in scarlet coats;
And how we live in such degen'rate times,
That men conceal their wants and show their crimes;
While vicious deeds are screen'd by fashion's name,
And what was once our pride is now our shame.
Dinah was musing, as her friends discoursed,
When these last words a sudden entrance forced
Upon her mind, and what was once her pride
And now her shame, some painful views supplied;
Thoughts of the past within her bosom press'd,
And there a change was felt, and was confess'd:
While thus the Virgin strove with secret pain,
Her mind was wandering o'er the troubled main;
Still she was silent, nothing seem'd to see,

But sat and sigh'd in pensive reverie.
The friends prepared new subjects to begin,
When tall Susannah, maiden starch, stalk'd in;
Not in her ancient mode, sedate and slow,
As when she came, the mind she knew, to know;
Nor as, when list'ning half an hour before,
She twice or thrice tapp'd gently at the door;
But all decorum cast in wrath aside,
"I think the devil's in the man!" she cried;
"A huge tall sailor, with his tawny cheek
And pitted face, will with my lady speak;
He grinn'd an ugly smile, and said he knew,
Please you, my lady, 't would be joy to you:
What must I answer?"—Trembling and distress'd
Sank the pale Dinah by her fears oppress'd;
When thus alarm'd and brooking no delay,
Swift to her room the stranger made his way.
"Revive, my love!" said he, "I've done thee harm;
Give me thy pardon," and he look'd alarm:
Meantime the prudent Dinah had contrived
Her soul to question, and she then revived.
"See! my good friend," and then she raised her head,
"The bloom of life, the strength of youth is fled;
Living we die; to us the world is dead;
We parted bless'd with health, and I am now
Age-struck and feeble—so I find art thou;
Thine eye is sunken, furrow'd is thy face,
And downward look'st thou—so we run our race;
And happier they whose race is nearly run,
Their troubles over, and their duties done."
"True, lady, true—we are not girl and boy,
But time has left us something to enjoy."
"What! hast thou learn'd my fortune?—yes, I live
To feel how poor the comforts wealth can give:
Thou too perhaps art wealthy; but our fate
Still mocks our wishes, wealth is come too late."
"To me nor late nor early; I am come
Poor as I left thee to my native home:
Nor yet," said Rupert, "will I grieve; 'tis mine
To share thy comforts, and the glory thine:
For thou wilt gladly take that generous part
That both exalts and gratifies the heart;
While mine rejoices"—"Heavens!" return'd the maid,
"This talk to one so wither'd and decay'd?
No! all my care is now to fit my mind
For other spousal, and to die resigned:
As friend and neighbour, I shall hope to see
These noble views, this pious love in thee;

That we together may the change await,
Guides and spectators in each other's fate;
When fellow pilgrims, we shall daily crave
The mutual prayer that arms us for the grave."
Half angry, half in doubt, the lover gazed
On the meek maiden, by her speech amazed;
"Dinah," said he, "dost thou respect thy vows?
What spousal mean'st thou?—thou art Rupert's spouse;
That chance is mine to take, and thine to give:
But, trifling this, if we together live:
Can I believe, that, after all the past,
Our vows, our loves, thou wilt be false at last?
Something thou hast—I know not what—in view;
I find thee pious—let me find thee true."
"Ah! cruel this; but do, my friend, depart;
And to its feelings leave my wounded heart."
"Nay, speak at once; and Dinah, let me know,
Mean'st thou to take me, now I'm wreck'd, in tow?
Be fair; nor longer keep me in the dark;
Am I forsaken for a trimmer spark?
Heaven's spouse thou art not; nor can I believe
That God accepts her who will man deceive:
True I am shatter'd, I have service seen,
And service done, and have in trouble been;
My cheek (it shames me not) has lost its red,
And the brown buff is o'er my features spread:
Perchance my speech is rude; for I among
Th' untamed have been, in temper and in tongue;
Have been trepann'd, have lived in toil and care,
And wrought for wealth I was not doom'd to share;
It touch'd me deeply, for I felt a pride
In gaining riches for my destin'd bride:
Speak then my fate; for these my sorrows past,
Time lost, youth fled, hope wearied, and at last
This doubt of thee—a childish thing to tell,
But certain truth—my very throat they swell:
They stop the breath, and but for shame could I
Give way to weakness, and with passion cry;
These are unmanly struggles, but I feel
This hour must end them, and perhaps will heal."
Here Dinah sigh'd, as if afraid to speak—
And then repeated—"They were frail and weak:
His soul she lov'd, and hoped he had the grace
To fix his thoughts upon a better place."
She ceased;—with steady glance, as if to see
The very root of this hypocrisy,—
He her small fingers moulded in his hard
And bronzed broad hand; then told her his regard,

His best respect were gone, but love had still
Hold in his heart, and govern'd yet the will—
Or he would curse her:—saying this, he threw
The hand in scorn away, and bade adieu
To every lingering hope, with every care in view.
Proud and indignant, suffering, sick, and poor,
He grieved unseen: and spoke of love no more—
Till all he felt in indignation died,
As hers had sunk in avarice and pride.
In health declining, as in mind distressed,
To some in power his troubles he confess'd,
And shares a parish-gift; at prayers he sees
The pious Dinah dropp'd upon her knees;
Thence as she walks the street with stately air
As chance directs, oft meet the parted pair;
When he, with thickset coat of badgeman's blue,
Moves near her shaded silk of changeful hue;
When his thin locks of gray approach her braid,
A costly purchase made in Beauty's aid;
When his frank air, and his unstudied pace,
Are seen with her soft manner, air, and grace;
And his plain artless look with her sharp meaning face;
It might some wonder in a stranger move,
How these together could have talk'd of love.
Behold them now!—see there a tradesman stands,
And humbly hearkens to some fresh commands;
He moves to speak, she interrupts him—"Stay,"
Her air expresses,—"Hark to what I say!"
Ten paces off, poor Rupert on a seat
Has taken refuge from the noon-day heat,
His eyes on her intent, as if to find
What were the movements of that subtle mind:
How still!—how earnest is he!—it appears
His thoughts are wand'ring through his earlier years;
Through years of fruitless labour, to the day
When all his earthly prospects died away:
"Had I," he thinks, "been wealthier of the two,
Would she have found me so unkind, untrue?
Or knows not man when poor, what man when rich will do?
Yes, yes! I feel that I had faithful proved,
And should have soothed and raised her, bless'd and loved."
But Dinah moves—she had observed before
The pensive Rupert at an humble door:
Some thoughts of pity raised by his distress,
Some feeling touch of ancient tenderness;
Religion, duty urged the maid to speak,
In terms of kindness to a man so weak:
But pride forbade, and to return would prove

She felt the shame of his neglected love;
Nor wrapp'd in silence could she pass, afraid
Each eye should see her, and each heart upbraid;
One way remain'd—the way the Levite took,
Who without mercy could on misery look;
(A way perceiv'd by craft, approved by pride),
She cross'd and pass'd him on the other side.

TALE V

THE PATRON

*It were all one,
That I should love a bright peculiar star,
And think to wed it; she is so much above me:
In her bright radiance and collateral heat
Must I be comforted, not in her sphere.*
SHAKESPEARE, All's Well that Ends Well.

*Poor wretches, that depend
On greatness' favours, dream as I have done,
Wake and find nothing.*
Cymbeline.

*And since—
Th' affliction of my mind amends, with which
I fear a madness held me.*
Tempest.

A Borough-Bailiff, who to law was train'd,
A wife and sons in decent state maintain'd,
He had his way in life's rough ocean steer'd
And many a rock and coast of danger clear'd;
He saw where others fail'd, and care had he,
Others in him should not such feelings see:
His sons in various busy states were placed,
And all began the sweets of gain to taste,
Save John, the younger, who, of sprightly parts,
Felt not a love for money-making arts:
In childhood feeble, he, for country air,
Had long resided with a rustic pair;
All round whose room were doleful ballads, songs,
Of lovers' sufferings and of ladies' wrongs;
Of peevish ghosts who came at dark midnight,
For breach of promise, guilty men to fright;

Love, marriage, murder, were the themes, with these,
All that on idle, ardent spirits seize;
Robbers at land and pirates on the main,
Enchanters foil'd, spells broken, giants slain;
Legends of love, with tales of halls and bowers,
Choice of rare songs, and garlands of choice flowers,
And all the hungry mind without a choice devours.
From village-children kept apart by pride,
With such enjoyments, and without a guide,
Inspired by feelings all such works infused,
John snatch'd a pen, and wrote as he perused:
With the like fancy he could make his knight
Slay half a host, and put the rest to flight;
With the like knowledge he could make him ride
From isle to isle at Parthenissa's side;
And with a heart yet free, no busy brain
Form'd wilder notions of delight and pain,
The raptures smiles create, the anguish of disdain.
Such were the fruits of John's poetic toil—
Weeds, but still proofs of vigour in the soil:
He nothing purposed but with vast delight,
Let Fancy loose, and wonder'd at her flight:
His notions of poetic worth were high,
And of his own still-hoarded poetry;—
These to his father's house he bore with pride,
A miser's treasure, in his room to hide;
Till spurr'd by glory, to a reading friend,
He kindly show'd the sonnets he had penn'd:
With erring judgment, though with heart sincere,
That friend exclaim'd, "These beauties must appear.'
In magazines they claim'd their share of fame,
Though undistinguish'd by their author's name;
And with delight the young enthusiast found
The muse of Marcus with applauses crown'd.
This heard the father, and with some alarm;
"The boy," said he, "will neither trade nor farm,
He for both law and physic is unfit,
Wit he may have, but cannot live on wit:
Let him his talents then to learning give,
Where verse is honour'd, and where poets live."
John kept his terms at college unreproved,
Took his degree, and left the life he loved;
Not yet ordain'd, his leisure he employ'd
In the light labours he so much enjoy'd;
His favourite notions and his daring views
Were cherish'd still, and he adored the Muse.
"A little time, and he should burst to light,
And admiration of the world excite;

And every friend, now cool and apt to blame
His fond pursuit, would wonder at his fame."
When led by fancy, and from view retired,
He call'd before him all his heart desired;
"Fame shall be mine, then wealth shall I possess,
And beauty next an ardent lover bless;
For me the maid shall leave her nobler state,
Happy to raise and share her poet's fate."
He saw each day his father's frugal board,
With simple fare by cautious prudence stored:
Where each indulgence was foreweigh'd with care,
And the grand maxims were to save and spare:
Yet in his walks, his closet, and his bed,
All frugal cares and prudent counsels fled;
And bounteous Fancy, for his glowing mind,
Wrought various scenes, and all of glorious kind:
Slaves of the ring and lamp! what need of you,
When Fancy's self such magic deeds can do?
Though rapt in visions of no vulgar kind,
To common subjects stoop'd our poet's mind;
And oft when wearied with more ardent flight,
He felt a spur satiric song to write;
A rival burgess his bold Muse attack'd,
And whipp'd severely for a well known fact;
For while he seem'd to all demure and shy,
Our poet gazed at what was passing by;
And e'en his father smiled when playful wit,
From his young bard, some haughty object hit.
From ancient times, the borough where they dwelt
Had mighty contests at elections felt;
Sir Godfrey Ball, 'tis true, had held in pay
Electors many for the trying day;
But in such golden chains to bind them all
Required too much for e'en Sir Godfrey Ball.
A member died, and to supply his place
Two heroes enter'd for th' important race;
Sir Godfrey's friend and Earl Fitzdonnel's son,
Lord Frederick Darner, both prepared to run;
And partial numbers saw with vast delight
Their good young lord oppose the proud old knight.
Our poet's father, at a first request,
Gave the young lord his vote and interest;
And what he could our poet, for he stung
The foe by verse satiric, said and sung.
Lord Frederick heard of all this youthful zeal,
And felt as lords upon a canvass feel;
He read the satire, and he saw the use
That such cool insult, and such keen abuse,

Might on the wavering minds of voting men produce;
Then too his praises were in contrast seen,
"A lord as noble as the knight was mean."
"I much rejoice," he cried, "such worth to find;
To this the world must be no longer blind:
His glory will descend from sire to son,
The Burns of English race, the happier Chatterton."
Our poet's mind now hurried and elate,
Alarm'd the anxious parent for his fate;
Who saw with sorrow, should their friend succeed,
That much discretion would the poet need.
Their friends succeeded, and repaid the zeal
The Poet felt, and made opposers feel,
By praise (from lords how soothing and how sweet!)
An invitation to his noble seat.
The father ponder'd, doubtful if the brain
Of his proud boy such honour could sustain;
Pleased with the favours offer'd to a son,
But seeing dangers few so ardent shun.
Thus when they parted, to the youthful breast
The father's fears were by his love impress'd:
"There will you find, my son, the courteous ease
That must subdue the soul it means to please;
That soft attention which e'en beauty pays
To wake our passions, or provoke our praise;
There all the eye beholds will give delight,
Where every sense is flatter'd like the sight;
This is your peril; can you from such scene
Of splendour part, and feel your mind serene,
And in the father's humble state resume
The frugal diet and the narrow room?"
To this the youth with cheerful heart replied,
Pleased with the trial, but as yet untried;
And while professing patience, should he fail,
He suffered hope o'er reason to prevail.
Impatient, by the morning mail conveyed,
The happy guest his promised visit paid;
And now arriving at the Hall, he tried
For air composed, serene and satisfied;
As he had practised in his room alone,
And there acquired a free and easy tone:
There he had said, "Whatever the degree
A man obtains, what more than man is he?"
And when arrived—"This room is but a room;
Can aught we see the steady soul o'ercome?
Let me in all a manly firmness show,
Upheld by talents, and their value know."
This reason urged; but it surpassed his skill

To be in act as manly as in will:
When he his Lordship and the Lady saw
Brave as he was, he felt oppress'd with awe;
And spite of verse, that so much praise had won,
The poet found he was the Bailiff's son.
But dinner came, and the succeeding hours
Fix'd his weak nerves, and raised his failing powers;
Praised and assured, he ventured once or twice
On some remark, and bravely broke the ice;
So that, at night, reflecting on his words,
He found, in time, he might converse with lords.
Now was the Sister of his Patron seen—
A lovely creature, with majestic mien;
Who, softly smiling, while she looked so fair,
Praised the young poet with such friendly air;
Such winning frankness in her looks express'd,
And such attention to her brother's guest;
That so much beauty, join'd with speech so kind,
Raised strong emotions in the poet's mind;
Till reason fail'd his bosom to defend,
From the sweet power of this enchanting friend.—
Rash boy! what hope thy frantic mind invades?
What love confuses, and what pride persuades?
Awake to truth! shouldst thou deluded feed
On hopes so groundless, thou art mad indeed.
What say'st thou, wise one?—"that all powerful Love
Can fortune's strong impediments remove;
Nor is it strange that worth should wed to worth,
The pride of genius with the pride of birth."
While thou art dreaming thus, the Beauty spies
Love in thy tremor, passion in thine eyes;
And with th' amusement pleased, of conquest vain,
She seeks her pleasure, careless of thy pain;
She gives thee praise to humble and confound,
Smiles to ensnare, and flatters thee to wound.
Why has she said that in the lowest state
The noble mind ensures a noble fate?
And why thy daring mind to glory call?—
That thou may'st dare and suffer, soar and fall.
Beauties are tyrants, and if they can reign,
They have no feeling for their subjects' pain:
Their victim's anguish gives their charms applause,
And their chief glory is the woe they cause:
Something of this was felt, in spite of love,
Which hope, in spite of reason, would remove.
Thus lived our youth, with conversation, books,
And Lady Emma's soul-subduing looks:
Lost in delight, astonish'd at his lot,

All prudence banish'd, all advice forgot—
Hopes, fears, and every thought, were fix'd upon the spot.
'Twas autumn yet, and many a day must frown
On Brandon-Hall, ere went my Lord to town;
Meantime the father, who had heard his boy
Lived in a round of luxury and joy,
And justly thinking that the youth was one
Who, meeting danger, was unskill'd to shun;
Knowing his temper, virtue, spirit, zeal,
How prone to hope and trust, believe and feel;
These on the parent's soul their weight impress'd,
And thus he wrote the counsels of his breast:—
"John, thou'rt a genius; thou hast some pretence,
I think, to wit,—but hast thou sterling sense?
That which, like gold, may through the world go forth,
And always pass for what 'tis truly worth:
Whereas this genius, like a bill must take
Only the value our opinions make.
"Men famed for wit, of dangerous talents vain.
Treat those of common parts with proud disdain;
The powers that wisdom would, improving, hide,
They blaze abroad with inconsid'rate pride;
While yet but mere probationers for fame,
They seize the honour they should then disclaim;
Honour so hurried to the light must fade,
The lasting laurels flourish in the shade.
"Genius is jealous: I have heard of some
Who, if unnoticed, grew perversely dumb;
Nay, different talents would their envy raise;
Poets have sicken'd at a dancer's praise;
And one, the happiest writer of his time,
Grew pale at hearing Reynolds was sublime;
That Rutland's Duchess wore a heavenly smile—
'And I,' said he, 'neglected all the while!'
"A waspish tribe are these, on gilded wings,
Humming their lays, and brandishing their stings:
And thus they move their friends and foes among,
Prepared for soothing or satiric song.
"Hear me, my Boy; thou hast a virtuous mind—
But be thy virtues of the sober kind;
Be not a Quixote, ever up in arms
To give the guilty and the great alarms:
If never heeded, thy attack is vain;
And if they heed thee, they'll attack again;
Then too in striking at that heedless rate,
Thou in an instant may'st decide thy fate.
"Leave admonition—let the vicar give
Rules how the nobles of his flock should live;

Nor take that simple fancy to thy brain,
That thou canst cure the wicked and the vain.
"Our Pope, they say, once entertain'd the whim,
Who fear'd not God should be afraid of him;
But grant they fear'd him, was it further said,
That he reform'd the hearts he made afraid?
Did Chartres mend? Ward, Waters, and a score
Of flagrant felons, with his floggings sore?
Was Cibber silenced? No; with vigour blest,
And brazen front, half earnest, half in jest,
He dared the bard to battle, and was seen
In all his glory match'd with Pope and spleen;
Himself he stripp'd, the harder blow to hit,
Then boldly match'd his ribaldry with wit;
The poet's conquest truth and time proclaim,
But yet the battle hurt his peace and fame.
"Strive not too much for favour; seem at ease.
And rather please thyself, than bent to please:
Upon thy lord with decent care attend,
But not too near; thou canst not be a friend;
And favourite be not, 'tis a dangerous post—
Is gain'd by labour, and by fortune lost:
Talents like thine may make a man approved,
But other talents trusted and beloved.
Look round, my son, and thou wilt early see
The kind of man thou art not form'd to be.
"The real favourites of the great are they
Who to their views and wants attention pay,
And pay it ever; who, with all their skill,
Dive to the heart, and learn the secret will;
If that be vicious, soon can they provide
The favourite ill, and o'er the soul preside,
For vice is weakness, and the artful know
Their power increases as the passions grow;
If indolent the pupil, hard their task;
Such minds will ever for amusement ask;
And great the labour! for a man to choose
Objects for one whom nothing can amuse;
For ere those objects can the soul delight,
They must to joy the soul herself excite;
Therefore it is, this patient, watchful kind
With gentle friction stir the drowsy mind:
Fix'd on their end, with caution they proceed,
And sometimes give, and sometimes take the lead;
Will now a hint convey, and then retire,
And let the spark awake the lingering fire;
Or seek new joys, and livelier pleasures bring
To give the jaded sense a quick'ning spring.

"These arts, indeed, my son must not pursue;
Nor must he quarrel with the tribe that do:
It is not safe another's crimes to know,
Nor is it wise our proper worth to show:—
'My lord,' you say, 'engaged me for that worth;'—
True, and preserve it ready to come forth:
If questioned, fairly answer,—and that done,
Shrink back, be silent, and thy father's son;
For they who doubt thy talents scorn thy boast,
But they who grant them will dislike thee most:
Observe the prudent; they in silence sit,
Display no learning, and affect no wit;
They hazard nothing, nothing they assume,
But know the useful art of acting dumb.
Yet to their eyes each varying look appears,
And every word finds entrance at their ears.
"Thou art Religion's advocate—take heed,
Hurt not the cause, thy pleasure 'tis to plead;
With wine before thee, and with wits beside,
Do not in strength of reasoning powers confide;
What seems to thee convincing, certain, plain,
They will deny, and dare thee to maintain;
And thus will triumph o'er thy eager youth,
While thou wilt grieve for so disgracing truth.
With pain I've seen, these wrangling wits among,
Faith's weak defenders, passionate and young;
Weak thou art not, yet not enough on guard,
Where wit and humour keep their watch and ward:
Men gay and noisy will o'erwhelm thy sense,
Then loudly laugh at truth's and thy expense;
While the kind ladies will do all they can
To check their mirth, and cry, 'The good young man!'
"Prudence, my Boy, forbids thee to commend
The cause or party of thy noble friend;
What are his praises worth, who must be known,
To take a Patron's maxims for his own?
When ladies sing, or in thy presence play,
Do not, dear John, in rapture melt away;
'Tis not thy part, there will be list'ners round,
To cry Divine! and dote upon the sound;
Remember, too, that though the poor have ears,
They take not in the music of the spheres;
They must not feel the warble and the thrill,
Or be dissolved in ecstasy at will;
Beside, 'tis freedom in a youth like thee
To drop his awe, and deal in ecstasy!
"In silent ease, at least in silence, dine,
Nor one opinion start of food or wine:

Thou knowest that all the science thou can boast,
Is of thy father's simple boil'd or roast;
Nor always these; he sometimes saved his cash,
By interlinear days of frugal hash:
Wine hadst thou seldom; wilt thou be so vain
As to decide on claret or champagne?
Dost thou from me derive this taste sublime,
Who order port the dozen at a time?
When (every glass held precious in our eyes)
We judged the value by the bottle's size:
Then never merit for thy praise assume,
Its worth well knows each servant in the room.
"Hard, Boy, thy task, to steer thy way among
That servile, supple, shrewd, insidious throng;
Who look upon thee as of doubtful race,
An interloper, one who wants a place:
Freedom with these, let thy free soul condemn,
Nor with thy heart's concerns associate them.
"Of all be cautious—but be most afraid
Of the pale charms that grace My Lady's Maid;
Of those sweet dimples, of that fraudful eye,
The frequent glance designed for thee to spy;
The soft bewitching look, the fond bewailing sigh:
Let others frown and envy; she the while
(Insidious syren!) will demurely smile;
And for her gentle purpose, every day
Inquire thy wants, and meet thee in thy way;
She has her blandishments, and, though so weak,
Her person pleases, and her actions speak:
At first her folly may her aim defeat;
But kindness shown, at length will kindness meet:
Have some offended? them will she disdain,
And, for thy sake, contempt and pity feign;
She hates the vulgar, she admires to look
On woods and groves, and dotes upon a book;
Let her once see thee on her features dwell,
And hear one sigh, then liberty farewell.
"But, John, remember we cannot maintain
A poor, proud girl, extravagant and vain.
"Doubt much of friendship: shouldst thou find a friend
Pleased to advise thee, anxious to commend;
Should he the praises he has heard report,
And confidence (in thee confiding) court;
Much of neglected Patrons should he say,
And then exclaim—'How long must merit stay!'
Then show how high thy modest hopes may stretch,
And point to stations far beyond thy reach;
Let such designer, by thy conduct, see

(Civil and cool) he makes no dupe of thee;
And he will quit thee, as a man too wise
For him to ruin first, and then despise.
"Such are thy dangers:—yet, if thou canst steer
Past all the perils, all the quicksands clear,
Then may'st thou profit; but if storms prevail,
If foes beset thee, if thy spirits fail,—
No more of winds or waters be the sport,
But in thy father's mansion, find a port."
Our poet read.—"It is in truth," said he,
"Correct in part, but what is this to me?
I love a foolish Abigail! in base
And sordid office! fear not such disgrace:
Am I so blind?" "Or thou wouldst surely see
That lady's fall, if she should stoop to thee!"
"The cases differ." "True! for what surprise
Could from thy marriage with the maid arise?
But through the island would the shame be spread,
Should the fair mistress deign with thee to wed."
John saw not this; and many a week had pass'd,
While the vain beauty held her victim fast;
The Noble Friend still condescension show'd,
And, as before, with praises overflowed;
But his grave Lady took a silent view
Of all that pass'd, and smiling, pitied too.
Cold grew the foggy morn, the day was brief,
Loose on the cherry hung the crimson leaf;
The dew dwelt ever on the herb; the woods
Roar'd with strong blasts, with mighty showers the floods:
All green was vanish'd, save of pine and yew,
That still displayed their melancholy hue;
Save the green holly with its berries red,
And the green moss that o'er the gravel spread.
To public views my Lord must soon attend;
And soon the ladies—would they leave their friend?
The time was fix'd—approach'd—was near—was come;
The trying time that fill'd his soul with gloom:
Thoughtful our poet in the morning rose,
And cried, "One hour my fortune will disclose;
Terrific hour! from thee have I to date
Life's loftier views, or my degraded state;
For now to be what I have been before
Is so to fall, that I can rise no more."
The morning meal was past; and all around
The mansion rang with each discordant sound;
Haste was in every foot, and every look
The trav'ller's joy for London-journey spoke:
Not so our youth; whose feelings at the noise

Of preparation, had no touch of joys:
He pensive stood, and saw each carriage drawn,
With lackeys mounted, ready on the lawn:
The ladies came; and John in terror threw
One painful glance, and then his eyes withdrew;
Not with such speed, but he in other eyes
With anguish read—"I pity, but despise—
Unhappy boy!—presumptuous scribbler!—you,
To dream such dreams!—be sober, and adieu!"
Then came the Noble Friend—"And will my Lord
Vouchsafe no comfort; drop no soothing word?
Yes, he must speak;" he speaks, "My good young friend,
You know my views; upon my care depend;
My hearty thanks to your good father pay,
And be a student.—Harry, drive away."
Stillness reign'd all around; of late so full
The busy scene, deserted now and dull:
Stern is his nature who forbears to feel
Gloom o'er his spirits on such trials steal;
Most keenly felt our poet as he went
From room to room without a fix'd intent;
"And here," he thought, "I was caress'd; admired
Were here my songs; she smiled, and I aspired.
The change how grievous!" As he mused, a dame
Busy and peevish to her duties came;
Aside the tables and the chairs she drew,
And sang and mutter'd in the poet's view:—
"This was her fortune; here they leave the poor;
Enjoy themselves, and think of us no more;
I had a promise"—here his pride and shame
Urged him to fly from this familiar dame;
He gave one farewell look, and by a coach
Reach'd his own mansion at the night's approach.
His father met him with an anxious air,
Heard his sad tale, and check'd what seem'd despair:
Hope was in him corrected, but alive;
My lord would something for a friend contrive;
His word was pledged: our hero's feverish mind
Admitted this, and half his grief resigned:
But, when three months had fled, and every day
Drew from the sickening hopes their strength away,
The youth became abstracted, pensive, dull;
He utter'd nothing, though his heart was full;
Teased by inquiring words and anxious looks,
And all forgetful of his Muse and books;
Awake he mourn'd, but in his sleep perceived
A lovely vision that his pain relieved:—
His soul, transported, hail'd the happy seat,

Where once his pleasure was so pure and sweet;
Where joys departed came in blissful view
Till reason waked, and not a joy he knew.
Questions now vex'd his spirit, most from those
Who are call'd friends, because they are not foes:
"John?" they would say; he, starting, turn'd around,
"John!" there was something shocking in the sound:
Ill brook'd he then the pert familiar phrase,
The untaught freedom and th' inquiring gaze;
Much was his temper touch'd, his spleen provoked,
When ask'd how ladies talk'd, or walk'd, or look'd?
"What said my Lord of politics! how spent
He there his time? and was he glad he went?"
At length a letter came, both cool and brief,
But still it gave the burden'd heart relief:
Though not inspired by lofty hopes, the youth
Placed much reliance on Lord Frederick's truth;
Summon'd to town, he thought the visit one
Where something fair and friendly would be done;
Although he judged not, as before his fall,
When all was love and promise at the hall.
Arrived in town, he early sought to know
The fate such dubious friendship would bestow;
At a tall building trembling he appear'd,
And his low rap was indistinctly heard;
A well-known servant came—"Awhile," said he,
"Be pleased to wait; my Lord has company."
Alone our hero sat; the news in hand,
Which though he read, he could not understand:
Cold was the day; in days so cold as these
There needs a fire, where minds and bodies freeze.
The vast and echoing room, the polish'd grate,
The crimson chairs, the sideboard with its plate;
The splendid sofa, which, though made for rest,
He then had thought it freedom to have press'd;
The shining tables, curiously inlaid,
Were all in comfortless proud style display'd;
And to the troubled feelings terror gave,
That made the once-dear friend the sick'ning slave.
"Was he forgotten?" Thrice upon his ear
Struck the loud clock, yet no relief was near:
Each rattling carriage, and each thundering stroke
On the loud door, the dream of fancy broke;
Oft as a servant chanced the way to come,
"Brings he a message?" no! he passed the room.'
At length 'tis certain; "Sir, you will attend
At twelve on Thursday!" Thus the day had end.
Vex'd by these tedious hours of needless pain,

John left the noble mansion with disdain;
For there was something in that still, cold place,
That seemed to threaten and portend disgrace.
Punctual again the modest rap declared
The youth attended; then was all prepared:
For the same servant, by his lord's command,
A paper offer'd to his trembling hand:
"No more!" he cried: "disdains he to afford
One kind expression, one consoling word?"
With troubled spirit he began to read
That "In the Church my lord could not succeed;"
Who had "to peers of either kind applied,
And was with dignity and grace denied;
While his own livings were by men possess'd,
Not likely in their chancels yet to rest;
And therefore, all things weigh'd (as he my lord,
Had done maturely, and he pledged his word),
Wisdom it seem'd for John to turn his view
To busier scenes, and bid the Church adieu!"
Here grieved the youth: he felt his father's pride
Must with his own be shocked and mortified;
But, when he found his future comforts placed
Where he, alas! conceived himself disgraced—
In some appointment on the London quays,
He bade farewell to honour and to ease;
His spirit fell, and from that hour assured
How vain his dreams, he suffer'd and was cured.
Our Poet hurried on, with wish to fly
From all mankind, to be conceal'd, and die.
Alas! what hopes, what high romantic views
Did that one visit to the soul infuse,
Which cherished with such love, 'twas worse than death to lose.
Still he would strive, though painful was the strife,
To walk in this appointed road of life;
On these low duties duteous he would wait,
And patient bear the anguish of his fate.
Thanks to the Patron, but of coldest kind,
Express'd the sadness of the Poet's mind;
Whose heavy hours were pass'd with busy men,
In the dull practice of th' official pen;
Who to superiors must in time impart;
(The custom this) his progress in their art:
But so had grief on his perception wrought,
That all unheeded were the duties taught;
No answers gave he when his trial came,
Silent he stood, but suffering without shame;
And they observed that words severe or kind
Made no impression on his wounded mind:

For all perceived from whence his failure rose,
Some grief, whose cause he deign'd not to disclose.
A soul averse from scenes and works so new,
Fear ever shrinking from the vulgar crew;
Distaste for each mechanic law and rule.
Thoughts of past honour and a patron cool;
A grieving parent, and a feeling mind,
Timid and ardent, tender and refined:
These all with mighty force the youth assail'd,
Till his soul fainted, and his reason fail'd:
When this was known, and some debate arose,
How they who saw it should the fact disclose,
He found their purpose, and in terror fled
From unseen kindness, with mistaken dread.
Meantime the parent was distress'd to find
His son no longer for a priest design'd;
But still he gain'd some comfort by the news
Of John's promotion, though with humbler views;
For he conceived that in no distant time
The boy would learn to scramble and to climb;
He little thought his son, his hope and pride,
His favour'd boy, was now a home denied:
Yes! while the parent was intent to trace
How men in office climb from place to place,
By day, by night, o'er moor and heath, and hill,
Roved the sad youth, with ever-changing will,
Of every aid bereft, exposed to every ill.
Thus as he sat, absorb'd in all the care
And all the hope that anxious fathers share,
A friend abruptly to his presence brought,
With trembling hand, the subject of his thought;
Whom he had found afflicted and subdued
By hunger, sorrow, cold, and solitude.
Silent he enter'd the forgotten room,
As ghostly forms may be conceived to come;
With sorrow-shrunken face and hair upright,
He look'd dismayed, neglect, despair, affright;
But dead to comfort, and on misery thrown,
His parent's loss he felt not, nor his own.
The good man, struck with horror, cried aloud,
And drew around him an astonish'd crowd;
The sons and servants to the father ran,
To share the feelings of the griev'd old man.
"Our brother, speak!" they all exclam'd "explain
Thy grief, thy suffering:"—but they ask'd in vain:
The friend told all he knew; and all was known,
Save the sad causes whence the ills had grown;
But, if obscure the cause, they all agreed

From rest and kindness must the cure proceed:
And he was cured; for quiet, love, and care,
Strove with the gloom, and broke on the despair;
Yet slow their progress, and as vapours move
Dense and reluctant from the wintry grove;
All is confusion, till the morning light
Gives the dim scene obscurely to the sight;
More and yet more defined the trunks appear,
Till the wild prospect stands distinct and clear;—
So the dark mind of our young poet grew
Clear and sedate; the dreadful mist withdrew;
And he resembled that bleak wintry scene,
Sad, though unclouded; dismal, though serene.
At times he utter'd, "What a dream was mine!
And what a prospect! glorious and divine!
Oh! in that room, and on that night to see
Those looks, that sweetness beaming all on me;
That syren-flattery—and to send me then,
Hope-raised and soften'd, to those heartless men;
That dark-brow'd stern Director, pleased to show
Knowledge of subjects I disdain'd to know;
Cold and controlling—but 'tis gone—'tis past;
I had my trial, and have peace at last."
Now grew the youth resigned: he bade adieu
To all that hope, to all that fancy drew;
His frame was languid, and the hectic heat
Flush'd on his pallid face, and countless beat
The quick'ning pulse, and faint the limbs that bore
The slender form that soon would breathe no more.
Then hope of holy kind the soul sustain'd,
And not a lingering thought of earth remain'd;
Now heaven had all, and he could smile at Love,
And the wild sallies of his youth reprove;
Then could he dwell upon the tempting days,
The proud aspiring thought, the partial praise;
Victorious now, his worldly views were closed,
And on the bed of death the youth reposed.
The father grieved—but as the poet's heart
Was all unfitted for his earthly part;
As, he conceived, some other haughty fair
Would, had he lived, have led him to despair;
As, with this fear, the silent grave shut out
All feverish hope, and all tormenting doubt;
While the strong faith the pious youth possess'd,
His hope enlivening gave his sorrows rest;
Soothed by these thoughts, he felt a mournful joy
For his aspiring and devoted boy.
Meantime the news through various channels spread,

The youth, once favour'd with such praise, was dead:
"Emma," the lady cried, "my words attend,
Your syren-smiles have kill'd your humble friend;
The hope you raised can now delude no more,
Nor charms, that once inspired, can now restore."
Faint was the flush of anger and of shame,
That o'er the cheek of conscious beauty came:
"You censure not," said she, "the sun's bright rays,
When fools imprudent dare the dangerous gaze;
And should a stripling look till he were blind,
You would not justly call the light unkind:
But is he dead? and am I to suppose
The power of poison in such looks as those?"
She spoke, and pointing to the mirror, cast
A pleased gay glance, and curtsied as she pass'd.
My Lord, to whom the poet's fate was told,
Was much affected, for a man so cold:
"Dead!" said his lordship, "run distracted, mad!
Upon my soul I'm sorry for the lad;
And now no doubt th' obliging world will say
That my harsh usage help'd him on his way:
What! I suppose, I should have nursed his muse,
And with champagne have brighten'd up his views;
Then had he made me famed my whole life long,
And stunn'd my ears with gratitude and song.
Still should the father bear that I regret
Our joint misfortune—Yes! I'll not forget."
Thus they:—the father to his grave convey'd
The son he loved, and his last duties paid.
"There lies my Boy," he cried, "of care bereft,
And heaven be praised, I've not a genius left:
No one among ye, sons! is doomed to live
On high-raised hopes of what the Great may give;
None, with exalted views and fortunes mean,
To die in anguish, or to live in spleen:
Your pious brother soon escaped the strife
Of such contention, but it cost his life;
You then, my sons, upon yourselves depend,
And in your own exertions find the friend."

TALE VI

THE FRANK COURTSHIP

Yes, faith, it is my cousin's duty to make a curtsy, and say, "Father, as it please you;" but for all that, cousin, let him be a handsome fellow, or else make another curtsy, and say, "Father, as it pleases me."

Grave Jonas Kindred, Sybil Kindred's sire,
Was six feet high, and look'd six inches higher;
Erect, morose, determined, solemn, slow,
Who knew the man could never cease to know:
His faithful spouse, when Jonas was not by,
Had a firm presence and a steady eye;
But with her husband dropp'd her look and tone,
And Jonas ruled unquestion'd and alone.
He read, and oft would quote the sacred words,
How pious husbands of their wives were lords;
Sarah called Abraham Lord! and who could be,
So Jonas thought, a greater man than he?
Himself he view'd with undisguised respect,
And never pardon'd freedom or neglect.
They had one daughter, and this favourite child
Had oft the father of his spleen beguiled;
Soothed by attention from her early years,
She gained all wishes by her smiles or tears;
But Sybil then was in that playful time,
When contradiction is not held a crime;
When parents yield their children idle praise
For faults corrected in their after days.
Peace in the sober house of Jonas dwelt,
Where each his duty and his station felt:
Yet not that peace some favour'd mortals find,
In equal views and harmony of mind;
Not the soft peace that blesses those who love,
Where all with one consent in union move;
But it was that which one superior will
Commands, by making all inferiors still;
Who bids all murmurs, all objections, cease,
And with imperious voice announces—Peace!
They were, to wit, a remnant of that crew,

Who, as their foes maintain, their Sovereign slew;
An independent race, precise, correct,
Who ever married in the kindred sect:
No son or daughter of their order wed
A friend to England's king who lost his head;
Cromwell was still their Saint, and when they met,
They mourn'd that Saints were not our rulers yet.
Fix'd were their habits; they arose betimes,
Then pray'd their hour, and sang their party-rhymes:
Their meals were plenteous, regular and plain;
The trade of Jonas brought him constant gain;
Vender of hops and malt, of coals and corn—
And, like his father, he was merchant born:
Neat was their house; each table, chair, and stool,
Stood in its place, or moving moved by rule;
No lively print or picture graced the room;
A plain brown paper lent its decent gloom;
But here the eye, in glancing round, survey'd
A small recess that seem'd for china made;
Such pleasing pictures seem'd this pencill'd ware,
That few would search for nobler objects there—
Yet, turn'd by chosen friends, and there appear'd
His stern, strong features, whom they all revered;
For there in lofty air was seen to stand
The bold Protector of the conquer'd land;
Drawn in that look with which he wept and swore,
Turn'd out the Members, and made fast the door,
Ridding the House of every knave and drone,
Forced, though it grieved his soul, to rule alone.
The stern still smile each friend approving gave,
Then turn'd the view, and all again were grave.
There stood a clock, though small the owner's need,
For habit told when all things should proceed;
Few their amusements, but when friends appear'd,
They with the world's distress their spirits cheer'd;
The nation's guilt, that would not long endure
The reign of men so modest and so pure:
Their town was large, and seldom pass'd a day
But some had fail'd, and others gone astray;
Clerks had absconded, wives eloped, girls flown
To Gretna-Green, or sons rebellious grown;
Quarrels and fires arose;—and it was plain
The times were bad; the Saints had ceased to reign!
A few yet lived, to languish and to mourn
For good old manners never to return.
Jonas had sisters, and of these was one
Who lost a husband and an only son:
Twelve months her sables she in sorrow wore,

And mourn'd so long that she could mourn no more.
Distant from Jonas, and from all her race,
She now resided in a lively place;
There, by the sect unseen, at whist she play'd,
Nor was of churchman or their church afraid:
If much of this the graver brother heard,
He something censured, but he little fear'd;
He knew her rich and frugal; for the rest,
He felt no care, or, if he felt, suppress'd:
Nor for companion when she ask'd her Niece,
Had he suspicions that disturb'd his peace;
Frugal and rich, these virtues as a charm
Preserved the thoughtful man from all alarm;
An infant yet, she soon would home return,
Nor stay the manners of the world to learn;
Meantime his boys would all his care engross,
And be his comforts if he felt the loss.
The sprightly Sybil, pleased and unconfined,
Felt the pure pleasure of the op'ning mind:
All here was gay and cheerful—all at home
Unvaried quiet and unruffled gloom:
There were no changes, and amusements few;—
Here all was varied, wonderful, and new;
There were plain meals, plain dresses, and grave looks—
Here, gay companions and amusing books;
And the young Beauty soon began to taste
The light vocations of the scene she graced.
A man of business feels it as a crime
On calls domestic to consume his time;
Yet this grave man had not so cold a heart,
But with his daughter he was grieved to part:
And he demanded that in every year
The Aunt and Niece should at his house appear.
"Yes! we must go, my child, and by our dress
A grave conformity of mind express;
Must sing at meeting, and from cards refrain,
The more t'enjoy when we return again."
Thus spake the Aunt, and the discerning child
Was pleased to learn how fathers are beguiled.
Her artful part the young dissembler took,
And from the matron caught th' approving look:
When thrice the friends had met, excuse was sent
For more delay, and Jonas was content;
Till a tall maiden by her sire was seen,
In all the bloom and beauty of sixteen;
He gazed admiring;—she, with visage prim,
Glanced an arch look of gravity on him;
For she was gay at heart, but wore disguise,

And stood a vestal in her father's eyes:
Pure, pensive, simple, sad; the damsel's heart,
When Jonas praised, reproved her for the part.
For Sybil, fond of pleasure, gay and light,
Had still a secret bias to the right;
Vain as she was—and flattery made her vain—
Her simulation gave her bosom pain.
Again return'd, the Matron and the Niece
Found the late quiet gave their joy increase;
The aunt infirm, no more her visits paid,
But still with her sojourn'd the favourite maid.
Letters were sent when franks could be procured,
And when they could not, silence was endured;
All were in health, and if they older grew,
It seem'd a fact that none among them knew;
The aunt and niece still led a pleasant life,
And quiet days had Jonas and his wife.
Near him a Widow dwelt of worthy fame,
Like his her manners, and her creed the same;
The wealth her husband left, her care retain'd
For one tall Youth, and widow she remain'd;
His love respectful all her care repaid,
Her wishes watch'd, and her commands obey'd.
Sober he was and grave from early youth,
Mindful of forms, but more intent on truth:
In a light drab he uniformly dress'd,
And look serene th' unruffled mind express'd;
A hat with ample verge his brows o'erspread,
And his brown locks curl'd graceful on his head;
Yet might observers in his speaking eye
Some observation, some acuteness spy;
The friendly thought it keen, the treacherous deem'd it sly.
Yet not a crime could foe or friend detect,
His actions all were, like his speech, correct;
And they who jested on a mind so sound,
Upon his virtues must their laughter found;
Chaste, sober, solemn, and devout they named
Him who was thus, and not of this ashamed.
Such were the virtues Jonas found in one
In whom he warmly wish'd to find a son:
Three years had pass'd since he had Sybil seen;
But she was doubtless what she once had been,
Lovely and mild, obedient and discreet;
The pair must love whenever they should meet;
Then ere the widow or her son should choose
Some happier maid, he would explain his views:
Now she, like him, was politic and shrewd,
With strong desire of lawful gain embued;

To all he said, she bow'd with much respect,
Pleased to comply, yet seeming to reject;
Cool and yet eager, each admired the strength
Of the opponent, and agreed at length:
As a drawn battle shows to each a force,
Powerful as his, he honours it of course;
So in these neighbours, each the power discern'd,
And gave the praise that was to each return'd.
Jonas now ask'd his daughter—and the Aunt,
Though loth to lose her, was obliged to grant:—
But would not Sybil to the matron cling,
And fear to leave the shelter of her wing?
No! in the young there lives a love of change,
And to the easy they prefer the strange!
Then, too, the joys she once pursued with zeal,
From whist and visits sprung, she ceased to feel:
When with the matrons Sybil first sat down,
To cut for partners and to stake her crown,
This to the youthful maid preferment seem'd,
Who thought what woman she was then esteem'd;
But in few years, when she perceived, indeed,
The real woman to the girl succeed,
No longer tricks and honours fill'd her mind,
But other feelings, not so well defined;
She then reluctant grew, and thought it hard
To sit and ponder o'er an ugly card;
Rather the nut-tree shade the nymph preferr'd,
Pleased with the pensive gloom and evening bird;
Thither, from company retired, she took
The silent walk, or read the fav'rite book.
The father's letter, sudden, short, and kind,
Awaked her wonder, and disturb'd her mind;
She found new dreams upon her fancy seize,
Wild roving thoughts and endless reveries.
The parting came;—and when the Aunt perceived
The tears of Sybil, and how much she grieved—
To love for her that tender grief she laid,
That various, soft, contending passions made.
When Sybil rested in her father's arms,
His pride exulted in a daughter's charms;
A maid accomplish'd he was pleased to find,
Nor seem'd the form more lovely than the mind:
But when the fit of pride and fondness fled,
He saw his judgment by his hopes misled;
High were the lady's spirits, far more free
Her mode of speaking than a maid's should be;
Too much, as Jonas thought, she seem'd to know,
And all her knowledge was disposed to show;

"Too gay her dress, like theirs who idly dote
On a young coxcomb or a coxcomb's coat;
In foolish spirits when our friends appear,
And vainly grave when not a man is near."
Thus Jonas, adding to his sorrow blame,
And terms disdainful to a Sister's name:
"The sinful wretch has by her arts denied
The ductile spirit of my darling child."
"The maid is virtuous," said the dame—Quoth he,
"Let her give proof, by acting virtuously:
Is it in gaping when the Elders pray?
In reading nonsense half a summer's day?
In those mock forms that she delights to trace,
Or her loud laughs in Hezekiah's face?
She—O Susannah!—to the world belongs;
She loves the follies of its idle throngs,
And reads soft tales of love, and sings love's soft'ning songs.
But, as our friend is yet delay'd in town,
We must prepare her till the Youth comes down:
You shall advise the maiden; I will threat;
Her fears and hopes may yield us comfort yet."
Now the grave father took the lass aside,
Demanding sternly, "Wilt thou be a bride?"
She answer'd, calling up an air sedate,
"I have not vow'd against the holy state."
"No folly, Sybil," said the parent; "know
What to their parents virtuous maidens owe:
A worthy, wealthy youth, whom I approve,
Must thou prepare to honour and to love.
Formal to thee his air and dress may seem,
But the good youth is worthy of esteem:
Shouldst thou with rudeness treat him; of disdain
Should he with justice or of slight complain,
Or of one taunting speech give certain proof,
Girl! I reject thee from my sober roof."
"My aunt," said Sybil," will with pride protect
One whom a father can for this reject;
Nor shall a formal, rigid, soul-less boy
My manners alter, or my views destroy!"
Jonas then lifted up his hands on high,
And, utt'ring something 'twixt a groan and sigh,
Left the determined maid, her doubtful mother by.
"Hear me," she said; "incline thy heart, my child,
And fix thy fancy on a man so mild:
Thy father, Sybil, never could be moved
By one who loved him, or by one he loved.
Union like ours is but a bargain made
By slave and tyrant—he will be obey'd;

Then calls the quiet, comfort—but thy Youth
Is mild by nature, and as frank as truth."
"But will he love?" said Sybil; "I am told
That these mild creatures are by nature cold."
"Alas!" the matron answer'd, "much I dread
That dangerous love by which the young are led!
That love is earthy; you the creature prize,
And trust your feelings and believe your eyes:
Can eyes and feelings inward worth descry?
No! my fair daughter, on our choice rely!
Your love, like that display'd upon the stage,
Indulged is folly, and opposed is rage;—
More prudent love our sober couples show,
All that to mortal beings, mortals owe;
All flesh is grass—before you give a heart,
Remember, Sybil, that in death you part;
And should your husband die before your love,
What needless anguish must a widow prove!
No! my fair child, let all such visions cease;
Yield but esteem, and only try for peace."
"I must be loved," said Sybil; "I must see
The man in terrors who aspires to me;
At my forbidding frown his heart must ache,
His tongue must falter, and his frame must shake:
And if I grant him at my feet to kneel,
What trembling, fearful pleasure must he feel;
Nay, such the raptures that my smiles inspire,
That reason's self must for a time retire."
"Alas! for good Josiah," said the dame,
"These wicked thoughts would fill his soul with shame;
He kneel and tremble at a thing of dust!
He cannot, child:"—the Child replied, "He must."
They ceased: the matron left her with a frown;
So Jonas met her when the Youth came down:
"Behold," said he, "thy future spouse attends;
Receive him, daughter, as the best of friends;
Observe, respect him—humble be each word,
That welcomes home thy husband and thy lord."
Forewarn'd, thought Sybil, with a bitter smile,
I shall prepare my manner and my style.
Ere yet Josiah enter'd on his task,
The father met him—"Deign to wear a mask
A few dull days, Josiah—but a few—
It is our duty, and the sex's due;
I wore it once, and every grateful wife
Repays it with obedience through her life:
Have no regard to Sybil's dress, have none
To her pert language, to her flippant tone:

Henceforward thou shalt rule unquestion'd and alone;
And she thy pleasure in thy looks shall seek—
How she shall dress, and whether she may speak."
A sober smile returned the Youth, and said,
"Can I cause fear, who am myself afraid?"
Sybil, meantime, sat thoughtful in her room,
And often wonder'd—"Will the creature come?
Nothing shall tempt, shall force me to bestow
My hand upon him,—yet I wish to know."
The door unclosed, and she beheld her sire
Lead in the Youth, then hasten to retire;
"Daughter, my friend—my daughter, friend," he cried,
And gave a meaning look, and stepp'd aside:
That look contained a mingled threat and prayer,
"Do take him, child,—offend him if you dare."
The couple gazed—were silent, and the maid
Look'd in his face, to make the man afraid;
The man, unmoved, upon the maiden cast
A steady view—so salutation pass'd:
But in this instant Sybil's eye had seen
The tall fair person, and the still staid mien;
The glow that temp'rance o'er the cheek had spread,
Where the soft down half veil'd the purest red;
And the serene deportment that proclaim'd
A heart unspotted, and a life unblamed:
But then with these she saw attire too plain,
The pale brown coat, though worn without a stain;
The formal air, and something of the pride
That indicates the wealth it seems to hide;
And looks that were not, she conceived, exempt
From a proud pity, or a sly contempt.
Josiah's eyes had their employment too,
Engaged and soften'd by so bright a view;
A fair and meaning face, an eye of fire,
That check'd the bold, and made the free retire:
But then with these he marked the studied dress
And lofty air, that scorn or pride express;
With that insidious look, that seem'd to hide
In an affected smile the scorn and pride;
And if his mind the virgin's meaning caught,
He saw a foe with treacherous purpose fraught—
Captive the heart to take, and to reject it, caught.
Silent they sat—thought Sybil, that he seeks
Something, no doubt; I wonder if he speaks:
Scarcely she wonder'd, when these accents fell
Slow in her ear—"Fair maiden, art thou well?"
"Art thou physician?" she replied; "my hand,
My pulse, at least, shall be at thy command."

She said—and saw, surprised, Josiah kneel,
And gave his lips the offer'd pulse to feel;
The rosy colour rising in her cheek,
Seem'd that surprise unmix'd with wrath to speak;
Then sternness she assumed, and—"Doctor, tell;
Thy words cannot alarm me—am I well?"
"Thou art," said he; "and yet thy dress so light,
I do conceive, some danger must excite:"
"In whom?" said Sybil, with a look demure:
"In more," said he, "than I expect to cure;—
I, in thy light luxuriant robe behold
Want and excess, abounding and yet cold;
Here needed, there display'd, in many a wanton fold;
Both health and beauty, learned authors show,
From a just medium in our clothing flow."
"Proceed, good doctor; if so great my need,
What is thy fee? Good doctor! pray proceed."
"Large is my fee, fair lady, but I take
None till some progress in my cure I make:
Thou hast disease, fair maiden; thou art vain;
Within that face sit insult and disdain;
Thou art enamour'd of thyself; my art
Can see the naughty malice of thy heart:
With a strong pleasure would thy bosom move,
Were I to own thy power, and ask thy love;
And such thy beauty, damsel, that I might,
But for thy pride, feel danger in thy sight,
And lose my present peace in dreams of vain delight."
"And can thy patients," said the nymph "endure
Physic like this? and will it work a cure?"
"Such is my hope, fair damsel; thou, I find,
Hast the true tokens of a noble mind;
But the world wins thee, Sybil, and thy joys
Are placed in trifles, fashions, follies, toys;
Thou hast sought pleasure in the world around,
That in thine own pure bosom should be found;
Did all that world admire thee, praise and love,
Could it the least of nature's pains remove?
Could it for errors, follies, sins atone,
Or give the comfort, thoughtful and alone?
It has, believe me, maid, no power to charm
Thy soul from sorrow, or thy flesh from harm:
Turn then, fair creature, from a world of sin,
And seek the jewel happiness within."
"Speak'st thou at meeting?" said the nymph; "thy speech
Is that of mortal very prone to teach;
But wouldst thou, doctor, from the patient learn
Thine own disease?—the cure is thy concern."

"Yea, with good will."—"Then know 'tis thy complaint,
That, for a sinner, thou'rt too much a saint;
Hast too much show of the sedate and pure,
And without cause art formal and demure:
This makes a man unsocial, unpolite;
Odious when wrong, and insolent if right.
Thou mayst be good, but why should goodness be
Wrapt in a garb of such formality?
Thy person well might please a damsel's eye,
In decent habit with a scarlet dye;
But, jest apart—what virtue canst thou trace
In that broad brim that hides thy sober face?
Does that long-skirted drab, that over-nice
And formal clothing, prove a scorn of vice?
Then for thine accent—what in sound can be
So void of grace as dull monotony?
Love has a thousand varied notes to move
The human heart:—thou mayest not speak of love
Till thou hast cast thy formal ways aside,
And those becoming youth and nature tried:
Not till exterior freedom, spirit, ease,
Prove it thy study and delight to please;
Not till these follies meet thy just disdain,
While yet thy virtues and thy worth remain."
"This is severe!—Oh! maiden wilt not thou
Something for habits, manners, modes, allow?"—
"Yes! but allowing much, I much require,
In my behalf, for manners, modes, attire!"
"True, lovely Sybil; and, this point agreed,
Let me to those of greater weight proceed:
Thy father!"—"Nay," she quickly interposed,
"Good doctor, here our conference is closed!"
Then left the Youth, who, lost in his retreat,
Pass'd the good matron on her garden-seat;
His looks were troubled, and his air, once mild
And calm, was hurried:—"My audacious child!"
Exclaim'd the dame, "I read what she has done
In thy displeasure—Ah! the thoughtless one:
But yet, Josiah, to my stern good man
Speak of the maid as mildly as you can:
Can you not seem to woo a little while
The daughter's will, the father to beguile?
So that his wrath in time may wear away;
Will you preserve our peace, Josiah? say."
"Yes! my good neighbour," said the gentle youth,
"Rely securely on my care and truth;
And should thy comfort with my efforts cease,
And only then,—perpetual is thy peace."

The dame had doubts: she well his virtues knew,
His deeds were friendly, and his words were true:
"But to address this vixen is a task
He is ashamed to take, and I to ask."
Soon as the father from Josiah learn'd
What pass'd with Sybil, he the truth discern'd.
"He loves," the man exclaim'd, "he loves, 'tis plain,
The thoughtless girl, and shall he love in vain?
She may be stubborn, but she shall be tried,
Born as she is of wilfulness and pride."
With anger fraught, but willing to persuade,
The wrathful father met the smiling maid:
"Sybil," said he, "I long, and yet I dread
To know thy conduct—hath Josiah fled?
And, grieved and fretted by thy scornful air,
For his lost peace, betaken him to prayer?
Couldst thou his pure and modest mind distress
By vile remarks upon his speech, address,
Attire, and voice?"—"All this I must confess."
"Unhappy child! what labour will it cost
To win him back!"—"I do not think him lost."
"Courts he then (trifler!) insult and disdain?"—
"No; but from these he courts me to refrain."
"Then hear me, Sybil: should Josiah leave
Thy father's house?"—"My father's child would grieve."
"That is of grace, and if he come again
To speak of love?"—"I might from grief refrain."
"Then wilt thou, daughter, our design embrace?"—
"Can I resist it, if it be of Grace?"
"Dear child in three plain words thy mind express:
Wilt thou have this good youth?"—"Dear Father! yes."

TALE VII

THE WIDOW'S TALE

Ah me! for aught that I could ever read,
Or ever hear by tale or history,
The course of true love never did run smooth:
But either it was different in blood,
Or else misgrafted in respect of years,
Or else it stood upon the choice of friends;
Or, if there were a sympathy in choice,
War, death, or sickness did lay siege to it.
SHAKESPEARE, Midsummer Night's Dream.

Oh! thou didst then ne'er love so heartily,
If thou rememberest not the slighest folly
That ever love did make thee run into.
As You Like It.

Cry the man mercy! love him, take his offer.
As You Like It.

To Farmer Moss, in Langar Vale, came down,
His only daughter, from her school in town;
A tender, timid maid! who knew not how
To pass a pig-sty, or to face a cow:
Smiling she came, with petty talents graced,
A fair complexion, and a slender waist.
Used to spare meals, disposed in manner pure,
Her father's kitchen she could ill endure:
Where by the steaming beef he hungry sat,
And laid at once a pound upon his plate;
Hot from the field, her eager brother seized
An equal part, and hunger's rage appeased;
The air surcharged with moisture, flagg'd around,
And the offended damsel sigh'd and frown'd;
The swelling fat in lumps conglomerate laid,
And fancy's sickness seized the loathing maid:
But when the men beside their station took,
The maidens with them, and with these the cook;
When one huge wooden bowl before them stood,
Fill'd with huge balls of farinaceous food;
With bacon, mass saline, where never lean
Beneath the brown and bristly rind was seen;
When from a single horn the party drew
Their copious draughts of heavy ale and new;
When the coarse cloth she saw, with many a stain
Soil'd by rude hinds who cut and came again—
She could not breathe; but with a heavy sigh,
Rein'd the fair neck, and shut th' offended eye;
She minced the sanguine flesh in frustums fine,
And wonder'd much to see the creatures dine;
When she resolved her father's heart to move,
If hearts of farmers were alive to love.
She now entreated by herself to sit
In the small parlour, if papa thought fit,
And there to dine, to read, to work alone—
"No!" said the Farmer in an angry tone;
"These are your school-taught airs; your mother's pride
Would send you there; but I am now your guide.—
Arise betimes, our early meal prepare,

And, this despatch'd, let business be your care;
Look to the lasses, let there not be one
Who lacks attention, till her tasks be done;
In every household work your portion take,
And what you make not, see that others make:
At leisure times attend the wheel, and see
The whit'ning web besprinkled on the lea;
When thus employ'd, should our young neighbours view,
A useful lass,—you may have more to do."
Dreadful were these commands; but worse than these
The parting hint—a Farmer could not please:
'Tis true she had without abhorrence seen
Young Harry Carr, when he was smart and clean:
But, to be married—be a farmer's wife—
A slave! a drudge!—she could not for her life.
With swimming eyes the fretful nymph withdrew,
And, deeply sighing, to her chamber flew;
There on her knees, to Heaven she grieving pray'd
For change of prospect to a tortured maid.
Harry, a youth whose late-departed sire
Had left him all industrious men require,
Saw the pale Beauty,—and her shape and air
Engaged him much, and yet he must forbear:
"For my small farm what can the damsel do?"
He said,—then stopp'd to take another view:
"Pity so sweet a lass will nothing learn
Of household cares,—for what can beauty earn
By those small arts which they at school attain,
That keep them useless, and yet make them vain?"
This luckless Damsel look'd the village round,
To find a friend, and one was quickly found:
A pensive Widow, whose mild air and dress
Pleased the sad nymph, who wish'd her soul's distress
To one so seeming kind, confiding, to confess.
"What Lady that?" the anxious lass inquired,
Who then beheld the one she most admired:
"Here," said the Brother, "are no ladies seen—
That is a widow dwelling on the Green;
A dainty dame, who can but barely live
On her poor pittance, yet contrives to give;
She happier days has known, but seems at ease,
And you may call her lady if you please:
But if you wish, good sister, to improve,
You shall see twenty better worth your love."
These Nancy met; but, spite of all they taught,
This useless Widow was the one she sought:
The father growl'd; but said he knew no harm
In such connexion that could give alarm;

"And if we thwart the trifler in her course,
'Tis odds against us she will take a worse."
Then met the friends; the Widow heard the sigh
That ask'd at once compassion and reply:—
"Would you, my child, converse with one so poor,
Yours were the kindness—yonder is my door:
And, save the time that we in public pray,
From that poor cottage I but rarely stray."
There went the nymph, and made her strong complaints,
Painting her woe as injured feeling paints.
"Oh, dearest friend! do think how one must feel,
Shock'd all day long, and sicken'd every meal;
Could you behold our kitchen (and to you
A scene so shocking must indeed be new),
A mind like yours, with true refinement graced,
Would let no vulgar scenes pollute your taste:
And yet, in truth, from such a polish'd mind
All base ideas must resistance find,
And sordid pictures from the fancy pass,
As the breath startles from the polish'd glass.
"Here you enjoy a sweet romantic scene,
Without so pleasant, and within so clean;
These twining jess'mines, what delicious gloom
And soothing fragrance yield they to the room!
What lovely garden! there you oft retire,
And tales of woe and tenderness admire.
In that neat case your books, in order placed,
Soothe the full soul, and charm the cultur'd taste;
And thus, while all about you wears a charm,
How must you scorn the Farmer and the Farm!"
The Widow smiled, and "Know you not," said she,
"How much these farmers scorn or pity me;
Who see what you admire, and laugh at all they see?
True, their opinion alters not my fate,
By falsely judging of an humble state:
This garden you with such delight behold,
Tempts not a feeble dame who dreads the cold;
These plants which please so well your livelier sense,
To mine but little of their sweets dispense:
Books soon are painful to my failing sight,
And oftener read from duty than delight;
(Yet let me own, that I can sometimes find
Both joy and duty in the act combined;)
But view me rightly, you will see no more
Than a poor female, willing to be poor;
Happy indeed, but not in books nor flowers,
Not in fair dreams, indulged in earlier hours,
Of never-tasted joys;—such visions shun,

My youthful friend, nor scorn the Farmer's Son."
"Nay," said the Damsel, nothing pleased to see
A friend's advice could like a Father's be,
"Bless'd in your cottage, you must surely smile
At those who live in our detested style:
To my Lucinda's sympathising heart
Could I my prospects and my griefs impart;,
She would console me; but I dare not show,
Ills that would wound her tender soul to know:
And I confess, it shocks my pride to tell
The secrets of the prison where I dwell;
For that dear maiden would be shock'd to feel
The secrets I should shudder to reveal;
When told her friend was by a parent ask'd,
'Fed you the swine?'—Good heaven! how I am task'd!—
What! can you smile? Ah! smile not at the grief
That woos your pity and demands relief."
"Trifles, my love: you take a false alarm;
Think, I beseech you, better of the Farm:
Duties in every state demand your care,
And light are those that will require it there.
Fix on the Youth a favouring eye, and these,
To him pertaining, or as his, will please."
"What words," the Lass replied, "offend my ear!
Try you my patience? Can you be sincere?
And am I told a willing hand to give
To a rude farmer, and with rustics live?
Far other fate was yours;—some gentle youth
Admir'd your beauty, and avow'd his truth;
The power of love prevail'd, and freely both
Gave the fond heart, and pledged the binding oath;
And then the rival's plot, the parent's power,
And jealous fears, drew on the happy hour:
Ah! let not memory lose the blissful view,
But fairly show what love has done for you."
"Agreed, my daughter; what my heart has known
Of Love's strange power, shall be with frankness shown:
But let me warn you, that experience finds
Few of the scenes that lively hope designs."
"Mysterious all," said Nancy; "you, I know,
Have suffered much; now deign the grief to show,—
I am your friend, and so prepare my heart
In all your sorrows to receive a part."
The Widow answer'd: "I had once, like you,
Such thoughts of love; no dream is more untrue;
You judge it fated, and decreed to dwell
In youthful hearts, which nothing can expel,
A passion doom'd to reign, and irresistible.

The struggling mind, when once subdued, in vain
Rejects the fury or defies the pain;
The strongest reason fails the flames t'allay,
And resolution droops and faints away:
Hence, when the destined lovers meet, they prove
At once the force of this all-powerful love;
Each from that period feels the mutual smart,
Nor seeks to cure it—heart is changed for heart;
Nor is there peace till they delighted stand,
And, at the altar—hand is join'd to hand.
"Alas! my child, there are who, dreaming so,
Waste their fresh youth, and waking feel the woe.
There is no spirit sent the heart to move
With such prevailing and alarming love;
Passion to reason will submit—or why
Should wealthy maids the poorest swains deny?
Or how could classes and degrees create
The slightest bar to such resistless fate?
Yet high and low, you see, forbear to mix;
No beggars' eyes the heart of kings transfix;
And who but am'rous peers or nobles sigh,
When titled beauties pass triumphant by?
For reason wakes, proud wishes to reprove;
You cannot hope, and therefore dare not love;
All would be safe, did we at first inquire—
'Does reason sanction what our hearts desire?'
But quitting precept, let example show
What joys from Love uncheck'd by prudence flow.
"A Youth my father in his office placed,
Of humble fortune, but with sense and taste;
But he was thin and pale, had downcast looks:
He studied much, and pored upon his books:
Confused he was when seen, and when he saw
Me or my sisters, would in haste withdraw;
And had this youth departed with the year,
His loss had cost us neither sigh nor tear.
"But with my father still the youth remain'd,
And more reward and kinder notice gain'd:
He often, reading, to the garden stray'd,
Where I by books or musing was delay'd;
This to discourse in summer evenings led,
Of these same evenings, or of what we read:
On such occasions we were much alone;
But, save the look, the manner, and the tone,
(These might have meaning,) all that we discuss'd
We could with pleasure to a parent trust.
"At length 'twas friendship—and my Friend and I
Said we were happy, and began to sigh;

My sisters first, and then my father, found
That we were wandering o'er enchanted ground:
But he had troubles in his own affairs,
And would not bear addition to his cares:
With pity moved, yet angry, 'Child,' said he,
'Will you embrace contempt and beggary?'
Can you endure to see each other cursed
By want, of every human woe the worst?
Warring for ever with distress, in dread
Either of begging or of wanting bread;
While poverty, with unrelenting force,
Will your own offspring from your love divorce;
They, through your folly, must be doom'd to pine,
And you deplore your passion, or resign;
For if it die, what good will then remain?
And if it live, it doubles every pain.'"
"But you were true," exclaim'd the Lass," and fled
The tyrant's power who fill'd your soul with dread?"
"But," said the smiling Friend, "he fill'd my mouth with bread:
And in what other place that bread to gain
We long consider'd, and we sought in vain:
This was my twentieth year,—at thirty-five
Our hope was fainter, yet our love alive;
So many years in anxious doubt had pass'd."
"Then," said the Damsel, "you were bless'd at last?"
A smile again adorn'd the Widow's face,
But soon a starting tear usurp'd its place.
"Slow pass'd the heavy years, and each had more
Pains and vexations than the years before.
My father fail'd; his family was rent,
And to new states his grieving daughters sent:
Each to more thriving kindred found a way,
Guests without welcome,—servants without pay;
Our parting hour was grievous; still I feel
The sad, sweet converse at our final meal;
Our father then reveal'd his former fears,
Cause of his sternness, and then join'd our tears:
Kindly he strove our feelings to repress,
But died, and left us heirs to his distress.
The rich, as humble friends, my sisters chose;
I with a wealthy widow sought repose;
Who with a chilling frown her friend received,
Bade me rejoice, and wonder'd that I grieved:
In vain my anxious lover tried his skill,
To rise in life, he was dependent still:
We met in grief, nor can I paint the fears
Of these unhappy, troubled, trying years:
Our dying hopes and stronger fears between,

We felt no season peaceful or serene;
Our fleeting joys, like meteors in the night,
Shone on our gloom with inauspicious light;
And then domestic sorrows, till the mind,
Worn with distresses, to despair inclined;
Add too the ill that from the passion flows,
When its contemptuous frown the world bestows,
The peevish spirit caused by long delay,
When, being gloomy, we contemn the gay,
When, being wretched, we incline to hate
And censure others in a happier state;
Yet loving still, and still compell'd to move
In the sad labyrinth of lingering love:
While you, exempt from want, despair, alarm,
May wed—oh! take the Farmer and the Farm."
"Nay," said the nymph, "joy smiled on you at last?"
"Smiled for a moment," she replied, "and pass'd:
My lover still the same dull means pursued,
Assistant call'd, but kept in servitude;
His spirits wearied in the prime of life,
By fears and wishes in eternal strife;
At length he urged impatient—'Now consent;
With thee united, Fortune may relent.'
I paused, consenting; but a Friend arose,
Pleased a fair view, though distant, to disclose;
From the rough ocean we beheld a gleam
Of joy, as transient as the joys we dream;
By lying hopes deceived, my friend retired,
And sail'd—was wounded—reach'd us—and expired!
You shall behold his grave; and when I die,
There—but 'tis folly—I request to lie."
"Thus," said the lass, "to joy you bade adieu!
But how a widow?—that cannot be true:
Or was it force, in some unhappy hour,
That placed you, grieving, in a tyrant's power?"
"Force, my young friend, when forty years are fled,
Is what a woman seldom has to dread;
She needs no brazen locks nor guarding walls,
And seldom comes a lover though she calls:
Yet, moved by fancy, one approved my face,
Though time and tears had wrought it much disgrace.
"The man I married was sedate and meek,
And spoke of love as men in earnest speak;
Poor as I was, he ceaseless sought for years,
A heart in sorrow and a face in tears:
That heart I gave not; and 'twas long before
I gave attention, and then nothing more:
But in my breast some grateful feeling rose,

For one whose love so sad a subject chose;
Till long delaying, fearing to repent,
But grateful still, I gave a cold assent.
Thus we were wed; no fault had I to find,
And he but one: my heart could not be kind:
Alas! of every early hope bereft,
There was no fondness in my bosom left;
So had I told him, but had told in vain,
He lived but to indulge me and complain:
His was this cottage; he inclosed this ground.
And planted all these blooming shrubs around;
He to my room these curious trifles brought,
And with assiduous love my pleasure sought;
He lived to please me, and I ofttimes strove,
Smiling, to thank his unrequited love:
'Teach me,' he cried, 'that pensive mind to ease,
For all my pleasure is the hope to please.'
Serene though heavy, were the days we spent,
Yet kind each word, and gen'rous each intent;
But his dejection lessen'd every day,
And to a placid kindness died away:
In tranquil ease we pass'd our latter years,
By griefs untroubled, unassail'd by fears.
Let not romantic views your bosom sway;
Yield to your duties, and their call obey:
Fly not a Youth, frank, honest, and sincere;
Observe his merits, and his passion hear!
'Tis true, no hero, but a farmer, sues—
Slow in his speech, but worthy in his views;
With him you cannot that affliction prove,
That rends the bosom of the poor in love:
Health, comfort, competence, and cheerful days,
Your friends' approval, and your father's praise,
Will crown the deed, and you escape their fate
Who plan so wildly, and are wise too late."
The Damsel heard; at first th' advice was strange,
Yet wrought a happy, nay, a speedy change:
"I have no care," she said, when next they met,
But one may wonder, he is silent yet;
He looks around him with his usual stare,
And utters nothing—not that I shall care."
This pettish humour pleased th' experienced Friend—
None need despair, whose silence can offend;
"Should I," resumed the thoughtful Lass, "consent
To hear the man, the man may now repent:
Think you my sighs shall call him from the plough,
Or give one hint, that 'You may woo me now?'"
"Persist, my love," replied the Friend, "and gain

A parent's praise, that cannot be in vain."
The father saw the change, but not the cause,
And gave the alter'd maid his fond applause:
The coarser manners she in part removed,
In part endured, improving and improved;
She spoke of household works, she rose betimes,
And said neglect and indolence were crimes;
The various duties of their life she weigh'd,
And strict attention to her dairy paid;
The names of servants now familiar grew,
And fair Lucinda's from her mind withdrew;
As prudent travellers for their ease assume
Their modes and language to whose lands they come;
So to the Farmer this fair Lass inclined,
Gave to the business of the Farm her mind;
To useful arts she turned her hand and eye;
And by her manners told him—"You may try."
Th' observing Lover more attention paid,
With growing pleasure, to the alter'd maid;
He fear'd to lose her, and began to see
That a slim beauty might a helpmate be:
'Twixt hope and fear he now the lass address'd,
And in his Sunday robe his love express'd:
She felt no chilling dread, no thrilling joy,
Nor was too quickly kind, too slowly coy;
But still she lent an unreluctant ear
To all the rural business of the year;
Till love's strong hopes endured no more delay,
And Harry ask'd, and Nancy named the day.
"A happy change! my Boy," the father cried:
"How lost your sister all her school-day pride?"
The Youth replied, "It is the Widow's deed;
The cure is perfect and was wrought with speed.
And comes there, Boy, this benefit of books,
Of that smart dress, and of those dainty looks?
We must be kind—some offerings from the Farm
To the White Cot will speak our feelings warm;
Will show that people, when they know the fact,
Where they have judged severely, can retract.
Oft have I smiled, when I beheld her pass
With cautious step as if she hurt the grass;
Where, if a snail's retreat she chanced to storm,
She look'd as begging pardon of the worm;
And what, said I, still laughing at the view,
Have these weak creatures in the world to do?
But some are made for action, some to speak;
And, while she looks so pitiful and meek,
Her words are weighty, though her nerves are weak.'

Soon told the village-bells the rite was done,
That joined the school-bred Miss and Farmer's Son;
Her former habits some slight scandal raised,
But real worth was soon perceived and praised;
She, her neat taste imparted to the Farm,
And he, th' improving skill and vigorous arm.

TALE VIII

THE MOTHER

What though you have beauty,
Must you be therefore proud and pitiless?
SHAKESPEARE, As You Like It.

I would not marry her, though she were endowed with all that
Adam had left him before he transgressed.
As You Like It.

Wilt thou love such a woman? What! to make thee an instrument, and play false strains upon
thee!—Not to be endured.
As You Like It.

Your son,
As mad in folly, lack'd the sense to know
Her estimation hence.
All's Well that Ends Well.

Be this sweet Helen's knell;
He left a wife whose words all ears took captive,
Whose dear perfections hearts that scorn'd to serve
Humbly call'd Mistress.
All's Well that Ends Well.

There was a worthy, but a simple Pair,
Who nursed a Daughter, fairest of the fair:
Sons they had lost, and she alone remain'd,
Heir to the kindness they had all obtain'd,
Heir to the fortune they design'd for all,
Nor had th' allotted portion then been small;
And now, by fate enrich'd with beauty rare,
They watch'd their treasure with peculiar care:
The fairest features they could early trace,
And, blind with love saw merit in her face—
Saw virtue, wisdom, dignity, and grace;

And Dorothea, from her infant years,
Gain'd all her wishes from their pride or fears;
She wrote a billet, and a novel read,
And with her fame her vanity was fed;
Each word, each look, each action was a cause
For flattering wonder and for fond applause;
She rode or danced, and ever glanced around,
Seeking for praise, and smiling when she found,
The yielding pair to her petitions gave
An humble friend to be a civil slave,
Who for a poor support herself resign'd
To the base toil of a dependant mind:
By nature cold, our Heiress stoop'd to art,
To gain the credit of a tender heart.
Hence at her door must suppliant paupers stand,
To bless the bounty of her beauteous hand:
And now, her education all complete,
She talk'd of virtuous love and union sweet;
She was indeed by no soft passion moved,
But wished with all her soul to be beloved.
Here, on the favour'd beauty Fortune smiled;
Her chosen Husband was a man so mild,
So humbly temper'd, so intent to please,
It quite distress'd her to remain at ease,
Without a cause to sigh, without pretence to tease:
She tried his patience on a thousand modes,
And tried it not upon the roughest roads.
Pleasure she sought, and disappointed, sigh'd
For joys, she said, "to her alone denied;"
And she was sure "her parents if alive
Would many comforts for their child contrive:"
The gentle Husband bade her name him one;
"No—that," she answered, "should for her be done;
How could she say what pleasures were around?
But she was certain many might be found."
"Would she some seaport, Weymouth, Scarborough, grace?"—
"He knew she hated every watering-place."
"The town?"—"What! now 'twas empty, joyless, dull?"
"In winter?"—"No; she liked it worse when full."
She talk'd of building—"Would she plan a room?"—
"No! she could live, as he desired, in gloom."
"Call then our friends and neighbours."—"He might call,
And they might come and fill his ugly hall;
A noisy vulgar set, he knew she scorn'd them all."
"Then might their two dear girls the time employ,
And their Improvement yield a solid joy."—
"Solid indeed! and heavy—oh! the bliss
Of teaching letters to a lisping miss!"

"My dear, my gentle Dorothea, say,
Can I oblige you?"—"You may go away."
Twelve heavy years this patient soul sustain'd
This wasp's attacks, and then her praise obtain'd,
Graved on a marble tomb, where he at peace remain'd.
Two daughters wept their loss; the one a child
With a plain face, strong sense, and temper mild,
Who keenly felt the Mother's angry taunt,
"Thou art the image of thy pious Aunt:"
Long time had Lucy wept her slighted face,
And then began to smile at her disgrace.
Her father's sister, who the world had seen
Near sixty years when Lucy saw sixteen,
Begg'd the plain girl: the gracious Mother smiled,
And freely gave her grieved but passive child;
And with her elder-born, the beauty bless'd,
This parent rested, if such minds can rest:
No miss her waxen babe could so admire,
Nurse with such care, or with such pride attire;
They were companions meet, with equal mind,
Bless'd with one love, and to one point inclined;
Beauty to keep, adorn, increase, and guard,
Was their sole care, and had its full reward:
In rising splendour with the one it reign'd,
And in the other was by care sustain'd,
The daughter's charms increased, the parent's yet remain'd.
Leave we these ladies to their daily care,
To see how meekness and discretion fare:—
A village maid, unvex'd by want or love,
Could not with more delight than Lucy move;
The village lark, high mounted in the spring,
Could not with purer joy than Lucy sing;
Her cares all light, her pleasures all sincere,
Her duty joy, and her companion dear;
In tender friendship and in true respect
Lived Aunt and Niece, no flattery, no neglect—
They read, walk'd, visited—together pray'd,
Together slept the matron and the maid:
There was such goodness, such pure nature seen
In Lucy's looks, a manner so serene;
Such harmony in motion, speech, and air,
That without fairness she was more than fair,
Had more than beauty in each speaking grace,
That lent their cloudless glory to the face;
Where mild good sense in placid looks were shown,
And felt in every bosom but her own;
The one presiding feature in her mind
Was the pure meekness of a will resign'd;

A tender spirit, freed from all pretence
Of wit, and pleased in mild benevolence;
Bless'd in protecting fondness she reposed
With every wish indulged though undisclosed;
But love, like zephyr on the limpid lake,
Was now the bosom of the maid to shake,
And in that gentle mind a gentle strife to make.
Among their chosen friends, a favoured few
The aunt and niece a youthful Rector knew;
Who, though a younger brother, might address
A younger sister, fearless of success;
His friends, a lofty race, their native pride
At first display'd, and their assent denied:
But, pleased such virtues and such love to trace,
They own'd she would adorn the loftiest race.
The Aunt, a mother's caution to supply,
Had watch'd the youthful priest with jealous eye;
And, anxious for her charge, had view'd unseen
The cautious life that keeps the conscience clean:
In all she found him all she wish'd to find,
With slight exception of a lofty mind:
A certain manner that express'd desire
To be received as brother to the 'Squire.
Lucy's meek eye had beam'd with many a tear,
Lucy's soft heart had beat with many a fear,
Before he told (although his looks, she thought,
Had oft confess'd) that he her favour sought;
But when he kneel'd, (she wish'd him not to kneel,)
And spoke the fears and hopes that lovers feel;
When too the prudent aunt herself confess'd
Her wishes on the gentle youth would rest;
The maiden's eye with tender passion beam'd,
She dwelt with fondness on the life she schemed;
The household cares, the soft and lasting ties
Of love, with all his binding charities;
Their village taught, consoled, assisted, fed,
Till the young zealot tears of pleasure shed.
But would her Mother? Ah! she fear'd it wrong
To have indulged these forward hopes so long,
Her mother loved, but was not used to grant
Favours so freely as her gentle aunt.—
Her gentle aunt, with smiles that angels wear,
Dispell'd her Lucy's apprehensive tear:
Her prudent foresight the request had made
To one whom none could govern, few persuade;
She doubted much if one in earnest woo'd
A girl with not a single charm endued;
The Sister's nobler views she then declared,

And what small sum for Lucy could be spared;
"If more than this the foolish priest requires,
Tell him," she wrote," to check his vain desires."
At length, with many a cold expression mix'd,
With many a sneer on girls so fondly fix'd,
There came a promise—should they not repent,
But take with grateful minds the portion meant,
And wait the Sister's day—the Mother might consent.
And here, might pitying hope o'er truth prevail,
Or love o'er fortune, we would end our tale;
For who more bless'd than youthful pair removed
From fear of want—by mutual friends approved—
Short time to wait, and in that time to live
With all the pleasures hope and fancy give;
Their equal passion raised on just esteem,
When reason sanctions all that love can dream?
Yes! reason sanctions what stern fate denies:
The early prospect in the glory dies,
As the soft smiles on dying infants play
In their mild features, and then pass away.
The Beauty died ere she could yield her hand
In the high marriage by the Mother plann'd;
Who grieved indeed, but found a vast relief
In a cold heart, that ever warr'd with grief.
Lucy was present when her sister died,
Heiress to duties that she ill supplied:
There were no mutual feelings, sister arts,
No kindred taste, nor intercourse of hearts:
When in the mirror play'd the matron's smile,
The maiden's thoughts were traveling all the while;
And when desired to speak, she sigh'd to find
Her pause offended; "Envy made her blind:
Tasteless she was, nor had a claim in life
Above the station of a rector's wife;
Yet as an heiress, she must shun disgrace,
Although no heiress to her mother's face:
It is your duty," said th' imperious dame,
"(Advanced your fortune,) to advance your name,
And with superior rank, superior offers claim:
Your sister's lover, when his sorrows die,
May look upon you, and for favour sigh;
Nor can you offer a reluctant hand;
His birth is noble, and his seat is grand."
Alarm'd was Lucy, was in tears—"A fool!
Was she a child in love?—a miss at school?
Doubts any mortal, if a change of state
Dissolves all claims and ties of earlier date?"
The Rector doubted, for he came to mourn

A sister dead, and with a wife return:
Lucy with heart unchanged received the youth,
True in herself, confiding in his truth;
But own'd her mother's change; the haughty dame
Pour'd strong contempt upon the youthful flame;
She firmly vow'd her purpose to pursue,
Judged her own cause, and bade the youth adieu!
The lover begg'd, insisted, urged his pain,
His brother wrote to threaten and complain;
Her sister reasoning proved the promise made,
Lucy appealing to a parent pray'd;
But all opposed the event that she design'd,
And all in vain—she never changed her mind;
But coldly answer'd in her wonted way,
That she "would rule, and Lucy must obey."
With peevish fear, she saw her health decline,
And cried, "Oh! monstrous, for a man to pine!
But if your foolish heart must yield to love,
Let him possess it whom I now approve;
This is my pleasure."—Still the Rector came
With larger offers and with bolder claim;
But the stern lady would attend no more—
She frown'd, and rudely pointed to the door;
Whate'er he wrote, he saw unread return'd,
And he, indignant, the dishonour spurn'd:
Nay, fix'd suspicion where he might confide,
And sacrificed his passion to his pride.
Lucy, meantime, though threaten'd and distress'd,
Against her marriage made a strong protest:
All was domestic war; the Aunt rebell'd
Against the sovereign will, and was expell'd;
And every power was tried, and every art,
To bend to falsehood one determined heart;
Assail'd, in patience it received the shock,
Soft as the wave, unshaken as the rock:
But while th' unconquer'd soul endures the storm
Of angry fate, it preys upon the form;
With conscious virtue she resisted still,
And conscious love gave vigour to her will;
But Lucy's trial was at hand; with joy
The Mother cried—"Behold your constant boy—
Thursday—was married:—take the paper, sweet,
And read the conduct of your reverend cheat;
See with what pomp of coaches, in what crowd
The creature married—of his falsehood proud!
False, did I say?—at least no whining fool;
And thus will hopeless passions ever cool:
But shall his bride your single state reproach?

No! give him crowd for crowd, and coach for coach.
Oh! you retire; reflect then, gentle miss,
And gain some spirit in a cause like this."
Some spirit Lucy gain'd; a steady soul,
Defying all persuasion, all control:
In vain reproach, derision, threats were tried;
The constant mind all outward force defied,
By vengeance vainly urged, in vain assail'd by pride;
Fix'd in her purpose, perfect in her part,
She felt the courage of a wounded heart;
The world receded from her rising view,
When heaven approach'd as earthly things withdrew;
Not strange before, for in the days of love,
Joy, hope, and pleasure, she had thoughts above,
Pious when most of worldly prospects fond,
When they best pleased her she could look beyond;
Had the young priest a faithful lover died,
Something had been her bosom to divide;
Now heaven had all, for in her holiest views
She saw the matron whom she fear'd to lose;
While from her parent, the dejected maid
Forced the unpleasant thought, or thinking pray'd.
Surprised, the mother saw the languid frame,
And felt indignant, yet forbore to blame;
Once with a frown she cried, "And do you mean
To die of love—the folly of fifteen?"
But as her anger met with no reply,
She let the gentle girl in quiet die;
And to her sister wrote, impell'd by pain,
"Come quickly, Martha, or you come in vain."
Lucy meantime profess'd with joy sincere,
That nothing held, employ'd, engaged her here.
"I am an humble actor, doom'd to play
A part obscure, and then to glide away:
Incurious how the great or happy shine,
Or who have parts obscure and sad as mine;
In its best prospect I but wish'd for life,
To be th' assiduous, gentle, useful wife;
That lost, with wearied mind, and spirit poor,
I drop my efforts, and can act no more;
With growing joy I feel my spirits tend
To that last scene where all my duties end."
Hope, ease, delight, the thoughts of dying gave,
Till Lucy spoke with fondness of the grave;
She smiled with wasted form, but spirit firm,
And said, "She left but little for the worm:"
As toll'd the bell, "There's one," she said, "hath press'd
Awhile before me to the bed of rest:"

And she beside her with attention spread
The decorations of the maiden dead.
While quickly thus the mortal part declin'd,
The happiest visions fill'd the active mind;
A soft, religious melancholy gain'd
Entire possession, and for ever reign'd:
On Holy Writ her mind reposing dwelt,
She saw the wonders, she the mercies felt;
Till, in a bless'd and glorious reverie,
She seem'd the Saviour as on earth to see,
And, fill'd with love divine, th' attending friend to be;
Or she who trembling, yet confiding, stole
Near to the garment, touch'd it, and was whole;
When, such the intenseness of the working thought,
On her it seem'd the very deed was wrought;
She the glad patient's fear and rapture found,
The holy transport, and the healing wound;
This was so fix'd, so grafted in the heart,
That she adopted, nay became the part:
But one chief scene was present to her sight,
Her Saviour resting in the tomb by night;
Her fever rose, and still her wedded mind
Was to that scene, that hallow'd cave, confin'd—
Where in the shade of death the body laid,
There watch'd the spirit of the wandering maid;
Her looks were fix'd, entranced, illumed, serene,
In the still glory of the midnight scene:
There at her Saviour's feet, in visions bless'd,
Th' enraptured maid a sacred joy possess'd;
In patience waiting for the first-born ray
Of that all-glorious and triumphant day:
To this idea all her soul she gave,
Her mind reposing by the sacred grave;
Then sleep would seal the eye, the vision close,
And steep the solemn thoughts in brief repose.
Then grew the soul serene, and all its powers
Again restored, illumed the dying hours;
But reason dwelt where fancy stray'd before,
And the mind wander'd from its views no more;
Till death approach'd, when every look express'd
A sense of bliss, till every sense had rest.
The mother lives, and has enough to buy
The attentive ear and the submissive eye
Of abject natures—these are daily told,
How triumph'd beauty in the days of old;
How, by her window seated, crowds have cast
Admiring glances, wondering as they pass'd;
How from her carriage as she stepp'd to pray,

Divided ranks would humbly make her way;
And how each voice in the astonish'd throng
Pronounced her peerless as she moved along.
Her picture then the greedy Dame displays;
Touch'd by no shame, she now demands its praise;
In her tall mirror then she shows a face,
Still coldly fair with unaffecting grace;
These she compares: "It has the form," she cries,
"But wants the air, the spirit, and the eyes;
This, as a likeness, is correct and true,
But there alone the living grace we view."
This said, th' applauding voice the Dame requir'd,
And, gazing, slowly from the glass retired.

TALE IX

ARABELLA

Thrice blessed they that master so their blood—
But earthly happier is the rose distill'd,
Than that which, withering on the virgin thorn,
Grows, lives, and dies in single blessedness.
SHAKESPEARE, Midsummer Night's Dream.

I something do excuse the thing I hate,
For his advantage whom I dearly love.
Measure for Measure.

Contempt, farewell! and maiden pride, adieu!
Much Ado about Nothing.

Of a fair town where Doctor Rack was guide,
His only daughter was the boast and pride—
Wise Arabella, yet not wise alone,
She like a bright and polish'd brilliant shone;
Her father own'd her for his prop and stay,
Able to guide, yet willing to obey;
Pleased with her learning while discourse could please,
And with her love in languor and disease:
To every mother were her virtues known,
And to their daughters as a pattern shown;
Who in her youth had all that age requires,
And with her prudence all that youth admires:
These odious praises made the damsels try
Not to obtain such merits, but deny;

For, whatsoever wise mammas might say,
To guide a daughter, this was not the way;
From such applause disdain and anger rise,
And envy lives where emulation dies.
In all his strength contends the noble horse
With one who just precedes him on the course,
But when the rival flies too far before,
His spirit fails, and he attempts no more.
This reasoning Maid, above her sex's dread,
Had dared to read, and dared to say she read;
Not the last novel, not the new-born play;
Not the mere trash and scandal of the day;
But (though her young companions felt the shock)
She studied Berkeley, Bacon, Hobbes and Locke:
Her mind within the maze of history dwelt,
And of the moral Muse the beauty felt;
The merits of the Roman page she knew,
And could converse with More and Montague:
Thus she became the wonder of the town,
From that she reap'd, to that she gave renown;
And strangers coming, all were taught t'admire
The learned lady, and the lofty spire.
Thus fame in public fix'd the Maid where all
Might throw their darts, and see the idol fall:
A hundred arrows came with vengeance keen,
From tongues envenom'd, and from arms unseen;
A thousand eyes were fix'd upon the place,
That, if she fell, she might not fly disgrace:
But malice vainly throws the poison'd dart,
Unless our frailty shows the peccant part;
And Arabella still preserved her name
Untouch'd, and shone with undisputed fame;
Her very notice some respect would cause,
And her esteem was honour and applause.
Men she avoided; not in childish fear,
As if she thought some savage foe was near;
Not as a prude, who hides that man should seek,
Or who by silence hints that they should speak;
But with discretion all the sex she view'd,
Ere yet engaged pursuing or pursued;
Ere love had made her to his vices blind,
Or hid the favourite's failings from her mind.
Thus was the picture of the man portray'd,
By merit destined for so rare a maid;
At whose request she might exchange her state,
Or still be happy in a virgin's fate:—
He must be one with manners like her own,
His life unquestion'd, his opinions known;

His stainless virtue must all tests endure,
His honour spotless, and his bosom pure;
She no allowance made for sex or times,
Of lax opinion—crimes were ever crimes;
No wretch forsaken must his frailty curse,
No spurious offspring drain his private purse;
He at all times his passions must command,
And yet possess—or be refused her hand.
All this without reserve the maiden told,
And some began to weigh the rector's gold;
To ask what sum a prudent man might gain,
Who had such store of virtues to maintain?
A Doctor Campbell, north of Tweed, came forth,
Declared his passion, and proclaim'd his worth;
Not unapproved, for he had much to say
On every cause, and in a pleasant way;
Not all his trust was in a pliant tongue,
His form was good, and ruddy he, and young:
But though the doctor was a man of parts,
He read not deeply male or female hearts;
But judged that all whom he esteem'd as wise
Must think alike, though some assumed disguise;
That every reasoning Brahmin, Christian, Jew,
Of all religions took their liberal view;
And of her own, no doubt, this learned Maid
Denied the substance, and the forms obey'd:
And thus persuaded, he his thoughts express'd
Of her opinions, and his own profess'd:
"All states demand this aid, the vulgar need
Their priests and prayers, their sermons and their creed;
And those of stronger minds should never speak
(In his opinion) what might hurt the weak:
A man may smile, but still he should attend
His hour at church, and be the Church's friend,
What there he thinks conceal, and what he hears commend."
Frank was the speech, but heard with high disdain,
Nor had the doctor leave to speak again;
A man who own'd, nay gloried in deceit,
"He might despise her, but he should not cheat."
The Vicar Holmes appear'd: he heard it said
That ancient men best pleased the prudent maid;
And true it was her ancient friends she loved,
Servants when old she favour'd and approved;
Age in her pious parents she revered,
And neighbours were by length of days endear'd;
But, if her husband too must ancient be,
The good old vicar found it was not he.
On Captain Bligh her mind in balance hung—

Though valiant, modest; and reserved, though young:
Against these merits must defects be set—
Though poor, imprudent; and though proud, in debt:
In vain the captain close attention paid;
She found him wanting, whom she fairly weigh'd.
Then came a youth, and all their friends agreed
That Edward Huntly was the man indeed;
Respectful duty he had paid awhile,
Then ask'd her hand, and had a gracious smile:
A lover now declared, he led the fair
To woods and fields, to visits, and to pray'r;
Then whisper'd softly—"Will you name the day?"
She softly whisper'd—"If you love me, stay."
"Oh! try me not beyond my strength," he cried:
"Oh! be not weak," the prudent Maid replied;
"But by some trial your affection prove—
Respect, and not impatience, argues love:
And love no more is by impatience known,
Than ocean's depth is by its tempests shown:
He whom a weak and fond impatience sways,
But for himself with all his fervour prays,
And not the maid he woos, but his own will obeys;
And will she love the being who prefers,
With so much ardour, his desire to hers?"
Young Edward grieved, but let not grief be seen;
He knew obedience pleased his fancy's queen:
Awhile he waited, and then cried—"Behold!
The year advancing, be no longer cold!"
For she had promised—"Let the flowers appear,
And I will pass with thee the smiling year:"
Then pressing grew the youth; the more he press'd,
The less inclined the maid to his request:
"Let June arrive." Alas! when April came,
It brought a stranger, and the stranger, shame;
Nor could the Lover from his house persuade
A stubborn lass whom he had mournful made;
Angry and weak, by thoughtless vengeance moved,
She told her story to the Fair beloved;
In strongest words th' unwelcome truth was shown,
To blight his prospects, careless of her own.
Our heroine grieved, but had too firm a heart
For him to soften, when she swore to part;
In vain his seeming penitence and pray'r,
His vows, his tears; she left him in despair:
His mother fondly laid her grief aside,
And to the reason of the nymph applied:—
"It well becomes thee, lady, to appear,
But not to be, in very truth, severe;

Although the crime be odious in thy sight,
That daring sex is taught such things to slight,
His heart is thine, although it once was frail;
Think of his grief, and let his love prevail!"
"Plead thou no more, "the lofty lass return'd;
"Forgiving woman is deceived and spurn'd:
Say that the crime is common—shall I take
A common man my wedded lord to make?
See? a weak woman by his arts betray'd,
An infant born his father to upbraid;
Shall I forgive his vileness, take his name,
Sanction his error, and partake his shame?
No! this assent would kindred frailty prove,
A love for him would be a vicious love:
Can a chaste maiden secret counsel hold
With one whose crime by every mouth is told?
Forbid it spirit, prudence, virtuous pride;
He must despise me, were he not denied:
The way from vice the erring mind to win
Is with presuming sinners to begin,
And show, by scorning them, a just contempt for sin."
The youth, repulsed, to one more mild convey'd
His heart, and smiled on the remorseless maid;
The maid, remorseless, in her pride, the while
Despised the insult, and return'd the smile.
First to admire, to praise her, and defend,
Was (now in years advanced) a virgin-friend:
Much she preferr'd, she cried the single state,
"It was her choice"—it surely was her fate;
And much it pleased her in the train to view
A maiden vot'ress, wise and lovely too.
Time to the yielding mind his change imparts,
He varies notions, and he alters hearts;
'Tis right, 'tis just to feel contempt for vice,
But he that shows it may be over-nice:
There are who feel, when young, the false sublime,
And proudly love to show disdain for crime;
To whom the future will new thoughts supply,
The pride will soften, and the scorn will die;
Nay, where they still the vice itself condemn,
They bear the vicious, and consort with them:
Young Captain Grove, when one had changed his side,
Despised the venal turncoat, and defied;
Old Colonel Grove now shakes him by the hand,
Though he who bribes may still his vote command.
Why would not Ellen to Belinda speak,
When she had flown to London for a week,
And then return'd, to every friend's surprise,

With twice the spirit, and with half the size?
She spoke not then—but, after years had flown,
A better friend had Ellen never known:
Was it the lady her mistake had seen?
Or had she too on such a journey been?
No: 'twas the gradual change in human hearts,
That time, in commerce with the world, imparts;
That on the roughest temper throws disguise,
And steals from virtue her asperities.
The young and ardent, who with glowing zeal
Felt wrath for trifles, and were proud to feel,
Now find those trifles all the mind engage,
To soothe dull hours, and cheat the cares of age;
As young Zelinda, in her quaker-dress,
Disdain'd each varying fashion's vile excess,
And now her friends on old Zelinda gaze,
Pleased in rich silks and orient gems to blaze:
Changes like these 'tis folly to condemn,
So virtue yields not, nor is changed with them.
Let us proceed:—Twelve brilliant years were past,
Yet each with less of glory than the last.
Whether these years to this fair virgin gave
A softer mind—effect they often have;
Whether the virgin-state was not so bless'd
As that good maiden in her zeal profess'd;
Or whether lovers falling from her train,
Gave greater price to those she could retain,
Is all unknown;—but Arabella now
Was kindly listening to a Merchant's vow,
Who offer'd terms so fair, against his love
To strive was folly, so she never strove.—
Man in his earlier days we often find
With a too easy and unguarded mind;
But by increasing years and prudence taught,
He grows reserved, and locks up every thought:
Not thus the maiden, for in blooming youth
She hides her thought and guards the tender truth:
This, when no longer young, no more she hides,
But frankly in the favour'd swain confides:
Man, stubborn man, is like the growing tree,
That, longer standing, still will harder be;
And like its fruit, the virgin, first austere,
Then kindly softening with the ripening year.
Now was the lover urgent, and the kind
And yielding lady to his suit inclined:
"A little time, my friend, is just, is right;
We must be decent in our neighbours' sight:"
Still she allow'd him of his hopes to speak,

And in compassion took off week by week;
Till few remain'd, when, wearied with delay,
She kindly meant to take off day by day.
That female Friend who gave our virgin praise
For flying man and all his treacherous ways,
Now heard with mingled anger, shame, and fear
Of one accepted, and a wedding near;
But she resolved again with friendly zeal
To make the maid her scorn of wedlock feel;
For she was grieved to find her work undone,
And like a sister mourn'd the failing nun.
Why are these gentle maidens prone to make
Their sister-doves the tempting world forsake?
Why all their triumph when a maid disdains
The tyrant sex, aud scorns to wear its chains?
Is it pure joy to see a sister flown
From the false pleasures they themselves have known:
Or do they, as the call-birds in the cage,
Try, in pure envy, others to engage?
And therefore paint their native woods and groves,
As scenes of dangerous joys and naughty loves?
Strong was the maiden's hope; her friend was proud,
And had her notions to the world avow'd;
And, could she find the Merchant weak and frail,
With power to prove it, then she must prevail:
For she aloud would publish his disgrace,
And save his victim from a man so base.
When all inquiries had been duly made,
Came the kind Friend her burthen to unlade:—
"Alas! my dear! not all our care and art
Can thread the maze of man's deceitful heart;
Look not surprised—nor let resentment swell
Those lovely features, all will yet be well;
And thou, from love's and man's deceptions free,
Wilt dwell in virgin-state, and walk to Heaven with me."
The Maiden frown'd, and then conceived "that wives
Could walk as well, and lead as holy lives,
As angry prudes who scorn'd the marriage-chain,
Or luckless maids, who sought it still in vain."
The Friend was vex'd—she paused; at length she cried,
"Know your own danger, then your lot decide:
That traitor Beswell, while he seeks your hand,
Has, I affirm, a wanton at command;
A slave, a creature from a foreign place,
The nurse and mother of a spurious race;
Brown ugly bastards (Heaven the word forgive,
And the deed punish!) in his cottage live;
To town if business calls him, there he stays

In sinful pleasures wasting countless days.
Nor doubt the facts, for I can witness call,
For every crime, and prove them one and all."
Here ceased th' informer; Arabella's look
Was like a schoolboy's puzzled by his book;
Intent she cast her eyes upon the floor,
Paused—then replied—
"I wish to know no more:
I question not your motive, zeal, or love,
But must decline such dubious points to prove.
All is not true, I judge, for who can guess
Those deeds of darkness men with care suppress?
He brought a slave perhaps to England's coast,
And made her free; it is our country's boast!
And she perchance too grateful—good and ill
Were sown at first, and grow together still;
The colour'd infants on the village green,
What are they more than we have often seen?
Children half-clothed who round their village stray,
In sun or rain, now starved, now beaten, they
Will the dark colour of their fate betray:
Let us in Christian love for all account,
And then behold to what such tales amount."
"His heart is evil," said the impatient Friend:
"My duty bids me try that heart to mend,"
Replied the virgin; "we may be too nice
And lose a soul in our contempt of vice;
If false the charge, I then shall show regard
For a good man, and be his just reward:
And what for virtue can I better do
Than to reclaim him, if the charge be true?"
She spoke, nor more her holy work delay'd;
'Twas time to lend an erring mortal aid:
"The noblest way," she judged, "a soul to win,
Was with an act of kindness to begin,
To make the sinner sure, and then t'attack the sin." [3]

TALE X

THE LOVER'S JOURNEY

The sun is in the heavens, and the proud day,
Attended with the pleasures of the world,
Is all too wanton.
SHAKESPEARE, King John.

The lunatic, the lover, and the poet.
Are of imagination all compact.
Midsummer Night's Dream.

Oh! how this spring of love resembleth
Th' uncertain glory of an April day,
Which now shows all her beauty to the sun,
And by and by a cloud takes all away.
Two Gentlemen of Verona.

And happily I have arrived at last
Unto the wished haven of my bliss.
Taming of the Shrew.

It is the Soul that sees: the outward eyes
Present the object, but the Mind descries;
And thence delight, disgust, or cool indiff'rence rise:
When minds are joyful, then we look around,
And what is seen is all on fairy ground;
Again they sicken, and on every view
Cast their own dull and melancholy hue;
Or, if absorb'd by their peculiar cares,
The vacant eye on viewless matter glares,
Our feelings still upon our views attend,
And their own natures to the objects lend:
Sorrow and joy are in their influence sure,
Long as the passion reigns th' effects endure;
But Love in minds his various changes makes,
And clothes each object with the change he takes;
His light and shade on every view he throws,
And on each object what he feels bestows.
Fair was the morning, and the month was June,
When rose a Lover;—love awakens soon:
Brief his repose, yet much he dreamt the while
Of that day's meeting, and his Laura's smile:
Fancy and love that name assign'd to her,
Call'd Susan in the parish-register;
And he no more was John—his Laura gave
The name Orlando to her faithful slave.
Bright shone the glory of the rising day,
When the fond traveller took his favourite way;
He mounted gaily, felt his bosom light,
And all he saw was pleasing in his sight.
"Ye hours of expectation, quickly fly,
And bring on hours of bless'd reality;
When I shall Laura see, beside her stand,
Hear her sweet voice, and press her yielded hand."

First o'er a barren heath beside the coast
Orlando rode, and joy began to boast.
"This neat low gorse," said he, "with golden bloom,
Delights each sense, is beauty, is perfume;
And this gay ling, with all its purple flowers,
A man at leisure might admire for hours;
This green-fringed cup-moss has a scarlet tip,
That yields to nothing but my Laura's lip;
And then how fine this herbage! men may say
A heath is barren; nothing is so gay:
Barren or bare to call such charming scene
Argues a mind possess'd by care and spleen."
Onward he went, and fiercer grew the heat,
Dust rose in clouds before the horse's feet;
For now he pass'd through lanes of burning sand,
Bounds to thin crops or yet uncultured land;
Where the dark poppy flourish'd on the dry
And sterile soil, and mock'd the thin-set rye.
"How lovely this!" the rapt Orlando said;
"With what delight is labouring man repaid!
The very lane has sweets that all admire,
The rambling suckling, and the vigorous brier;
See! wholesome wormwood grows beside the way,
Where dew-press'd yet the dog-rose bends the spray;
Fresh herbs the fields, fair shrubs the banks adorn,
And snow-white bloom falls flaky from the thorn;
No fostering hand they need, no sheltering wall,
They spring uncultured, and they bloom for all."
The Lover rode as hasty lovers ride,
And reach'd a common pasture wild and wide;
Small black-legg'd sheep devour with hunger keen
The meagre herbage, fleshless, lank, and lean:
Such o'er thy level turf, Newmarket! stray,
And there, with other black-legs, find their prey.
He saw some scatter'd hovels; turf was piled
In square brown stacks; a prospect bleak and wild!
A mill, indeed, was in the centre found,
With short sear herbage withering all around;
A smith's black shed opposed a wright's long shop,
And join'd an inn where humble travellers stop.
"Ay, this is Nature," said the gentle 'Squire;
"This ease, peace, pleasure—who would not admire?
With what delight these sturdy children play,
And joyful rustics at the close of day;
Sport follows labour; on this even space
Will soon commence the wrestling and the race;
Then will the village-maidens leave their home,
And to the dance with buoyant spirits come;

No affectation in their looks is seen,
Nor know they what disguise aud flattery mean;
Nor aught to move an envious pang they see,
Easy their service, and their love is free;
Hence early springs that love, it long endures,
And life's first comfort, while they live, ensures:
They the low roof and rustic comforts prize,
Nor cast on prouder mansions envying eyes:
Sometimes the news at yonder town they hear,
And learn what busier mortals feel and fear;
Secure themselves, although by tales amazed
Of towns bombarded and of cities razed;
As if they doubted, in their still retreat,
The very news that makes their quiet sweet,
And their days happy—happier only knows
He on whom Laura her regard bestows."
On rode Orlando, counting all the while
The miles he pass'd, and every coming mile;
Like all attracted things, he quicker flies,
The place approaching where th' attraction lies;
When next appear'd a dam—so call the place—
Where lies a road confined in narrow space;
A work of labour, for on either side
Is level fen, a prospect wild and wide,
With dikes on either hand by ocean's self supplied:
Far on the right the distant sea is seen,
And salt the springs that feed the marsh between:
Beneath an ancient bridge, the straiten'd flood
Rolls through its sloping banks of slimy mud;
Near it a sunken boat resists the tide,
That frets and hurries to th' opposing side;
The rushes sharp, that on the borders grow,
Bend their brown flow'rets to the stream below,
Impure in all its course, in all its progress slow:
Here a grave Flora scarcely deigns to bloom,
Nor wears a rosy blush, nor sheds perfume:
The few dull flowers that o'er the place are spread
Partake the nature of their fenny bed;
Here on its wiry stem, in rigid bloom,
Grows the salt lavender that lacks perfume;
Here the dwarf sallows creep, the septfoil harsh,
And the soft slimy mallow of the marsh;
Low on the ear the distant billows sound,
And just in view appears their stony bound;
No hedge nor tree conceals the glowing sun,
Birds, save a wat'ry tribe, the district shun,
Nor chirp among the reeds where bitter waters run.
"Various as beauteous, Nature, is thy face,"

Exclaim'd Orlando: "all that grows has grace:
All are appropriate—bog, and marsh, and fen,
Are only poor to undiscerning men;
Here may the nice and curious eye explore
How Nature's hand adorns the rushy moor;
Here the rare moss in secret shade is found,
Here the sweet myrtle of the shaking ground;
Beauties are these that from the view retire,
But well repay th' attention they require;
For these my Laura will her home forsake,
And all the pleasures they afford partake."
Again, the country was enclosed, a wide
And sandy road has banks on either side;
Where, lo! a hollow on the left appear'd,
And there a gipsy tribe their tent had rear'd;
'Twas open spread, to catch the morning sun,
And they had now their early meal begun,
When two brown boys just left their grassy seat,
The early Trav'ller with their prayers to greet:
While yet Orlando held his pence in hand,
He saw their sister on her duty stand;
Some twelve years old, demure, affected, sly,
Prepared the force of early powers to try;
Sudden a look of languor he descries,
And well-feign'd apprehension in her eyes;
Train'd but yet savage, in her speaking face
He mark'd the features of her vagrant race;
When a light laugh and roguish leer express'd
The vice implanted in her youthful breast:
Forth from the tent her elder brother came,
Who seem'd offended, yet forbore to blame
The young designer, but could only trace
The looks of pity in the trav'ller's face:
Within, the Father, who from fences nigh
Had brought the fuel for the fire's supply,
Watch'd now the feeble blaze, and stood dejected by.
On ragged rug, just borrow'd from the bed,
And by the hand of coarse indulgence fed,
In dirty patchwork negligently dress'd,
Reclined the Wife, an infant at her breast;
In her wild face some touch of grace remain'd,
Of vigour palsied and of beauty stain'd;
Her bloodshot eyes on her unheeding mate
Were wrathful turn'd, and seem'd her wants to state,
Cursing his tardy aid—her Mother there
With gipsy-state engross'd the only chair;
Solemn and dull her look; with such she stands,
And reads the milk-maid's fortune in her hands,

Tracing the lines of life; assumed through years,
Each feature now the steady falsehood wears;
With hard and savage eye she views the food,
And grudging pinches their intruding brood;
Last in the group, the worn-out Grandsire sits
Neglected, lost, and living but by fits:
Useless, despised, his worthless labours done,
And half protected by the vicious Son,
Who half supports him; he with heavy glance
Views the young ruffians who around him dance;
And, by the sadness in his face, appears
To trace the progress of their future years:
Through what strange course of misery, vice, deceit,
Must wildly wander each unpractised cheat!
What shame and grief, what punishment and pain,
Sport of fierce passions, must each child sustain—
Ere they like him approach their latter end,
Without a hope, a comfort, or a friend!
But this Orlando felt not; "Rogues," said he,
"Doubtless they are, but merry rogues they be;
They wander round the land, and be it true
They break the laws—then let the laws pursue
The wanton idlers; for the life they live,
Acquit I cannot, but I can forgive."
This said, a portion from his purse was thrown,
And every heart seem'd happy like his own.
He hurried forth, for now the town was nigh—
"The happiest man of mortal men am I."
Thou art! but change in every state is near
(So while the wretched hope, the bless'd may fear):
"Say, Where is Laura?"—"That her words must show,"
A lass replied; "read this, and thou shalt know!"
"What, gone!—'Her friend insisted—forced to go:
Is vex'd, was teased, could not refuse her'—No?
'But you can follow.' Yes! 'The miles are few,
The way is pleasant; will you come?—Adieu!
Thy Laura!' No! I feel I must resign
The pleasing hope; thou hadst been here, if mine.
A lady was it?—Was no brother there?
But why should I afflict me, if there were?
'The way is pleasant.' What to me the way?
I cannot reach her till the close of day.
My dumb companion! Is it thus we speed?
Not I from grief nor thou from toil art freed;
Still art thou doom'd to travel and to pine,
For my vexation—What a fate is mine!
"Gone to a friend, she tells me;—I commend
Her purpose: means she to a female friend?

By Heaven, I wish she suffer'd half the pain
Of hope protracted through the day in vain.
Shall I persist to see th' ungrateful maid?
Yes, I will see her, slight her, and upbraid.
What! in the very hour? She knew the time,
And doubtless chose it to increase her crime."
Forth rode Orlando by a river's side,
Inland and winding, smooth, and full, and wide,
That roll'd majestic on, in one soft-flowing tide;
The bottom gravel, flow'ry were the banks,
Tall willows waving in their broken ranks;
The road, now near, now distant, winding led
By lovely meadows which the waters fed;
He pass'd the way-side inn, the village spire,
Nor stopp'd to gaze, to question or admire;
On either side the rural mansions stood,
With hedge-row trees, and hills, high-crown'd with wood,
And many a devious stream that reach'd the nobler flood.
"I hate these scenes," Orlando angry cried,
"And these proud farmers! yes I hate their pride,
See! that sleek fellow, how he strides along,
Strong as an ox, and ignorant as strong;
Can yon close crops a single eye detain
But he who counts the profits of the grain?
And these vile beans with deleterious smell,
Where is there beauty? can a mortal tell?
These deep fat meadows I detest; it shocks
One's feelings there to see the grazing ox;—
For slaughter fatted, as a lady's smile
Rejoices man, and means his death the while.
Lo! now the sons of labour! every day
Employ'd in toil and vex'd in every way;
Theirs is but mirth assumed, and they conceal,
In their affected joys, the ills they feel:
I hate these long green lanes; there's nothing sees
In this vile country but eternal green;
Woods! waters! meadows! Will they never end?
'Tis a vile prospect:—Gone to see a friend?"
Still on he rode! a mansion fair and tall
Rose on his view—the pride of Loddon Hall:
Spread o'er the park he saw the grazing steer,
The full-fed steed, and herds of bounding deer:
On a clear stream the vivid sunbeams play'd,
Through noble elms, and on the surface made
That moving picture, checker'd light and shade;
Th' attended children, there indulged to stray,
Enjoy'd and gave new beauty to the day;
Whose happy parents from their room were seen

Pleased with the sportive idlers on the green.
"Well!" said Orlando, "and for one so bless'd,
A thousand reasoning wretches are distressed;
Nay, these, so seeming glad, are grieving like the rest:
Man is a cheat—and all but strive to hide
Their inward misery by their outward pride.
What do yon lofty gates and walls contain,
But fruitless means to sooth unconquer'd pain?
The parents read each infant daughter's smile,
Form'd to seduce, encouraged to beguile;
They view the boys unconscious of their fate,
Sure to be tempted, sure to take the bait;
These will be Lauras, sad Orlandos these—
There's guilt and grief in all one hears and sees."
Our Trav'ller, lab'ring up a hill, look'd down
Upon a lively, busy, pleasant town;
All he beheld were there alert, alive,
The busiest bees that ever stock'd a hive:
A pair were married, and the bells aloud
Proclaim'd their joy, and joyful seem'd the crowd;
And now, proceeding on his way, he spied,
Bound by strong ties, the bridegroom and the bride,
Each by some friends attended, near they drew,
And spleen beheld them with prophetic view.
"Married! nay mad!" Orlando cried in scorn;
"Another wretch on this unlucky morn:
What are this foolish mirth, these idle joys?
Attempts to stifle doubt and fear by noise:
To me these robes, expressive of delight,
Foreshow distress, and only grief excite;
And for these cheerful friends, will they behold
Their wailing brood in sickness, want, and cold;
And his proud look, and her soft languid air
Will—but I spare you—go, unhappy pair!"
And now, approaching to the Journey's end,
His anger fails, his thoughts to kindness tend,
He less offended feels, and rather fears t'offend:
Now gently rising, hope contends with doubt,
And casts a sunshine on the views without;
And still reviving joy and lingering gloom
Alternate empire o'er his soul assume;
Till, long perplex'd he now began to find
The softer thoughts engross the settling mind:
He saw the mansion, and should quickly see
His Laura's self—and angry could he be?
No! the resentment melted all away—
"For this my grief a single smile will pay,"
Our trav'ller cried;—"And why should it offend,

That one so good should have a pressing friend?
Grieve not, my heart! to find a favourite guest
Thy pride and boast—ye selfish sorrows rest;
She will be kind, and I again be bless'd."
While gentler passions thus his bosom sway'd
He reach'd the mansion, and he saw the maid;
"My Laura!"—"My Orlando!—this is kind;
In truth I came persuaded, not inclined:
Our friends' amusement let us now pursue,
And I to-morrow will return with you."
Like man entranced the happy Lover stood—
"As Laura wills, for she is kind and good;
Ever the truest, gentlest, fairest, best—
As Laura wills: I see her and am bless'd."
Home went the Lovers through that busy place,
By Loddon Hall, the country's pride and grace;
By the rich meadows where the oxen fed,
Through the green vale that form'd the river's bed;
And by unnumber'd cottages and farms,
That have for musing minds unnumbered charms;
And how affected by the view of these
Was then Orlando? did they pain or please?
Nor pain nor pleasure could they yield—and why?
The mind was fill'd, was happy, and the eye
Roved o'er the fleeting views, that but appear'd to die.
Alone Orlando on the morrow paced
The well-known road; the gipsy-tent he traced;
The dam high-raised, the reedy dikes between,
The scatter'd hovels on the barren green,
The burning sand, the fields of thin-set rye,
Mock'd by the useless Flora blooming by;
And last the heath with all its various bloom,
And the close lanes that led the trav'ller home.
Then could these scenes the former joys renew?
Or was there now dejection in the view?—
Nor one or other would they yield—and why?
The mind was absent, and the vacant eye
Wander'd o'er viewless scenes, that but appear'd to die.

TALE XI

EDWARD SHORE

Seem they grave or learned?
Why, so didst thou.—Seem they religious?
Why, so didst thou; or are they spare in diet,

Free from gross passion, or of mirth or anger,
Constant in spirit, not swerving with the blood,
Garnish'd and deck'd in modest compliment,
Not working with the eye without the ear,
And but with purged judgment trusting neither?
Such and so finely bolted didst thou seem.
SHAKESPEARE, Henry V.

Better I were distract,
So should my thoughts be sever'd from my griefs,
And woes by strong imagination lose
The knowledge of themselves.
King Lear.

Genius! thou gift of Heav'n! thou light divine!
Amid what dangers art thou doom'd to shine!
Oft will the body's weakness check thy force,
Oft damp thy vigour, and impede thy course;
And trembling nerves compel thee to restrain
Thy nobler efforts, to contend with pain;
Or want (sad guest!) will in thy presence come,
And breathe around her melancholy gloom:
To life's low cares will thy proud thought confine,
And make her sufferings, her impatience, thine.
Evil and strong, seducing passions prey
On soaring minds, and win them from their way,
Who then to Vice the subject spirits give,
And in the service of the conqu'ror live;
Like captive Samson making sport for all,
Who fear'd their strength, and glory in their fall.
Genius, with virtue, still may lack the aid
Implored by humble minds, and hearts afraid;
May leave to timid souls the shield and sword
Of the tried Faith, and the resistless Word;
Amid a world of dangers venturing forth,
Frail, but yet fearless, proud in conscious worth,
Till strong temptation, in some fatal time,
Assails the heart, and wins the soul to crime,
When left by honour, and by sorrow spent,
Unused to pray, unable to repent,
The nobler powers, that once exalted high
Th' aspiring man, shall then degraded lie:
Reason, through anguish, shall her throne forsake,
And strength of mind but stronger madness make.
When Edward Shore had reach'd his twentieth year,
He felt his bosom light, his conscience clear;
Applause at school the youthful hero gain'd,

And trials there with manly strength sustain'd:
With prospects bright upon the world he came,
Pure love of virtue, strong desire of fame:
Men watch'd the way his lofty mind would take,
And all foretold the progress he would make.
Boast of these friends, to older men a guide,
Proud of his parts, but gracious in his pride;
He bore a gay good-nature in his face,
And in his air were dignity and grace;
Dress that became his state and years he wore,
And sense and spirit shone in Edward Shore.
Thus, while admiring friends the Youth beheld,
His own disgust their forward hopes repell'd;
For he unfix'd, unfixing, look'd around,
And no employment but in seeking found;
He gave his restless thoughts to views refined,
And shrank from worldly cares with wounded mind.
Rejecting trade, awhile he dwelt on laws,
"But who could plead, if unapproved the cause?"
A doubting, dismal tribe physicians seem'd;
Divines o'er texts and disputations dream'd,
War and its glory he perhaps could love,
But there again he must the cause approve.
Our hero thought no deed should gain applause
Where timid virtue found support in laws;
He to all good would soar, would fly all sin,
By the pure prompting of the will within;
"Who needs a law that binds him not to steal,"
Ask'd the young teacher, "can he rightly feel?
To curb the will, or arm in honour's cause,
Or aid the weak—are these enforced by laws?
Should we a foul, ungenerous action dread,
Because a law condemns th' adulterous bed?
Or fly pollution, not for fear of stain,
But that some statute tells us to refrain?
The grosser herd in ties like these we bind,
In virtue's freedom moves th' enlighten'd mind."
"Man's heart deceives him," said a friend.—"Of course,"
Replied the Youth; "but has it power to force?
Unless it forces, call it as you will,
It is but wish, and proneness to the ill."
"Art thou not tempted?"—"Do I fall?" said Shore.
"The pure have fallen."—"Then are pure no more.
While reason guides me, I shall walk aright,
Nor need a steadier hand, or stronger light;
Nor this in dread of awful threats, design'd
For the weak spirit and the grov'ling mind;
But that, engaged by thoughts and views sublime,

I wage free war with grossness and with crime."
Thus look'd he proudly on the vulgar crew,
Whom statutes govern, and whom fears subdue.
Faith, with his virtue, he indeed profess'd,
But doubts deprived his ardent mind of rest;
Reason, his sovereign mistress, fail'd to show
Light through the mazes of the world below:
Questions arose, and they surpass'd the skill
Of his sole aid, and would be dubious still;
These to discuss he sought no common guide,
But to the doubters in his doubts applied;
When all together might in freedom speak,
And their loved truth with mutual ardour seek.
Alas! though men who feel their eyes decay
Take more than common pains to find their way,
Yet, when for this they ask each other's aid,
Their mutual purpose is the more delay'd:
Of all their doubts, their reasoning clear'd not one,
Still the same spots were present in the sun:
Still the same scruples haunted Edward's mind,
Who found no rest, nor took the means to find.
But though with shaken faith, and slave to fame,
Vain and aspiring on the world he came,
Yet was he studious, serious, moral, grave,
No passion's victim, and no system's slave:
Vice he opposed, indulgence he disdain'd,
And o'er each sense in conscious triumph reign'd.
Who often reads will sometimes wish to write,
And Shore would yield instruction and delight:
A serious drama he design'd, but found
'Twas tedious travelling in that gloomy ground;
A deep and solemn story he would try,
But grew ashamed of ghosts, and laid it by;
Sermons he wrote, but they who knew his creed,
Or knew it not, were ill-disposed to read;
And he would lastly be the nation's guide,
But, studying, fail'd to fix upon a side;
Fame he desired, and talents he possess'd,
But loved not labour, though he could not rest,
Nor firmly fix the vacillating mind,
That, ever working, could no centre find.
'Tis thus a sanguine reader loves to trace
The Nile forth rushing on his glorious race;
Calm and secure the fancied traveller goes
Through sterile deserts and by threat'ning foes;
He thinks not then of Afric's scorching sands,
Th' Arabian sea, the Abyssinian bands;
Fasils and Michaels, and the robbers all, [4]

Whom we politely chiefs and heroes call:
He of success alone delights to think,
He views that fount, he stands upon the brink,
And drinks a fancied draught, exulting so to drink.
In his own room, and with his books around,
His lively mind its chief employment found;
Then idly busy, quietly employ'd,
And, lost to life, his visions were enjoy'd:
Yet still he took a keen inquiring view
Of all that crowds neglect, desire, pursue;
And thus abstracted, curious, still, serene,
He, unemploy'd, beheld life's shifting scene:
Still more averse from vulgar joys and cares,
Still more unfitted for the world's affairs.
There was a house where Edward ofttimes went,
And social hours in pleasant trifling spent;
He read, conversed, and reason'd, sang and play'd,
And all were happy while the idler stay'd;
Too happy one! for thence arose the pain,
Till this engaging trifler came again.
But did he love? We answer, day by day,
The loving feet would take th' accustom'd way,
The amorous eye would rove as if in quest
Of something rare, and on the mansion rest;
The same soft passion touch'd the gentle tongue,
And Anna's charms in tender notes were sung;
The ear, too, seem'd to feel the common flame,
Soothed and delighted with the fair one's name;
And thus, as love each other part possess'd,
The heart, no doubt, its sovereign power confess'd.
Pleased in her sight, the Youth required no more;
Not rich himself, he saw the damsel poor;
And he too wisely, nay, too kindly loved,
To pain the being whom his soul approved.
A serious Friend our cautious Youth possess'd,
And at his table sat a welcome guest;
Both unemploy'd, it was their chief delight
To read what free and daring authors write;
Authors who loved from common views to soar,
And seek the fountains never traced before:
Truth they profess'd, yet often left the true
And beaten prospect, for the wild and new.
His chosen friend his fiftieth year had seen,
His fortune easy, and his air serene;
Deist and atheist call'd; for few agreed
What were his notions, principles, or creed;
His mind reposed not, for he hated rest,
But all things made a query or a jest;

Perplex'd himself, he ever sought to prove
That man is doom'd in endless doubt to rove;
Himself in darkness he profess'd to be,
And would maintain that not a man could see.
The youthful Friend, dissentient, reason'd still
Of the soul's prowess, and the subject-will;
Of virtue's beauty, and of honour's force,
And a warm zeal gave life to his discourse:
Since from his feelings all his fire arose,
And he had interest in the themes he chose.
The Friend, indulging a sarcastic smile,
Said, "Dear enthusiast! thou wilt change thy style,
When man's delusions, errors, crimes, deceit,
No more distress thee, and no longer cheat."
Yet, lo! this cautious man, so coolly wise,
On a young Beauty fix'd unguarded eyes;
And her he married: Edward at the view
Bade to his cheerful visits long adieu;
But haply err'd, for this engaging bride
No mirth suppress'd, but rather cause supplied:
And when she saw the friends, by reasoning long,
Confused if right, and positive if wrong,
With playful speech, and smile that spoke delight,
She made them careless both of wrong and right.
This gentle damsel gave consent to wed,
With school and school-day dinners in her head:
She now was promised choice of daintiest food,
And costly dress, that made her sovereign good;
With walks on hilly heath to banish spleen,
And summer-visits when the roads were clean.
All these she loved, to these she gave consent,
And she was married to her heart's content.
Their manner this—the Friends together read,
Till books a cause for disputation bred;
Debate then follow'd, and the vapour'd child
Declared they argued till her head was wild;
And strange to her it was that mortal brain
Could seek the trial, or endure the pain.
Then, as the Friend reposed, the younger pair
Sat down to cards, and play'd beside his chair;
Till he, awaking, to his books applied,
Or heard the music of th' obedient bride:
If mild the evening, in the fields they stray'd,
And their own flock with partial eye survey'd;
But oft the husband, to indulgence prone,
Resumed his book, and bade them walk alone.
"Do, my kind Edward—I must take mine ease—
Name the dear girl the planets and the trees:

Tell her what warblers pour their evening song,
What insects flutter, as you walk along;
Teach her to fix the roving thoughts, to bind
The wandering sense, and methodize the mind."
This was obey'd; and oft when this was done,
They calmly gazed on the declining sun;
In silence saw the glowing landscape fade,
Or, sitting, sang beneath the arbour's shade:
Till rose the moon, and on each youthful face
Shed a soft beauty and a dangerous grace.
When the young Wife beheld in long debate
Tho friends, all careless as she seeming sate,
It soon appear'd there was in one combined
The nobler person and the richer mind:
He wore no wig, no grisly beard was seen,
And none beheld him careless or unclean,
Or watch'd him sleeping. We indeed have heard
Of sleeping beauty, and it has appear'd;
'Tis seen in infants—there indeed we find
The features soften'd by the slumbering mind;
But other beauties, when disposed to sleep,
Should from the eye of keen inspector keep:
The lovely nymph who would her swain surprise,
May close her mouth, but not conceal her eyes;
Sleep from the fairest face some beauty takes,
And all the homely features homelier makes:
So thought our wife, beholding with a sigh
Her sleeping spouse, and Edward smiling by.
A sick relation for the husband sent;
Without delay the friendly sceptic went;
Nor fear'd the youthful pair, for he had seen
The wife untroubled, and the friend serene;
No selfish purpose in his roving eyes,
No vile deception in her fond replies:
So judged the husband, and with judgment true,
For neither yet the guilt or danger knew.
What now remain'd? but they again should play
Th' accustom'd game, and walk th' accustom'd way;
With careless freedom should converse or read,
And the Friend's absence neither fear nor heed:
But rather now they seem'd confused, constrain'd;
Within their room still restless they remain'd,
And painfully they felt, and knew each other pain'd.
Ah, foolish men! how could ye thus depend,
One on himself, the other on his friend?
The Youth with troubled eye the lady saw,
Yet felt too brave, too daring to withdraw;
While she, with tuneless hand the jarring keys

Touching, was not one moment at her ease:
Now would she walk, and call her friendly guide,
Now speak of rain, and cast her cloak aside;
Seize on a book, unconscious what she read,
And restless still to new resources fled;
Then laugh'd aloud, then tried to look serene;
And ever changed, and every change was seen.
Painful it is to dwell on deeds of shame—
The trying day was past, another came;
The third was all remorse, confusion, dread,
And (all too late!) the fallen hero fled.
Then felt the Youth, in that seducing time,
How feebly Honour guards the heart from crime:
Small is his native strength; man needs the stay,
The strength imparted in the trying day;
For all that Honour brings against the force
Of headlong passion, aids its rapid course;
Its slight resistance but provokes the fire,
As wood-work stops the flame, and then conveys it higher.
The Husband came; a wife by guilt made bold
Had, meeting, soothed him, as in days of old;
But soon this fact transpired; her strong distress,
And his Friend's absence, left him nought to guess.
Still cool, though grieved, thus prudence bade him write—
"I cannot pardon, and I will not fight;
Thou art too poor a culprit for the laws,
And I too faulty to support my cause:
All must be punish'd; I must sigh alone,
At home thy victim for her guilt atone;
And thou, unhappy! virtuous now no more,
Must loss of fame, peace, purity deplore;
Sinners with praise will pierce thee to the heart,
And saints, deriding, tell thee what thou art."
Such was his fall; and Edward, from that time,
Felt in full force the censure and the crime—
Despised, ashamed; his noble views before,
And his proud thoughts, degraded him the more:
Should he repent—would that conceal his shame?
Could peace be his? It perish'd with his fame:
Himself he scorn'd, nor could his crime forgive;
He fear'd to die, yet felt ashamed to live:
Grieved, but not contrite, was his heart; oppress'd,
Not broken; not converted, but distress'd;
He wanted will to bend the stubborn knee,
He wanted light the cause of ill to see,
To learn how frail is man, how humble then should be;
For faith he had not, or a faith too weak
To gain the help that humble sinners seek;

Else had he pray'd—to an offended God
His tears had flown a penitential flood;
Though far astray, he would have heard the call
Of mercy—"Come! return, thou prodigal:"
Then, though confused, distress'd, ashamed, afraid,
Still had the trembling penitent obey'd;
Though faith had fainted, when assail'd by fear,
Hope to the soul had whisper'd, "Persevere!"
Till in his Father's house, an humbled guest,
He would have found forgiveness, comfort, rest.
But all this joy was to our Youth denied
By his fierce passions and his daring pride;
And shame and doubt impell'd him in a course,
Once so abhorr'd, with unresisted force,
Proud minds and guilty, whom their crimes oppress,
Fly to new crimes for comfort and redress;
So found our fallen Youth a short relief
In wine, the opiate guilt applies to grief,—
From fleeting mirth that o'er the bottle lives,
From the false joy its inspiration gives,—
And from associates pleased to find a friend
With powers to lead them, gladden, and defend,
In all those scenes where transient ease is found,
For minds whom sins oppress and sorrows wound.
Wine is like anger; for it makes us strong,
Blind, and impatient, and it leads us wrong;
The strength is quickly lost, we feel the error long:
Thus led, thus strengthen'd, in an evil cause,
For folly pleading, sought the Youth applause;
Sad for a time, then eloquently wild,
He gaily spoke as his companions smiled;
Lightly he rose, and with his former grace
Proposed some doubt, and argued on the case;
Fate and foreknowledge were his favourite themes—
How vain man's purpose, how absurd his schemes:
"Whatever is, was ere our birth decreed;
We think our actions from ourselves proceed,
And idly we lament th' inevitable deed;
It seems our own, but there's a power above
Directs the motion, nay, that makes us move;
Nor good nor evil can you beings name,
Who are but rooks and castles in the game;
Superior natures with their puppets play,
Till, bagg'd or buried, all are swept away."
Such were the notions of a mind to ill
Now prone, but ardent and determined still:
Of joy now eager, as before of fame,
And screen'd by folly when assail'd by shame,

Deeply he sank; obey'd each passion's call,
And used his reason to defend them all.
Shall I proceed, and step by step relate
The odious progress of a Sinner's fate?
No—let me rather hasten to the time
(Sure to arrive!) when misery waits on crime.
With Virtue, prudence fled; what Shore possessed
Was sold, was spent, and he was now distressed:
And Want, unwelcome stranger, pale and wan,
Met with her haggard looks the hurried man:
His pride felt keenly what he must expect
From useless pity and from cold neglect.
Struck by new terrors, from his friends he fled,
And wept his woes upon a restless bed;
Retiring late, at early hour to rise,
With shrunken features, and with bloodshot eyes:
If sleep one moment closed the dismal view,
Fancy her terrors built upon the true:
And night and day had their alternate woes,
That baffled pleasure, and that mock'd repose;
Till to despair and anguish was consign'd
The wreck and ruin of a noble mind.
Now seized for debt, and lodged within a jail,
He tried his friendships, and he found them fail;
Then fail'd his spirits, and his thoughts were all
Fix'd on his sins, his sufferings, and his fall:
His ruffled mind was pictured in his face,
Once the fair seat of dignity and grace:
Great was the danger of a man so prone
To think of madness, and to think alone;
Yet pride still lived, and struggled to sustain
The drooping spirit and the roving brain;
But this too fail'd: a Friend his freedom gave,
And sent him help the threat'ning world to brave;
Gave solid counsel what to seek or flee,
But still would stranger to his person be:
In vain! the truth determined to explore,
He traced the Friend whom he had wrong'd before.
This was too much; both aided and advised
By one who shunn'd him, pitied, and despised:
He bore it not; 'twas a deciding stroke,
And on his reason like a torrent broke:
In dreadful stillness he appear'd a while,
With vacant horror and a ghastly smile;
Then rose at once into the frantic rage,
That force controlled not, nor could love assuage.
Friends now appear'd, but in the Man was seen
The angry Maniac, with vindictive mien;

Too late their pity gave to care and skill
The hurried mind and ever-wandering will:
Unnoticed pass'd all time, and not a ray
Of reason broke on his benighted way;
But now he spurn'd the straw in pure disdain,
And now laugh'd loudly at the clinking chain.
Then, as its wrath subsided by degrees,
The mind sank slowly to infantine ease,
To playful folly, and to causeless joy,
Speech without aim, and without end, employ;
He drew fantastic figures on the wall,
And gave some wild relation of them all;
With brutal shape he join'd the human face,
And idiot smiles approved the motley race.
Harmless at length th' unhappy man was found,
The spirit settled, but the reason drown'd;
And all the dreadful tempest died away
To the dull stillness of the misty day.
And now his freedom he attain'd—if free
The lost to reason, truth, and hope, can be;
His friends, or wearied with the charge, or sure
The harmless wretch was now beyond a cure,
Gave him to wander where he pleased, and find
His own resources for the eager mind:
The playful children of the place he meets,
Playful with them he rambles through the streets;
In all they need, his stronger arm he lends,
And his lost mind to these approving friends.
That gentle Maid, whom once the Youth had loved,
Is now with mild religious pity moved;
Kindly she chides his boyish flights, while he
Will for a moment fix'd and pensive be;
And as she trembling speaks, his lively eyes
Explore her looks, he listens to her sighs;
Charm'd by her voice, th' harmonious sounds invade
His clouded mind, and for a time persuade:
Like a pleased infant, who has newly caught
From the maternal glance a gleam of thought,
He stands enrapt, the half-known voice to hear,
And starts, half conscious, at the falling tear.
Rarely from town, nor then unwatch'd, he goes,
In darker mood, as if to hide his woes;
Returning soon, he with impatience seeks
His youthful friends, and shouts, and sings, and speaks;
Speaks a wild speech with action all is wild—
The children's leader, and himself a child;
He spins their top, or, at their bidding, bends
His back, while o'er it leap his laughing friends;

Simple and weak, he acts the boy once more,
And heedless children call him Silly Shore.

TALE XII

'SQUIRE THOMAS; OR THE PRECIPITATE CHOICE

Such smiling rogues as these,
Like rats, oft bite the holy cords in twain.
Too intrinsicate t'unloose.
SHAKESPEARE, King Lear.

My other self, my counsel's consistory,
My oracle, my prophet,
I as a child will go by thy direction.
Richard III.

If I do not have pitv upon her, I'm a villain:
If I do not love her, I am a Jew.
Much Ado about Nothing.

Women are soft, mild, pitiable, flexible;
But thou art obdurate, flinty, rough, remorseless.
Henry VI.

He must be told of it, and he shall; the office
Becomes a woman best; I'll take it upon me;
If I prove honey-mouth'd, let my tongue blister.
Winter's Tale.

Disguise, I see thou art a wickedness.
Twelfth Night.

'Squire Thomas flatter'd long a wealthy Aunt,
Who left him all that she could give or grant;
Ten years he tried, with all his craft and skill,
To fix the sovereign lady's varying will;
Ten years enduring at her board to sit,
He meekly listen'd to her tales and wit:
He took the meanest office man can take,
And his aunt's vices for her money's sake:
By many a threat'ning hint she waked his fear,
And he was pain'd to see a rival near:
Yet all the taunts of her contemptuous pride
He bore, nor found his grov'ling spirit tried:

Nay, when she wish'd his parents to traduce,
Fawning he smiled, and justice call'd th' abuse:
"They taught you nothing: are you not at best,"
Said the proud Dame, "a trifler, and a jest?
Confess you are a fool!"—he bow'd and he confess'd.
This vex'd him much, but could not always last:
The dame is buried, and the trial past.
There was a female, who had courted long
Her cousin's gifts, and deeply felt the wrong;
By a vain boy forbidden to attend
The private councils of her wealthy friend,
She vow'd revenge, nor should that crafty boy
In triumph undisturb'd his spoils enjoy:
He heard, he smiled, and when the Will was read,
Kindly dismiss'd the Kindred of the dead;
"The dear deceased" he call'd her, and the crowd
Moved off with curses deep and threat'nings loud.
The youth retired, and, with a mind at ease,
Found he was rich, and fancied he must please:
He might have pleased, and to his comfort found
The wife he wish'd, if he had sought around,
For there were lasses of his own degree,
With no more hatred to the state than he;
But he had courted spleen and age so long,
His heart refused to woo the fair and young;
So long attended on caprice and whim,
He thought attention now was due to him;
And as his flattery pleased the wealthy Dame,
Heir to the wealth, he might the flattery claim:
But this the fair, with one accord, denied,
Nor waived for man's caprice the sex's pride.
There is a season when to them is due
Worship and awe, and they will claim it too:
"Fathers," they cry, "long hold us in their chain,
Nay, tyrant brothers claim a right to reign:
Uncles and guardians we in turn obey,
And husbands rule with ever-during sway;
Short is the time when lovers at the feet
Of beauty kneel, and own the slavery sweet;
And shall we thus our triumph, this the aim
And boast of female power, forbear to claim?
No! we demand that homage, that respect,
Or the proud rebel punish and reject."
Our Hero, still too indolent, too nice,
To pay for beauty the accustom'd price,
No less forbore t'address the humbler maid,
Who might have yielded with the price unpaid;
But lived, himself to humour and to please,

To count his money, and enjoy his ease.
It pleased a neighbouring 'squire to recommend
A faithful youth as servant to his friend;
Nay, more than servant, whom he praised for parts
Ductile yet strong, and for the best of hearts:
One who might ease him in his small affairs,
With tenants, tradesmen, taxes, and repairs;
Answer his letters, look to all his dues,
And entertain him with discourse and news.
The 'Squire believed, and found the trusted youth
A very pattern for his care and truth;
Not for his virtues to be praised alone,
But for a modest mien and humble tone;
Assenting always, but as if he meant
Only to strength of reasons to assent:
For was he stubborn, and retain'd his doubt,
Till the more subtle 'Squire had forced it out;
Nay, still was right, but he perceived that strong
And powerful minds could make the right the wrong.
When the 'Squire's thoughts on some fair damsel dwelt,
The faithful Friend his apprehensions felt;
It would rejoice his faithful heart to find
A lady suited to his master's mind;
But who deserved that master? who would prove
That hers was pure, uninterested love?
Although a servant, he would scorn to take
A countess, till she suffer'd for his sake;
Some tender spirit, humble, faithful, true,
Such, my dear master! must be sought for you.
Six months had pass'd, and not a lady seen,
With just this love, 'twixt fifty and fifteen;
All seem'd his doctrine or his pride to shun,
All would be woo'd before they would be won;
When the chance naming of a race and fair
Our 'Squire disposed to take his pleasure there,
The Friend profess'd, "although he first began
To hint the thing, it seem'd a thoughtless plan;
The roads, he fear'd, were foul, the days were short,
The village far, and yet there might be sport."
"What! you of roads and starless nights afraid?
You think to govern! you to be obey'd!"
Smiling he spoke: the humble Friend declared
His soul's obedience, and to go prepared.
The place was distant, but with great delight
They saw a race, and hail'd the glorious sight:
The 'Squire exulted, and declared the ride
Had amply paid, and he was satisfied.
They gazed, they feasted, and, in happy mood,

Homeward return'd, and hastening as they rode;
For short the day, and sudden was the change
From light to darkness, and the way was strange:
Our hero soon grew peevish, then distress'd;
He dreaded darkness, and he sigh'd for rest:
Going, they pass'd a village; but alas!
Returning saw no village to repass;
The 'Squire remember'd too a noble hall,
Large as a church, and whiter than its wall:
This he had noticed as they rode along,
And justly reason'd that their road was wrong,
George, full of awe, was modest in reply—
"The fault was his, 'twas folly to deny;
And of his master's safety were he sure,
There was no grievance he would not endure."
This made his peace with the relenting 'Squire,
Whose thoughts yet dwelt on supper and a fire;
When, as they reach'd a long and pleasant green,
Dwellings of men, and next a man, were seen.
"My friend," said George, "to travellers astray
Point out an inn, and guide us on the way."
The man look'd up; "Surprising! can it be
My master's son? as I'm alive, 'tis he!"
"How! Robin?" George replied, "and are we near
My father's house? how strangely things appear!—
Dear sir, though wanderers, we at last are right:
Let us proceed, and glad my father's sight:
We shall at least be fairly lodged and fed,
I can ensure a supper and a bed;
Let us this night as one of pleasure date,
And of surprise: it is an act of Fate."
"Go on," the 'Squire in happy temper cried;
"I like such blunder! I approve such guide."
They ride, they halt, the farmer comes in haste,
Then tells his wife how much their house is graced;
They bless the chance, they praise the lucky son.
That caused the error—Nay! it was not one,
But their good fortune: cheerful grew the 'Squire,
Who found dependants, flattery, wine, and fire;
He heard the jack turn round; the busy dame
Produced her damask; and with supper came
The Daughter, dress'd with care, and full of maiden shame.
Surprised, our hero saw the air and dress,
And strove his admiration to express;
Nay! felt it too—for Harriot was in truth
A tall fair beauty in the bloom of youth;
And from the pleasure and surprise, a grace
Adorn'd the blooming damsel's form and face;

Then, too, such high respect and duty paid
By all—such silent reverence in the maid;
Vent'ring with caution, yet with haste, a glance,
Loth to retire, yet trembling to advance,
Appear'd the nymph, and in her gentle guest
Stirr'd soft emotions till the hour of rest;
Sweet was his sleep, and in the morn again
He felt a mixture of delight and pain:
"How fair, how gentle," said the 'Squire, "how meek,
And yet how sprightly, when disposed to speak!
Nature has bless'd her form, and heaven her mind,
But in her favours Fortune is unkind;
Poor is the maid—nay, poor she cannot prove
Who is enrich'd with beauty, worth, and love."
The 'Squire arose, with no precise intent
To go or stay—uncertain what he meant:
He moved to part—they begg'd him first to dine;
And who could then escape from Love and Wine?
As came the night, more charming grew the Fair,
And seem'd to watch him with a twofold care:
On the third morn, resolving not to stay,
Though urged by Love, he bravely rode away.
Arrived at home, three pensive days he gave
To feelings fond and meditations grave;
Lovely she was, and, if he did not err,
As fond of him as his fond heart of her;
Still he delay'd, unable to decide,
Which was the master-passion, Love or Pride:
He sometimes wonder'd how his friend could make,
And then exulted in, the night's mistake;
Had she but fortune, "Doubtless then," he cried,
"Some happier man had won the wealthy bride."
While thus he hung in balance, now inclined
To change his state, and then to change his mind,
That careless George dropp'd idly on the ground
A letter, which his crafty master found;
The stupid youth confess'd his fault, and pray'd
The generous 'Squire to spare a gentle maid,
Of whom her tender mother, full of fears,
Had written much—"she caught her oft in tears,
For ever thinking on a youth above
Her humble fortune—still she own'd not love;
Nor can define, dear girl! the cherish'd pain,
But would rejoice to see the cause again:
That neighbouring youth, whom she endured before,
She now rejects, and will behold no more;
Raised by her passion, she no longer stoops
To her own equals, but she pines and droops,

Like to a lily on whose sweets the sun
Has withering gazed—she saw and was undone;
His wealth allured her not—nor was she moved
By his superior state, himself she loved;
So mild, so good, so gracious, so genteel,—
But spare your sister, and her love conceal;
We must the fault forgive, since she the pain must feel."
"Fault!" said the 'Squire, "there's coarseness in the mind
That thus conceives of feelings so refined;
Here end my doubts, nor blame yourself, my friend,
Fate made you careless—here my doubts have end."
The way is plain before us—there is now
The Lover's visit first, and then the vow,
Mutual and fond, the marriage-rite, the Bride
Brought to her home with all a husband's pride:
The 'Squire receives the prize his merits won,
And the glad parents leave the patron-son.
But in short time he saw, with much surprise,
First gloom, then grief, and then resentment rise,
From proud, commanding frowns, and anger-darting eyes:
"Is there in Harriot's humble mind this fire,
This fierce impatience?" ask'd the puzzled 'Squire:
"Has marriage changed her? or the mask she wore
Has she thrown by, and is herself once more?"
Hour after hour, when clouds on clouds appear,
Dark and more dark, we know the tempest near;
And thus the frowning brow, the restless form,
And threat'ning glance, forerun domestic storm:
So read the Husband, and, with troubled mind,
Reveal'd his fears—"My Love, I hope you find
All here is pleasant—but I must confess
You seem offended, or in some distress:
Explain the grief you feel, and leave me to redress."
"Leave it to you?" replied the Nymph—"indeed!
What to the cause from whence the ills proceed?
Good Heaven! to take me from a place where I
Had every comfort underneath the sky;
And then immure me in a gloomy place,
With the grim monsters of your ugly race,
That from their canvas staring, make me dread
Through the dark chambers, where they hang, to tread.
No friend nor neighbour comes to give that joy
Which all things here must banish or destroy.
Where is the promised coach? the pleasant ride?
Oh! what a fortune has a Farmer's bride!
Your sordid pride has placed me just above
Your hired domestics—and what pays me? Love!
A selfish fondness I endure each hour,

And share unwitness'd pomp, unenvied power.
I hear your folly, smile at your parade,
And see your favourite dishes duly made;
Then am I richly dress'd for you t'admire,
Such is my duty and my Lord's desire:
Is this a life for youth, for health, for joy?
Are these my duties—this my base employ?
No! to my father's house will I repair,
And make your idle wealth support me there.
Was it your wish to have an humble bride,
For bondage thankful? Curse upon your pride!
Was it a slave you wanted? You shall see,
That, if not happy, I at least am free:
Well, sir! your answer."—Silent stood the 'Squire,
As looks a miser at his house on fire;
Where all he deems is vanish'd in that flame,
Swept from the earth his substance and his name,
So, lost to every promised joy of life,
Our 'Squire stood gaping at his angry wife;—
His fate, his ruin, where he saw it vain
To hope for peace, pray, threaten, or complain;
And thus, betwixt his wonder at the ill
And his despair, there stood he gaping still.
"Your answer, sir!—Shall I depart a spot
I thus detest?"—"Oh, miserable lot!"
Exclaim'd the man. "Go, serpent! nor remain
To sharpen woe by insult and disdain;
A nest of harpies was I doom'd to meet;
What plots, what combinations of deceit!
I see it now—all plann'd, design'd, contrived;
Served by that villain—by this fury wived—
What fate is mine! What wisdom, virtue truth,
Can stand if demons set their traps for youth?
He lose his way? vile dog! he cannot lose
The way a villain through his life pursues;
And thou, deceiver! thou afraid to move,
And hiding close the serpent in the dove!
I saw—but, fated to endure disgrace,
Unheeding saw—the fury in thy face,
And call'd it spirit. Oh: I might have found
Fraud and imposture all the kindred round!
A nest of vipers"—
"Sir, I'll not admit
These wild effusions of your angry wit:
Have you that value, that we all should use
Such mighty arts for such important views?
Are you such prize—and is my state so fair,
That they should sell their souls to get me there?

Think you that we alone our thoughts disguise?
When, in pursuit of some contended prize,
Mask we alone the heart, and soothe whom we despise?
Speak you of craft and subtle schemes, who know
That all your wealth you to deception owe;
Who play'd for ten dull years a scoundrel part,
To worm yourself into a Widow's heart?
Now, when you guarded, with superior skill,
That lady's closet, and preserved her Will,
Blind in your craft, you saw not one of those
Opposed by you might you in turn oppose,
Or watch your motions, and by art obtain
Share of that wealth you gave your peace to gain.
Did conscience never"—
"Cease, tormentor, cease—
Or reach me poison;—let me rest in peace!"
"Agreed—but hear me—let the truth appear."
"Then state your purpose—I'll be calm and hear."
"Know then, this wealth, sole object of your care,
I had some right, without your hand, to share;
My mother's claim was just—but soon she saw
Your power, compell'd, insulted, to withdraw:
'Twas then my father, in his anger, swore
You should divide the fortune, or restore.
Long we debated—and you find me now
Heroic victim to a father's vow;
Like Jephtha's daughter, but in different state,
And both decreed to mourn our early fate:
Hence was my brother servant to your pride,
Vengeance made him your slave, and me your bride.
Now all is known—a dreadful price I pay
For our revenge—but still we have our day:
All that you love you must with others share,
Or all you dread from their resentment dare:—
Yet terms I offer—let contention cease;
Divide the spoil, and let us part in peace."
Our hero trembling heard—he sat, he rose—
Nor could his motions nor his mind compose;
He paced the room—and, stalking to her side,
Gazed on the face of his undaunted bride,
And nothing there but scorn and calm aversion spied.
He would have vengeance, yet he fear'd the law;
Her friends would threaten, and their power he saw;
"Then let her go:" but, oh! a mighty sum
Would that demand, since he had let her come;
Nor from his sorrows could he find redress,
Save that which led him to a like distress;
And all his ease was in his wife to see

A wretch as anxious and distress'd as he:
Her strongest wish, the fortune to divide,
And part in peace, his avarice denied;
And thus it happen'd, as in all deceit,
The cheater found the evil of the cheat;
The Husband griev'd—nor was the Wife at rest;
Him she could vex, and he could her molest;
She could his passion into frenzy raise,
But, when the fire was kindled, fear'd the blaze;
As much they studied, so in time they found
The easiest way to give the deepest wound;
But then, like fencers, they were equal still,—
Both lost in danger what they gain'd in skill;
Each heart a keener kind of rancour gain'd,
And, paining more, was more severely pain'd,
And thus by both was equal vengeance dealt,
And both the anguish they inflicted felt.

TALE XIII

JESSE AND COLIN

*Then she plots, then she ruminates, then she devises; and what they think in their hearts they may effect,
they will break their hearts but they will effect.
SHAKESPEARE, Merry Wives of Windsor.*

*She hath spoken that she should not, I am sure of that; Heaven knows what she hath known.
Macbeth.*

*Our house is hell, and thou a merry devil.
Merchant of Venice.*

*And yet, for aught I see, they are as sick that surfeit of too much, as they that starve with nothing; it is no
mean happiness, therefore, to be seated in the mean.
Merchant of Venice.*

A Vicar died and left his Daughter poor—
It hurt her not, she was not rich before:
Her humble share of worldly goods she sold,
Paid every debt, and then her fortune told;
And found, with youth and beauty, hope and health,
Two hundred guineas was her worldly wealth;
It then remain'd to choose her path in life,
And first, said Jesse, "Shall I be a wife?—
Colin is mild and civil, kind and just,

I know his love, his temper I can trust;
But small his farm, it asks perpetual care,
And we must toil as well as trouble share:
True, he was taught in all the gentle arts
That raise the soul and soften human hearts;
And boasts a parent, who deserves to shine
In higher class, and I could wish her mine;
Nor wants he will his station to improve,
A just ambition waked by faithful love;
Still is he poor—and here my Father's Friend
Deigns for his Daughter, as her own, to send:
A worthy lady, who it seems has known
A world of griefs and troubles of her own:
I was an infant when she came a guest
Beneath my father's humble roof to rest;
Her kindred all unfeeling, vast her woes,
Such her complaint, and there she found repose;
Enrich'd by fortune, now she nobly lives,
And nobly, from the bless'd abundance, gives;
The grief, the want, of human life she knows,
And comfort there and here relief bestows:
But are they not dependants?—Foolish pride!
Am I not honour'd by such friend and guide?
Have I a home" (here Jesse dropp'd a tear),
"Or friend beside?"—A faithful friend was near.
Now Colin came, at length resolved to lay
His heart before her, and to urge her stay:
True, his own plough the gentle Colin drove,
An humble farmer with aspiring love;
Who, urged by passion, never dared till now,
Thus urged by fears, his trembling hopes avow:
Her father's glebe he managed; every year
The grateful Vicar held the youth more dear;
He saw indeed the prize in Colin's view,
And wish'd his Jesse with a man so true:
Timid as true, he urged with anxious air
His tender hope, and made the trembling prayer,
When Jesse saw, nor could with coldness see,
Such fond respect, such tried sincerity;
Grateful for favours to her father dealt,
She more than grateful for his passion felt;
Nor could she frown on one so good and kind,
Yet fear'd to smile, and was unfix'd in mind;
But prudence placed the Female Friend in view—
What might not one so rich and grateful do?
So lately, too, the good old Vicar died,
His faithful daughter must not cast aside
The signs of filial grief, and be a ready bride.

Thus, led by prudence, to the Lady's seat
The Village-Beauty purposed to retreat;
But, as in hard-fought fields the victor knows
What to the vanquish'd he in honour owes,
So, in this conquest over powerful love,
Prudence resolved a generous foe to prove,
And Jesse felt a mingled fear and pain
In her dismission of a faithful swain,
Gave her kind thanks, and when she saw his woe,
Kindly betray'd that she was loth to go;
"But would she promise, if abroad she met
A frowning world, she would remember yet
Where dwelt a friend?"—"That could she not forget."
And thus they parted; but each faithful heart
Felt the compulsion, and refused to part.
Now, by the morning mail the timid Maid
Was to that kind and wealthy Dame conveyed;
Whose invitation, when her father died,
Jesse as comfort to her heart applied;
She knew the days her generous Friend had seen—
As wife and widow, evil days had been;
She married early, and for half her life
Was an insulted and forsaken wife;
Widow'd and poor, her angry father gave,
Mix'd with reproach, the pittance of a slave;
Forgetful brothers pass'd her, but she knew
Her humbler friends, and to their home withdrew:
The good old Vicar to her sire applied
For help, and help'd her when her sire denied.
When in few years Death stalk'd through bower and hall,
Sires, sons, and sons of sons, were buried all,
She then abounded, and had wealth to spare
For softening grief she once was doom'd to share;
Thus train'd in misery's school, and taught to feel,
She would rejoice an orphan's woes to heal:—
So Jesse thought, who look'd within her breast,
And thence conceived how bounteous minds are bless'd.
From her vast mansion look'd the Lady down
On humbler buildings of a busy town;
Thence came her friends of either sex, and all
With whom she lived on terms reciprocal:
They pass'd the hours with their accustom'd ease,
As guests inclined, but not compelled, to please;
But there were others in the mansion found,
For office chosen, and by duties bound;
Three female rivals, each of power possess'd,
Th' attendant Maid, poor Friend, and kindred Guest.
To these came Jesse, as a seaman thrown

By the rude storm upon a coast unknown:
The view was flattering, civil seem'd the race,
But all unknown the dangers of the place.
Few hours had pass'd, when, from attendants freed
The Lady utter'd, "This is kind indeed;
Believe me, love! that I for one like you
Have daily pray'd, a friend discreet and true;
Oh! wonder not that I on you depend,
You are mine own hereditary friend:
Hearken, my Jesse, never can I trust
Beings ungrateful, selfish, and unjust;
But you are present, and my load of care
Your love will serve to lighten and to share:
Come near me, Jesse—let not those below
Of my reliance on your friendship know;
Look as they look, be in their freedoms free—
But all they say do you convey to me."
Here Jesse's thoughts to Colin's cottage flew,
And with such speed she scarce their absence knew.
"Jane loves her mistress, and should she depart,
I lose her service, and she breaks her heart;
My ways and wishes, looks and thoughts, she knows,
And duteous care by close attention shows:
But is she faithful? in temptation strong,
Will she not wrong me? ah! I fear the wrong;
Your father loved me; now, in time of need,
Watch for my good, and to his place succeed.
"Blood doesn't bind—that Girl, who every day
Eats of my bread, would wish my life away;
I am her dear relation, and she thinks
To make her fortune, an ambitious minx!
She only courts me for the prospect's sake,
Because she knows I have a Will to make;
Yes, love! my Will delay'd, I know not how—
But you are here, and I will make it now.
"That idle creature, keep her in your view,
See what she does, what she desires to do;
On her young mind may artful villains prey,
And to my plate and jewels find a way:
A pleasant humour has the girl; her smile,
And cheerful manner, tedious hours beguile:
But well observe her, ever near her be,
Close in your thoughts, in your professions free.
"Again, my Jesse, hear what I advise,
And watch a woman ever in disguise;
Issop, that widow, serious, subtle, sly—
But what of this?—I must have company:
She markets for me, and although she makes

Profit, no doubt, of all she undertakes,
Yet she is one I can to all produce,
And all her talents are in daily use:
Deprived of her, I may another find
As sly and selfish, with a weaker mind:
But never trust her, she is full of art,
And worms herself into the closest heart;
Seem then, I pray you, careless in her sight,
Nor let her know, my love, how we unite.
"Do, my good Jesse, cast a view around,
And let no wrong within my house be found;
That Girl associates with—I know not who
Are her companions, nor what ill they do;
'Tis then the Widow plans, 'tis then she tries
Her various arts and schemes for fresh supplies;
'Tis then, if ever, Jane her duty quits,
And, whom I know not, favours and admits:
Oh! watch their movements all; for me 'tis hard,
Indeed is vain, but you may keep a guard;
And I, when none your watchful glance deceive,
May make my Will, and think what I shall leave."
Jesse, with fear, disgust, alarm, surprise,
Heard of these duties for her ears and eyes;
Heard by what service she must gain her bread,
And went with scorn and sorrow to her bed.
Jane was a servant fitted for her place,
Experienced, cunning, fraudful, selfish, base;
Skill'd in those mean humiliating arts
That make their way to proud and selfish hearts:
By instinct taught, she felt an awe, a fear,
For Jesse's upright, simple character;
Whom with gross flattery she awhile assail'd,
And then beheld with hatred when it fail'd;
Yet, trying still upon her mind for hold,
She all the secrets of the mansion told;
And, to invite an equal trust, she drew
Of every mind a bold and rapid view;
But on the widow'd Friend with deep disdain,
And rancorous envy, dwelt the treacherous Jane:
In vain such arts;—without deceit or pride,
With a just taste and feeling for her guide,
From all contagion Jesse kept apart,
Free in her manners, guarded in her heart.
Jesse one morn was thoughtful, and her sigh
The Widow heard as she was passing by;
And—"Well!" she said, "is that some distant swain,
Or aught with us, that gives your bosom pain?
Come, we are fellow-sufferers, slaves in thrall,

And tasks and griefs are common to us all;
Think not my frankness strange: they love to paint
Their state with freedom, who endure restraint;
And there is something in that speaking eye
And sober mien that prove I may rely:
You came a stranger; to my words attend,
Accept my offer, and you find a friend;
It is a labyrinth in which you stray,
Come, hold my clue, and I will lead the way.
"Good Heav'n! that one so jealous, envious, base,
Should be the mistress of so sweet a place;
She, who so long herself was low and poor,
Now broods suspicious on her useless store;
She loves to see us abject, loves to deal
Her insult round, and then pretends to feel:
Prepare to cast all dignity aside,
For know, your talents will be quickly tried;
Nor think, from favours past a friend to gain,—
'Tis but by duties we our posts maintain:
I read her novels, gossip through the town,
And daily go, for idle stories down;
I cheapen all she buys, and bear the curse
Of honest tradesmen for my niggard purse;
And, when for her this meanness I display,
She cries, 'I heed not what I throw away;'
Of secret bargains I endure the shame,
And stake my credit for our fish and game;
Oft has she smiled to hear 'her generous soul
Would gladly give, but stoops to my control:'
Nay! I have heard her, when she chanced to come
Where I contended for a petty sum,
Affirm 'twas painful to behold such care,
'But Issop's nature is to pinch and spare:'
Thus all the meanness of the house is mine,
And my reward—to scorn her, and to dine.
"See next that giddy thing, with neither pride
To keep her safe, nor principle to guide:
Poor, idle, simple flirt! as sure as fate
Her maiden-fame will have an early date:
Of her beware; for all who live below
Have faults they wish not all the world to know,
And she is fond of listening, full of doubt,
And stoops to guilt to find an error out.
"And now once more observe the artful Maid,
A lying, prying, jilting, thievish jade;
I think, my love, you would not condescend
To call a low, illiterate girl your friend:
But in our troubles we are apt, you know,

To lean on all who some compassion show;
And she has flexile features, acting eyes,
And seems with every look to sympathise;
No mirror can a mortal's grief express
With more precision, or can feel it less;
That proud, mean spirit, she by fawning courts
By vulgar flattery, and by vile reports;
And by that proof she every instant gives
To one so mean, that yet a meaner lives.
"Come, I have drawn the curtain, and you see
Your fellow-actors, all our company;
Should you incline to throw reserve aside,
And in my judgment and my love confide,
I could some prospects open to your view,
That ask attention—and, till then, adieu."
"Farewell!" said Jesse, hastening to her room,
Where all she saw within, without, was gloom:
Confused, perplex'd, she pass'd a dreary hour,
Before her reason could exert its power;
To her all seem'd mysterious, all allied
To avarice, meanness, folly, craft, and pride;
Wearied with thought, she breathed the garden's air,
Then came the laughing Lass, and join'd her thore.
"My sweetest friend has dwelt with us a week,
And does she love us? be sincere and speak;
My Aunt you cannot—Lord! how I should hate
To be like her, all misery and state;
Proud, and yet envious, she disgusted sees
All who are happy, and who look at ease.
Let friendship bind us, I will quickly show
Some favourites near us you'll be bless'd to know;
My aunt forbids it—but, can she expect,
To soothe her spleen, we shall ourselves neglect?
Jane and the Widow were to watch and stay
My free-born feet; I watch'd as well as they:
Lo! what is this?—this simple key explores
The dark recess that holds the Spinster's stores:
And, led by her ill star, I chanced to see
Where Issop keeps her stock of ratafie;
Used in the hours of anger and alarm,
It makes her civil, and it keeps her warm:
Thus bless'd with secrets both would choose to hide,
Their fears now grant me what their scorn denied.
"My freedom thus by their assent secured,
Bad as it is, the place may be endured;
And bad it is, but her estates, you know,
And her beloved hoards, she must bestow;
So we can slily our amusements take,

And friends of demons, if they help us, make."
"Strange creatures these," thought Jesse, half inclined
To smile at one malicious and yet kind;
Frank and yet cunning, with a heart to love
And malice prompt—the serpent and the dove;
Here could she dwell? or could she yet depart?
Could she be artful? could she bear with art?—
This splendid mansion gave the cottage grace,
She thought a dungeon was a happier place;
And Colin pleading, when he pleaded best,
Wrought not such sudden change in Jesse's breast.
The wondering maiden, who had only read
Of such vile beings, saw them now with dread;
Safe in themselves—for nature has design'd
The creature's poison harmless to the kind;
But all beside who in the haunts are found
Must dread the poison, and must feel the wound.
Days full of care, slow weary weeks pass'd on,
Eager to go, still Jesse was not gone;
Her time in trifling, or in tears, she spent,
She never gave, she never felt, content:
The Lady wonder'd that her humble guest
Strove not to please, would neither lie nor jest;
She sought no news, no scandal would convey,
But walk'd for health, and was at church to pray:
All this displeased, and soon the Widow cried,
"Let me be frank—I am not satisfied;
You know my wishes, I your judgment trust;
You can be useful, Jesse, and you must:
Let me be plainer, child—I want an ear,
When I am deaf, instead of mine to hear;
When mine is sleeping let your eye awake;
When I observe not, observation take:
Alas! I rest not on my pillow laid,
Then threat'ning whispers make my soul afraid;
The tread of strangers to my ear ascends,
Fed at my cost, the minions of my friends;
While you, without a care, a wish to please,
Eat the vile bread of idleness and ease."
Th' indignant Girl, astonish'd, answer'd—"Nay!
This instant, madam, let me haste away:
Thus speaks my father's, thus an orphan's friend?
This instant, lady, let your bounty end."
The Lady frown'd indignant—"What!" she cried,
"A vicar's daughter with a princess' pride
And pauper's lot! but pitying I forgive;
How, simple Jesse, do you think to live?
Have I not power to help you, foolish maid?

To my concerns be your attention paid;
With cheerful mind th' allotted duties take,
And recollect I have a Will to make."
Jesse, who felt as liberal natures feel,
When thus the baser their designs reveal,
Replied—"Those duties were to her unfit,
Nor would her spirit to her tasks submit."
In silent scorn the Lady sat awhile,
And then replied with stern contemptuous smile—
"Think you, fair madam, that you came to share
Fortunes like mine without a thought or care?
A guest, indeed! from every trouble free,
Dress'd by my help, with not a care for me;
When I a visit to your father made,
I for the poor assistance largely paid;
To his domestics I their tasks assign'd,
I fix'd the portion for his hungry hind;
And had your father (simple man!) obey'd
My good advice, and watch'd as well as pray'd,
He might have left you something with his prayers,
And lent some colour for these lofty airs.—
"In tears, my love! Oh, then my soften'd heart
Cannot resist—we never more will part;
I need your friendship—I will be your friend,
And, thus determined, to my Will attend."
Jesse went forth, but with determined soul
To fly such love, to break from such control:
"I hear enough," the trembling damsel cried;
Flight be my care, and Providence my guide:
Ere yet a prisoner, I escape will make;
Will, thus display'd, th' insidious arts forsake,
And, as the rattle sounds, will fly the fatal snake."
Jesse her thanks upon the morrow paid,
Prepared to go, determined though afraid.
"Ungrateful creature!" said the Lady, "this
Could I imagine?—are you frantic, miss?
What! leave your friend, your prospects—is it true?"
This Jesse answer'd by a mild "Adieu?"
The Dame replied "Then houseless may you rove,
The starving victim to a guilty love;
Branded with shame, in sickness doom'd to nurse
An ill-form'd cub, your scandal and your curse;
Spurn'd by its scoundrel father, and ill fed
By surly rustics with the parish-bread!—
Relent you not?—speak—yet I can forgive;
Still live with me."—"With you," said Jesse, "live?
No! I would first endure what you describe,
Rather than breathe with your detested tribe;

Who long have feign'd, till now their very hearts
Are firmly fix'd in their accursed parts;
Who all profess esteem, and feel disdain,
And all, with justice, of deceit complain;
Whom I could pity, but that, while I stay,
My terror drives all kinder thoughts away;
Grateful for this, that, when I think of you,
I little fear what poverty can do."
The angry matron her attendant Jane
Summon'd in haste to soothe the fierce disdain:—
"A vile detested wretch!" the Lady cried,
"Yet shall she be by many an effort tried,
And, clogg'd with debt and fear, against her will abide;
And, once secured, she never shall depart
Till I have proved the firmness of her heart:
Then when she dares not, would not, cannot go
I'll make her feel what 'tis to use me so."
The pensive Colin in his garden stray'd,
But felt not then the beauties it display'd;
There many a pleasant object met his view,
A rising wood of oaks behind it grew;
A stream ran by it, and the village-green
And public road were from the garden seen;
Save where the pine and larch the bound'ry made,
And on the rose-beds threw a softening shade.
The Mother sat beside the garden-door,
Dress'd as in times ere she and hers were poor;
The broad-laced cap was known in ancient days,
When madam's dress compell'd the village praise;
And still she look'd as in the times of old,
Ere his last farm the erring husband sold;
While yet the mansion stood in decent state,
And paupers waited at the well-known gate.
"Alas, my son!" the Mother cried, "and why
That silent grief and oft-repeated sigh?
True we are poor, but thou hast never felt
Pangs to thy father for his error dealt;
Pangs from strong hopes of visionary gain,
For ever raised, and ever found in vain.
He rose unhappy from his fruitless schemes,
As guilty wretches from their blissful dreams;
But thou wert then, my son, a playful child,
Wondering at grief, gay, innocent, and wild;
Listening at times to thy poor mother's sighs
With curious looks and innocent surprise;
Thy father dying, thou my virtuous boy,
My comfort always, waked my soul to joy;
With the poor remnant of our fortune left,

Thou hast our station of its gloom bereft:
Thy lively temper, and thy cheerful air,
Have cast a smile on sadness and despair;
Thy active hand has dealt to this poor space
The bliss of plenty and the charm of grace;
And all around us wonder when they find
Such taste and strength, such skill and power combined;
There is no mother, Colin, no not one,
But envies me so kind, so good a son;
By thee supported on this failing side,
Weakness itself awakes a parent's pride:
I bless the stroke that was my grief before,
And feel such joy that 'tis disease no more;
Shielded by thee, my want becomes my wealth,
And, soothed by Colin, sickness smiles at health;
The old men love thee, they repeat thy praise,
And say, like thee were youth in earlier days;
While every village-maiden cries, 'How gay,
How smart, how brave, how good is Colin Grey!'
"Yet art thou sad; alas! my son, I know
Thy heart is wounded, and the cure is slow;
Fain would I think that Jesse still may come
To share the comforts of our rustic home:
She surely loved thee; I have seen the maid,
When thou hast kindly brought the Vicar aid—
When thou hast eased his bosom of its pain,
Oh! I have seen her—she will come again."
The Matron ceased; and Colin stood the while
Silent, but striving for a grateful smile;
He then replied—"Ah! sure, had Jesse stay'd,
And shared the comforts of our sylvan shade,
The tenderest duty and the fondest love
Would not have fail'd that generous heart to move;
A grateful pity would have ruled her breast,
And my distresses would have made me bless'd.
"But she is gone, and ever has in view
Grandeur and taste,—and what will then ensue?
Surprise and then delight in scenes so fair and new;
For many a day, perhaps for many a week,
Home will have charms, and to her bosom speak;
But thoughtless ease, and affluence, and pride,
Seen day by day, will draw the heart aside:
And she at length, though gentle and sincere,
Will think no more of our enjoyments here."
Sighing he spake—but hark! he hears th' approach
Of rattling wheels! and, lo! the evening coach;
Once more the movement of the horses' feet
Makes the fond heart with strong emotion beat:

Faint were his hopes, but ever had the sight
Drawn him to gaze beside his gate at night;
And when with rapid wheels it hurried by,
He grieved his parent with a hopeless sigh;
And could the blessing have been bought—what sum
Had he not offer'd to have Jesse come!
She came—he saw her bending from the door,
Her face, her smile, and he beheld no more;
Lost in his joy—the mother lent her aid
T'assist and to detain the willing Maid;
Who thought her late, her present home to make,
Sure of a welcome for the Vicar's sake:
But the good parent was so pleased, so kind,
So pressing Colin, she so much inclined,
That night advanced; and then, so long detain'd,
No wishes to depart she felt, or feign'd;
Yet long in doubt she stood, and then perforce remain'd.
Here was a lover fond, a friend sincere;
Here was content and joy, for she was here:
In the mild evening, in the scene around,
The Maid, now free, peculiar beauties found;
Blended with village-tones, the evening gale
Gave the sweet night-bird's warblings to the vale:
The Youth, embolden'd, yet abash'd, now told
His fondest wish, nor found the maiden cold;
The Mother smiling whisper'd, "Let him go
And seek the licence!" Jesse answer'd "No:"
But Colin went.—I know not if they live
With all the comforts wealth and plenty give;
But with pure joy to envious souls denied,
To suppliant meanness and suspicious pride;
And village-maids of happy couples say,
"They live like Jesse Bourn and Colin Grey."

TALE XIV

THE STRUGGLES OF CONSCIENCE

I am a villain; yet I lie, I am not:
Fool! of thyself speak well:—Fool! do not flatter.
My conscience hath a thousand several tongues,
And every tongue brings in a several tale.
SHAKESPEARE, Richard III.

My conscience is but a kind of hard conscience . . . The fiend gives the more friendly counsel.
Merchant of Venice.

Thou hast it now—and I fear
Thou play'dst most foully for it.
Macbeth.

Canst thou not minister to a mind diseased,
Pluck from the memory a rooted sorrow,
Rase out the written troubles of the brain,
And with some sweet oblivious antidote
Cleanse the foul bosom of that perilous stuff
Which weighs upon the heart?
Macbeth.

Soft! I did but dream.
Oh! coward conscience, how thou dost afflict me.
Richard III.

A serious Toyman in the city dwelt,
Who much concern for his religion felt;
Reading, he changed his tenets, read again,
And various questions could with skill maintain;
Papist and Quaker if we set aside,
He had the road of every traveller tried;
There walk'd a while, and on a sudden turn'd
Into some by-way he had just discern'd:
He had a nephew, Fulham:—Fulham went
His Uncle's way, with every turn content;
He saw his pious kinsman's watchful care,
And thought such anxious pains his own might spare,
And he the truth obtain'd, without the toil, might share.
In fact, young Fulham, though he little read,
Perceived his uncle was by fancy led;
And smiled to see the constant care he took,
Collating creed with creed, and book with book.
At length the senior fix'd; I pass the sect
He call'd a Church, 'twas precious and elect;
Yet the seed fell not in the richest soil,
For few disciples paid the preacher's toil;
All in an attic room were wont to meet,
These few disciples, at their pastor's feet;
With these went Fulham, who, discreet and grave,
Follow'd the light his worthy uncle gave;
Till a warm Preacher found the way t'impart
Awakening feelings to his torpid heart:
Some weighty truths, and of unpleasant kind,
Sank, though resisted, in his struggling mind:
He wish'd to fly them, but, compell'd to stay,
Truth to the waking Conscience found her way;

For though the Youth was call'd a prudent lad,
And prudent was, yet serious faults he had—
Who now reflected—"Much am I surprised;
I find these notions cannot be despised:
No! there is something I perceive at last,
Although my uncle cannot hold it fast;
Though I the strictness of these men reject,
Yet I determine to be circumspect:
This man alarms me, and I must begin
To look more closely to the things within:
These sons of zeal have I derided long,
But now begin to think the laugher's wrong!
Nay, my good uncle, by all teachers moved,
Will be preferr'd to him who none approved;—
Better to love amiss than nothing to have loved."
Such were his thoughts, when Conscience first began
To hold close converse with th' awaken'd man:
He from that time reserved and cautious grew,
And for his duties felt obedience due;
Pious he was not, but he fear'd the pain
Of sins committed, nor would sin again:
Whene'er he stray'd, he found his Conscience rose,
Like one determined what was ill t'oppose,
What wrong t'accuse, what secret to disclose;
To drag forth every latent act to light,
And fix them fully in the actor's sight:
This gave him trouble, but he still confess'd
The labour useful, for it brought him rest.
The Uncle died, and when the Nephew read
The will, and saw the substance of the dead—
Five hundred guineas, with a stock in trade—
He much rejoiced, and thought his fortune made;
Yet felt aspiring pleasure at the sight,
And for increase, increasing appetite;
Desire of profit idle habits check'd
(For Fulham's virtue was to be correct);
He and his Conscience had their compact made—
"Urge me with truth, and you will soon persuade;
But not," he cried, "for mere ideal things
Give me to feel those terror-breeding stings."
"Let not such thoughts," she said, "your mind confound;
Trifles may wake me, but they never wound;
In them indeed there is a wrong and right,
But you will find me pliant and polite;
Not like a Conscience of the dotard kind,
Awake to dreams, to dire offences blind:
Let all within be pure, in all beside
Be your own master, governor, and guide;

Alive to danger, in temptation strong,
And I shall sleep our whole existence long."
"Sweet be thy sleep," said Fulham; "strong must be
The tempting ill that gains access to me:
Never will I to evil deed consent;
Or, if surprised, oh! how will I repent!
Should gain be doubtful, soon would I restore
The dangerous good, or give it to the poor;
Repose for them my growing wealth shall buy,
Or build—who knows?—an hospital like Guy.
Yet why such means to soothe the smart within,
While firmly purposed to renounce the sin?"
Thus our young Trader and his Conscience dwelt
In mutual love, and great the joy they felt;
But yet in small concerns, in trivial things,
"She was," he said, "too ready with the stings;"
And he too apt, in search of growing gains,
To lose the fear of penalties and pains:
Yet these were trifling bickerings, petty jars,
Domestic strifes, preliminary wars;
He ventured little, little she express'd
Of indignation, and they both had rest.
Thus was he fix d to walk the worthy way,
When profit urged him to a bold essay:—
A time was that when all at pleasure gamed
In lottery chances, yet a law unblamed:
This Fulham tried; who would to him advance
A pound or crown, he gave in turn a chance
For weighty prize—and should they nothing share,
They had their crown or pound in Fulham's ware;
Thus the old stores within the shop were sold
For that which none refuses, new or old.
Was this unjust? yet Conscience could not rest,
But made a mighty struggle in the breast,
And gave th' aspiring man an early proof
That should they war he would have work enough:
"Suppose," said she, "your vended numbers rise
The same with those which gain each real prize,
(Such your proposal), can you ruin shun?"—
"A hundred thousand," he replied, "to one."
"Still it may happen."—"I the sum must pay."
"You know you cannot."—"I can run away."
"That is dishonest."—"Nay, but you must wink
At a chance hit: it cannot be, I think.
Upon my conduct as a whole decide,
Such trifling errors let my virtues hide.
Fail I at meeting? am I sleepy there?
My purse refuse I with the priest to share?

Do I deny the poor a helping hand?
Or stop the wicked women in the Strand?
Or drink at club beyond a certain pitch?
Which are your charges? Conscience, tell me which?"
"'Tis well," said she, "but—" "Nay, I pray, have done:
Trust me, I will not into danger run."
The lottery drawn, not one demand was made;
Fulham gain'd profit and increase of trade.
"See now," said he—for Conscience yet arose—
"How foolish 'tis such measures to oppose:
Have I not blameless thus my state advanced?"
"Still," mutter'd Conscience, "still it might have chanced."
"Might!" said our hero: "who is so exact
As to inquire what might have been a fact?"
Now Fulham's shop contain'd a curious view
Of costly trifles, elegant and new:
The papers told where kind mammas might buy
The gayest toys to charm an infant's eye;
Where generous beaux might gentle damsels please,
And travellers call who cross the land or seas,
And find the curious art, the neat device,
Of precious value and of trifling price.
Here Conscience rested, she was pleased to find
No less an active than an honest mind;
But when he named his price, and when he swore
His Conscience check'd him that he ask'd no more,
When half he sought had been a large increase
On fair demand, she could not rest in peace;
(Beside th' affront to call th' adviser in,
Who would prevent, to justify the sin):
She therefore told him that "he vainly tried
To soothe her anger, conscious that he lied;
If thus he grasp'd at such usurious gains,
He must deserve, and should expect her pains."
The charge was strong; he would in part confess
Offence there was—But, who offended less?
"What! is a mere assertion call'd a lie?
And if it be, are men compell'd to buy?
'Twas strange that Conscience on such points should dwell,
While he was acting (he would call it) well;
He bought as others buy, he sold as others sell;
There was no fraud, and he demanded cause
Why he was troubled when he kept the laws?"
"My laws!" said Conscience. "What," said he, "are thine?
Oral or written, human or divine?
Show me the chapter, let me see the text;
By laws uncertain subjects are perplex'd:
Let me my finger on the statute lay,

And I shall feel it duty to obey."
"Reflect," said Conscience, "'twas your own desire
That I should warn you—does the compact tire?
Repent you this?—then bid me not advise,
And rather hear your passions as they rise:
So you may counsel and remonstrance shun;
But then remember it is war begun;
And you may judge from some attacks, my friend,
What serious conflicts will on war attend."
"Nay, but," at length the thoughtful man replied,
"I say not that; I wish you for my guide;
Wish for your checks and your reproofs—but then
Be like a conscience of my fellow-men;
Worthy I mean, and men of good report,
And not the wretches who with Conscience sport:
There's Bice, my friend, who passes off his grease
Of pigs for bears', in pots a crown apiece;
His Conscience never checks him when he swears
The fat he sells is honest fat of bears;
And so it is, for he contrives to give
A drachm to each—'tis thus that tradesmen live;
Now why should you and I be over-nice?
What man is held in more repute than Bice?"
Here ended the dispute; but yet 'twas plain
The parties both expected strife again:
Their friendship cool'd, he look'd about and saw
Numbers who seem'd unshackled by his awe;
While like a schoolboy he was threatened still,
Now for the deed, now only for the will:
Here Conscience answered "To thy neighbour's guide
Thy neighbour leave, and in thine own confide."
Such were each day the charges and replies,
When a new object caught the trader's eyes;
A Vestry-patriot, could he gain the name,
Would famous make him, and would pay the fame.
He knew full well the sums bequeath'd in charge
For schools, for almsmen, for the poor, were large;
Report had told, and he could feel it true,
That most unfairly dealt the trusted few;
No partners would they in their office take,
Nor clear accounts at annual meetings make.
Aloud our hero in the vestry spoke
Of hidden deeds, and vow'd to draw the cloak;
It was the poor man's cause, and he for one
Was quite determined to see justice done:
His foes affected, laughter, then disdain,
They too were loud; and threat'ning, but in vain;
The pauper's friend, their foe, arose and spoke again;

Fiercely he cried, "Your garbled statements show
That you determine we shall nothing know;
But we shall bring your hidden crimes to light,
Give you to shame, and to the poor their right."
Virtue like this might some approval ask—
But Conscience sternly said, "You wear a mask!"
"At least," said Fulham, "if I have a view
To serve myself, I serve the public too."
Fulham, though check'd, retain'd his former zeal,
And this the cautious rogues began to feel:
"Thus will he ever bark," in peevish tone
An elder cried—"the cur must have a bone."
They then began to hint, and to begin
Was all they needed—it was felt within:
In terms less veil'd an offer then was made;
Though distant still, it fail'd not to persuade:
More plainly then was every point proposed,
Approved, accepted, and the bargain closed.
The exulting paupers hail'd their Friend's success,
And bade adieu to murmurs and distress.
Alas! their Friend had now superior light,
And, view'd by that, he found that all was right;
"There were no errors, the disbursements small;
This was the truth, and truth was due to all."
And rested Conscience? No! she would not rest,
Yet was content with making a protest:
Some acts she now with less resistance bore,
Nor took alarm so quickly as before:
Like those in towns besieged, who every ball
At first with terror view, and dread them all;
But, grown familiar with the scenes, they fear
The clanger less, as it approaches near;
So Conscience, more familiar with the view
Of growing evils, less attentive grew:
Yet he, who felt some pain and dreaded more,
Gave a peace-offering to the angry poor.
Thus had he quiet—but the time was brief;
From his new triumph sprang a cause of grief;
In office join'd, and acting with the rest,
He must admit the sacramental test.
Now, as a sectary, he had all his life,
As he supposed, been with the Church at strife:—
No rules of hers, no laws had he perused,
Nor knew the tenets he by rote abused;
Yet Conscience here arose more fierce and strong
Than when she told of robbery and wrong.
"Change his religion! No! he must be sure
That was a blow no Conscience eould endure."

Though friend to Virtue, yet she oft abides
In early notions, fix'd by erring guides;
And is more startled by a call from those,
Than when the foulest crimes her rest oppose:
By error taught, by prejudice misled,
She yields her rights, and Fancy rules instead;
When Conscience all her stings and terror deals,
Not as Truth dictates, but as Fancy feels:
And thus within our hero's troubled breast,
Crime was less torture than the odious test.
New forms, new measures, he must now embrace,
With sad conviction that they warr'd with grace;
To his new church no former friend would come,
They scarce preferr'd her to the Church of Rome;
But thinking much, and weighing guilt and gain,
Conscience and he commuted for her pain;
Then promised Fulham to retain his creed,
And their peculiar paupers still to feed;
Their attic-room (in secret) to attend,
And not forget he was the preacher's friend:
Thus he proposed, and Conscience, troubled, tried,
And wanting peace, reluctantly complied.
Now, care subdued, and apprehensions gone,
In peace our hero went aspiring on;
But short the period—soon a quarrel rose,
Fierce in the birth, and fatal in the close;
With times of truce between, which rather proved
That both were weary, than that either loved.
Fulham e'en now disliked the heavy thrall,
And for her death would in his anguish call,
As Rome's mistaken friend exclaimed, 'Let Carthage fall,'
So felt our hero, so his wish express'd,
Against this powerful sprite—delenda est:
Rome in her conquest saw not danger near,
Freed from her rival and without a fear;
So, Conscience conquer'd, men perceive how free,
But not how fatal, such a state must be.
Fatal, not free, our hero's; foe or friend,
Conscience on him was destined to attend:
She dozed indeed, grew dull, nor seem'd to spy
Crime following crime, and each of deeper dye;
But all were noticed, and the reckoning time
With her account came on—crime following crime.
This, once a foe, now Brother in the Trust,
Whom Fulham late described as fair and just,
Was the sole Guardian of a wealthy maid,
Placed in his power, and of his frown afraid:
Not quite an idiot, for her busy brain

Sought, by poor cunning, trifling points to gain;
Success in childish projects her delight,
She took no heed of each important right.
The friendly parties met—the Guardian cried,
"I am too old; my sons have each a bride:
Martha, my ward, would make an easy wife:
On easy terms I'll make her yours for life;
And then the creature is so weak and mild.
She may be soothed and threaten'd as a child."
"Yet not obey," said Fulham, "for your fools,
Female and male, are obstinate as mules."
Some points adjusted, these new friends agreed,
Proposed the day, and hurried on the deed.
"'Tis a vile act," said Conscience. "It will prove,"
Replied the bolder man, "an act of love:
Her wicked guardian might the girl have sold
To endless misery for a tyrant's gold;
Now may her life be happy—for I mean
To keep my temper even and serene."
"I cannot thus compound," the spirit cried,
"Nor have my laws thus broken and defied:
This is a fraud, a bargain for a wife;
Expect my vengeance, or amend your life."
The Wife was pretty, trifling, childish, weak;
She could not think, but would not cease to speak.
This he forbade—she took the caution ill,
And boldly rose against his sovereign will;
With idiot-cunning she would watch the hour,
When friends were present, to dispute his power:
With tyrant-craft, he then was still and calm,
But raised in private terror and alarm:
By many trials, she perceived how far
To vex and tease, without an open war;
And he discovered that so weak a mind
No art could lead, and no compulsion bind;
The rudest force would fail such mind to tame,
And she was callous to rebuke and shame;
Proud of her wealth, the power of law she knew,
And would assist him in the spending too:
His threat'ning words with insult she defied,
To all his reasoning with a stare replied;
And when he begg'd her to attend, would say,
"Attend I will—but let me have my way."
Nor rest had Conscience: "While you merit pain
From me," she cried, "you seek redress in vain."
His thoughts were grievous: "All that I possess
From this vile bargain adds to my distress;
To pass a life with one who will not mend,

Who cannot love, nor save, nor wisely spend,
Is a vile prospect, and I see no end:
For if we part, I must of course restore
Much of her money, and must wed no more.
"Is there no way?"—Here Conscience rose in power,—
"Oh! fly the danger of this fatal hour;
I am thy Conscience, faithful, fond, and true:
Ah, fly this thought, or evil must ensue;
Fall on thy knees, and pray with all thy soul,
Thy purpose banish, thy design control:
Let every hope of such advantage cease,
Or never more expect a moment's peace."
Th' affrighten'd man a due attention paid,
Felt the rebuke, and the command obey'd.
Again the wife rebell'd, again express'd
A love for pleasure—a contempt of rest;
"She whom she pleased would visit, would receive
Those who pleased her, nor deign to ask for leave."
"One way there is," said he; "I might contrive
Into a trap this foolish thing to drive:
Who pleased her, said she?—I'll be certain who."
"Take heed," said Conscience "what thou mean'st to do;
Ensnare thy wife?"—"Why, yes," he must confess,
"It might be wrong, but there was no redress;
Beside to think," said he, "is not to sin."
"Mistaken man!" replied the power within.
No guest unnoticed to the lady came,
He judged th' event with mingled joy and shame;
Oft he withdrew, and seem'd to leave her free,
But still as watchful as a lynx was he;
Meanwhile the wife was thoughtless, cool, and gay,
And, without virtue, had no wish to stray.
Though thus opposed, his plans were not resign'd;
"Revenge," said he, "will prompt that daring mind;
Refused supplies, insulted and distress'd,
Enraged with me, and near a favourite guest—
Then will her vengeance prompt the daring deed,
And I shall watch, detect her, and be freed."
There was a youth—but let me hide the name,
With all the progress of this deed of shame;
He had his views—on him the husband cast
His net, and saw him in his trammels fast.
"Pause but a moment—think what you intend,"
Said the roused Sleeper: "I am yet a friend.
Must all our days in enmity be spent?"
"No!" and he paused—"I surely shall repent:"
Then hurried on—the evil plan was laid,
The wife was guilty, and her friend betray'd,

And Fulham gain'd his wish, and for his will was paid.
Had crimes less weighty on the spirit press'd,
This troubled Conscience might have sunk to rest;
And, like a foolish guard, been bribed to peace,
By a false promise, that offence should cease;
Past faults had seem'd familiar to the view,
Confused if many, and obscure though true;
And Conscience, troubled with the dull account,
Had dropp'd her tale, and slumber'd o'er th' amount:
But, struck by daring guilt, alert she rose,
Disturb'd, alarm'd, and could no more repose:
All hopes of friendship and of peace were past,
And every view with gloom was overcast.
Hence from that day, that day of shame and sin,
Arose the restless enmity within:
On no resource could Fulham now rely,
Doom'd all expedients, and in vain, to try;
For Conscience, roused, sat boldly on her throne,
Watch'd every thought, attack'd the foe alone,
And with envenom'd sting drew forth the inward groan:
Expedients fail'd that brought relief before,
In vain his alms gave comfort to the poor,
Give what he would, to him the comfort came no more:
Not prayer avail'd, and when (his crimes confess'd)
He felt some ease, she said, "Are they redress'd?
You still retain the profit, and be sure,
Long as it lasts, this anguish shall endure."
Fulham still tried to soothe her, cheat, mislead,
But Conscience laid her finger on the deed,
And read the crime with power, and all that must succeed:
He tried t'expel her, but was sure to find
Her strength increased by all that he design'd;
Nor ever was his groan more loud and deep
Than when refresh'd she rose from momentary sleep.
Now desperate grown, weak, harass'd, and afraid,
From new allies he sought for doubtful aid;
To thought itself he strove to bid adieu,
And from devotions to diversions flew;
He took a poor domestic for a slave
(Though avarice grieved to see the price he gave);
Upon his board, once frugal, press'd a load
Of viands rich the appetite to goad;
The long protracted meal, the sparkling cup,
Fought with his gloom, and kept his courage up:
Soon as the morning came, there met his eyes
Accounts of wealth, that he might reading rise;
To profit then he gave some active hours,
Till food and wine again should renovate his powers:

Yet, spite of all defence, of every aid,
The watchful Foe her close attention paid;
In every thoughtful moment on she press'd,
And gave at once her dagger to his breast;
He waked at midnight, and the fears of sin,
As waters through a bursten dam, broke in;
Nay, in the banquet, with his friends around,
When all their cares and half their crimes were drown'd,
Would some chance act awake the slumbering fear,
And care and crime in all their strength appear:
The news is read, a guilty victim swings,
And troubled looks proclaim the bosom-stings:
Some pair are wed; this brings the wife in view;
And some divorced; this shows the parting too:
Nor can he hear of evil word or deed,
But they to thought, and thought to sufferings lead.
Such was his life—no other changes came,
The hurrying day, the conscious night the same;
The night of horror—when he starting cried
To the poor startled sinner at his side,
"Is it in law? am I condemned to die?
Let me escape!—I'll give—oh! let me fly—
How! but a dream!—no judges! dungeon! chain!
Or these grim men!—I will not sleep again—
Wilt thou, dread being! thus thy promise keep?
Day is thy time—and wilt thou murder sleep?
Sorrow and want repose, and wilt thou come,
Nor give one hour of pure untroubled gloom?
"Oh! Conscience! Conscience! man's most faithful friend,
Him canst thou comfort, ease, relieve, defend;
But if he will thy friendly checks forego,
Thou art, oh? woe for me, his deadliest foe?"

TALE XV

ADVICE; OR THE 'SQUIRE AND THE PRIEST

His hours fill'd up with riots, banquets, sports—
And never noted in him any study,
Any retirement, any sequestration.
SHAKESPEARE, Henry V.

I will converse with iron-witted fools,
With unrespective boys: none are for me,
Who look into me with considerate eyes.
Richard III.

You cram these words into mine ears, against
The stomach of my sense.
Tempest.

A wealthy Lord of far-extended land
Had all that pleased him placed at his command;
Widow'd of late, but finding much relief
In the world's comforts, he dismiss'd his grief;
He was by marriage of his daughters eased,
And knew his sons could marry if they pleased;
Meantime in travel he indulged the boys,
And kept no spy nor partner of his joys.
These joys, indeed, were of the grosser kind,
That fed the cravings of an earthly mind;
A mind that, conscious of its own excess,
Felt the reproach his neighbours would express.
Long at th' indulgent board he loved to sit,
Where joy was laughter, and profaneness wit;
And such the guest and manners of the hall,
No wedded lady on the 'Squire would call:
Here reign'd a Favourite, and her triumph gain'd
O'er other favourites who before had reign'd;
Reserved and modest seemed the nymph to be,
Knowing her lord was charm'd with modesty;
For he, a sportsman keen, the more enjoy'd,
The greater value had the thing destroyed.
Our 'Squire declared, that from a wife released,
He would no more give trouble to a Priest;
Seem'd it not, then, ungrateful and unkind
That he should trouble from the priesthood find?
The Church he honour'd, and he gave the due
And full respect to every son he knew;
But envied those who had the luck to meet
A gentle pastor, civil and discreet;
Who never bold and hostile sermon penned,
To wound a sinner, or to shame a friend;
One whom no being either shunn'd or fear'd:
Such must be loved wherever they appear'd.
Not such the stern old Rector of the time,
Who soothed no culprit, and who spared no crime;
Who would his fears and his contempt express
For irreligion and licentiousness;
Of him our Village Lord, his guests among,
By speech vindictive proved his feelings stung.
"Were he a bigot," said the 'Squire, "whose zeal
Condemn'd us all, I should disdain to feel:

But when a man of parts, in college train'd,
Prates of our conduct, who would not be pain'd?
While he declaims (where no one dares reply)
On men abandon'd, grov'ling in the sty
(Like beasts in human shape) of shameless luxury.
Yet with a patriot's zeal I stand the shock
Of vile rebuke, example to his flock:
But let this Rector, thus severe and proud,
Change his wide surplice for a narrow shroud,
And I will place within his seat a youth,
Train'd by the Graces to explain the Truth;
Then shall the flock with gentle hand be led,
By wisdom won, and by compassion fed."
This purposed Teacher was a sister's son,
Who of her children gave the priesthood one;
And she had early train'd for this employ
The pliant talents of her college-boy:
At various times her letters painted all
Her brother's views—the manners of the Hall;
The rector's harshness, and the mischief made
By chiding those whom preachers should persuade:
This led the youth to views of easy life,
A friendly patron, an obliging wife;
His tithe, his glebe, the garden, and the steed,
With books as many as he wish'd to read.
All this accorded with the Uncle's will:
He loved a priest compliant, easy, still;
Sums he had often to his favourite sent,
"To be," he wrote, "in manly freedom spent;
For well it pleased his spirit to assist
An honest lad, who scorn'd a Methodist."
His mother, too, in her maternal care,
Bade him of canting hypocrites beware:
Who from his duties would his heart seduce,
And make his talents of no earthly use.
Soon must a trial of his worth be made—
The ancient priest is to the tomb convey'd;
And the Youth summon'd from a serious friend,
His guide and host, new duties to attend.
Three months before, the nephew and the 'Squire
Saw mutual worth to praise and to admire;
And though the one too early left his wine,
The other still exclaim'd—"My boy will shine:
Yes, I perceive that he will soon improve,
And I shall form the very guide I love;
Decent abroad, he will my name defend,
And when at home, be social and unbend."
The plan was specious, for the mind of James

Accorded duly with his uncle's schemes;
He then aspired not to a higher name
Than sober clerks of moderate talents claim;
Gravely to pray, and rev'rendly to preach,
Was all he saw, good youth! within his reach:
Thus may a mass of sulphur long abide,
Cold and inert, but, to the flame applied,
Kindling it blazes, and consuming turns
To smoke and poison, as it boils and burns.
James, leaving college, to a Preacher stray'd;
What call'd he knew not—but the call obey'd;
Mild, idle, pensive, ever led by those
Who could some specious novelty propose;
Humbly he listen'd, while the preacher dwelt
On touching themes, and strong emotions felt;
And in this night was fix'd that pliant will
To one sole point, and he retains it still.
At first his care was to himself confined;
Himself assured, he gave it to mankind:
His zeal grew active—honest, earnest zeal,
And comfort dealt to him, he long'd to deal;
He to his favourite preacher now withdrew,
Was taught to teach, instructed to subdue,
And train'd for ghostly warfare, when the call
Of his new duties reach'd him from the Hall.
Now to the 'Squire, although alert and stout,
Came unexpected an attack of gout;
And the grieved patron felt such serious pain,
He never thought to see a church again:
Thrice had the youthful rector taught the crowd,
Whose growing numbers spoke his powers aloud,
Before the patron could himself rejoice
(His pain still lingering) in the general voice;
For he imputed all this early fame
To graceful manner and the well-known name;
And to himself assumed a share of praise,
For worth and talents he was pleased to raise.
A month had flown, and with it fled disease;
What pleased before, began again to please;
Emerging daily from his chamber's gloom,
He found his old sensations hurrying home;
Then call'd his nephew, and exclaim'd, "My boy,
Let us again the balm of life enjoy;
The foe has left me, and I deem it right,
Should he return, to arm me for the fight."
Thus spoke the 'Squire, the favourite nymph stood by,
And view'd the priest with insult in her eye;
She thrice had heard him when he boldly spoke

On dangerous points, and fear'd he would revoke:
For James she ioved not—and her manner told,
"This warm affection will be quickly cold:"
And still she fear'd impression might be made
Upon a subject nervous and decay'd;
She knew her danger, and had no desire
Of reformation in the gallant 'Squire;
And felt an envious pleasure in her breast
To see the rector daunted and distress'd.
Again the Uncle to the youth applied—
"Cast, my dear lad, that cursed gloom aside:
There are for all things time and place; appear
Grave in your pulpit, and be merry here:
Now take your wine—for woes a sure resource,
And the best prelude to a long discourse."
James half obey'd, but cast an angry eye
On the fair lass, who still stood watchful by;
Resolving thus, "I have my fears—but still
I must perform my duties, and I will:
No love, no interest, shall my mind control;
Better to lose my comforts than my soul;
Better my uncle's favour to abjure,
Than the upbraidings of my heart endure."
He took his glass, and then address'd the 'Squire:
"I feel not well, permit me to retire."
The 'Squire conceived that the ensuing day
Gave him these terrors for the grand essay,
When he himself should this young preacher try,
And stand before him with observant eye;
This raised compassion in his manly breast,
And he would send the rector to his rest;
Yet first, in soothing voice—"A moment stay,
And these suggestions of a friend obey;
Treasure these hints, if fame or peace you prize,—
The bottle emptied, I shall close my eyes.
"On every priest a twofold care attends,
To prove his talents, and insure his friends:
First, of the first—your stores at once produce;
And bring your reading to its proper use:
On doctrines dwell, and every point enforce
By quoting much, the scholar's sure resource;
For he alone can show us on each head
What ancient schoolmen and sage fathers said.
No worth has knowledge, if you fail to show
How well you studied and how much you know:
Is faith your subject, and you judge it right
On theme so dark to cast a ray of light,
Be it that faith the orthodox maintain,

Found in the rubric, what the creeds explain;
Fail not to show us on this ancient faith
(And quote the passage) what some martyr saith:
Dwell not one moment on a faith that shocks
The minds of men sincere and orthodox;
That gloomy faith, that robs the wounded mind
Of all the comfort it was wont to find
From virtuous acts, and to the soul denies
Its proper due for alms and charities;
That partial faith, that, weighing sins alone,
Lets not a virtue for a fault atone;
That partial faith, that would our tables clear,
And make one dreadful Lent of all the year;
And cruel too, for this is faith that rends
Confiding beauties from protecting friends;
A faith that all embracing, what a gloom
Deep and terrific o'er the land would come!
What scenes of horror would that time disclose!
No sight but misery, and no sound but woes;
Your nobler faith, in loftier style convey'd,
Shall be with praise and admiration paid:
On points like these your hearers all admire
A preacher's depth, and nothing more require.
Shall we a studious youth to college send,
That every clown his words may comprehend?
'Tis for your glory, when your hearers own
Your learning matchless, but the sense unknown.
"Thus honour gain'd, learn now to gain a friend,
And the sure way is—never to offend;
For, James, consider—what your neighbours do
Is their own business, and concerns not you:
Shun all resemblance to that forward race
Who preach of sins before a sinner's face;
And seem as if they overlook'd a pew,
Only to drag a failing man in view:
Much should I feel, when groaning in disease,
If a rough hand upon my limb should seize;
But great my anger, if this hand were found
The very doctor's who should make it sound:
So feel our minds, young Priest, so doubly feel,
When hurt by those whose office is to heal.
"Yet of our duties you must something tell,
And must at times on sin and frailty dwell;
Here you may preach in easy, flowing style,
How errors cloud us, and how sins defile:
Here bring persuasive tropes and figures forth,
To show the poor that wealth is nothing worth;
That they, in fact, possess an ample share

Of the world's good, and feel not half its care:
Give them this comfort, and, indeed, my gout
In its full vigour causes me some doubt;
And let it always, for your zeal, suffice
That vice you combat, in the abstract—vice:
The very captious will be quiet then;
We all confess we are offending men:
In lashing sin, of every stroke beware,
For sinners feel, and sinners you must spare;
In general satire, every man perceives
A slight attack, yet neither fears nor grieves;
But name th' offence, and you absolve the rest,
And point the dagger at a single breast.
"Yet are there sinners of a class so low,
That you with safety may the lash bestow;
Poachers, and drunkards, idle rogues, who feed
At others' cost, a mark'd correction need:
And all the better sort, who see your zeal,
Will love and reverence for their pastor feel;
Reverence for one who can inflict the smart,
And love, because he deals them not a part.
"Remember well what love and age advise:
A quiet rector is a parish prize,
Who in his learning has a decent pride;
Who to his people is a gentle guide;
Who only hints at failings that he sees;
Who loves his glebe, his patron, and his ease,
And finds the way to fame and profit is to please."
The Nephew answer'd not, except a sigh
And look of sorrow might be term'd reply;
He saw the fearful hazard of his state,
And held with truth and safety strong debate;
Nor long he reason'd, for the zealous youth
Resolved, though timid, to profess the truth;
And though his friend should like a lion roar,
Truth would he preach, and neither less nor more.
The bells had toll'd—arrived the time of prayer,
The flock assembled, and the 'Squire was there:
And now can poet sing, or proseman say,
The disappointment of that trying day?
As he who long had train'd a favourite steed,
(Whose blood and bone gave promise of his speed,)
Sanguine with hope, he runs with partial eye
O'er every feature, and his bets are high;
Of triumph sure, he sees the rivals start,
And waits their coming with exulting heart;
Forestalling glory, with impatient glance,
And sure to see his conquering steed advance:

The conquering steed advances—luckless day!
A rival's Herod bears the prize away,
Nor second his, nor third, but lagging last,
With hanging head he comes, by all surpass'd:
Surprise and wrath the owner's mind inflame,
Love turns to scorn, and glory ends in shame;—
Thus waited, high in hope, the partial 'Squire,
Eager to hear, impatient to admire;
When the young Preacher, in the tones that find
A certain passage to the kindling mind,
With air and accent strange, impressive, sad,
Alarm'd the judge—he trembled for the lad;
But when the text announced the power of grace,
Amazement scowl'd upon his clouded face
At this degenerate son of his illustrious race;
Staring he stood, till hope again arose
That James might well define the words he chose:
For this he listen'd—but, alas! he found
The preacher always on forbidden ground.
And now the Uncle left the hated pew,
With James, and James's conduct, in his view;
A long farewell to all his favourite schemes!
For now no crazed fanatic's frantic dreams
Seem'd vile as James's conduct, or as James:
All he had long derided, hated, fear'd,
This, from the chosen youth, the uncle heard;—
The needless pause, the fierce disorder'd air,
The groan for sin, the vehemence of prayer,
Gave birth to wrath, that, in a long discourse
Of grace triumphant, rose to fourfold force:
He found his thoughts despised, his rules transgress'd,
And while the anger kindled in his breast,
The pain must be endured that could not be expressed:
Each new idea more inflamed his ire,
As fuel thrown upon a rising fire:
A hearer yet, he sought by threatening sign
To ease his heart, and awe the young divine;
But James refused those angry looks to meet,
Till he dismiss'd his flock, and left his seat:
Exhausted then he felt his trembling frame,
But fix'd his soul,—his sentiments the same;
And therefore wise it seem'd to fly from rage,
And seek for shelter in his parsonage:
There, if forsaken, yet consoled to find
Some comforts left, though not a few resign'd;
There, if he lost an erring parent's love,
An honest conscience must the cause approve;
If the nice palate were no longer fed,

The mind enjoy'd delicious thoughts instead;
And if some part of earthly good was flown,
Still was the tithe of ten good farms his own.
Fear now, and discord, in the village reign,
The cool remonstrate, and the meek complain;
But there is war within, and wisdom pleads in vain.
Now dreads the Uncle, and proclaims his dread,
Lest the Boy-priest should turn each rustic head;
The certain converts cost him certain woe,
The doubtful fear lest they should join the foe:
Matrons of old, with whom he used to joke,
Now pass his Honour with a pious look;
Lasses, who met him once with lively airs,
Now cross his way, and gravely walk to prayers:
An old companion, whom he long has loved,
By coward fears confess'd his conscience moved;
As the third bottle gave its spirit forth,
And they bore witness to departing worth,
The friend arose, and he too would depart:
"Man," said the 'Squire, "thou wert not wont to start;
Hast thou attended to that foolish boy,
Who would abridge all comforts, or destroy?"
Yes, he had listen'd, who had slumber'd long,
And was convinced that something must be wrong:
But, though affected, still his yielding heart,
And craving palate, took the Uncle's part;
Wine now oppress'd him, who, when free from wine,
Could seldom clearly utter his design;
But though by nature and indulgence weak,
Yet, half converted, he resolved to speak;
And, speaking, own'd, "that in his mind the Youth
Had gifts and learning, and that truth was truth:
The 'Squire he honour'd, and for his poor part,
He hated nothing like a hollow heart:
But 'twas a maxim he had often tried,
That right was right, and there he would abide;
He honoured learning, and he would confess
The preacher had his talents—more or less:
Why not agree? he thought the young divine
Had no such strictness—they might drink and dine;
For them sufficient—but he said before
That truth was truth, and he would drink no more."
This heard the 'Squire with mix'd contempt and pain;
He fear'd the Priest this recreant sot would gain.
The favourite Nymph, though not a convert made,
Conceived the man she scorn'd her cause would aid,
And when the spirits of her lord were low,
The lass presumed the wicked cause to show;

"It was the wretched life his Honour led,
And would draw vengeance on his guilty head;
Their loves (Heav'n knew how dreadfully distressed
The thought had made her!) were as yet unbless'd:
And till the church had sanction'd"—Here she saw
The wrath that forced her trembling to withdraw.
Add to these outward ills some inward light,
That showed him all was not correct and right:
Though now he less indulged—and to the poor,
From day to day, sent alms from door to door;
Though he some ease from easy virtues found,
Yet conscience told him he could not compound,
But must himself the darling sin deny,
Change the whole heart,—but here a heavy sigh
Proclaim'd, "How vast the toil! and, ah! how weak am I!"
James too has trouble—he divided sees
A parish, once harmonious and at ease;
With him united are the simply meek,
The warm, the sad, the nervous, and the weak;
The rest his Uncle's, save the few beside,
Who own no doctrine, and obey no guide;
With stragglers of each adverse camp, who lend
Their aid to both, but each in turn offend.
Though zealous still, yet he begins to feel
The heat too fierce that glows in vulgar zeal;
With pain he hears his simple friends relate
Their week's experience, and their woful state;
With small temptation struggling every hour,
And bravely battling with the tempting power:
His native sense is hurt by strange complaints
Of inward motions in these warring saints;
Who never cast on sinful bait a look,
But they perceive the devil at the hook:
Grieved, yet compell'd to smile, he finds it hard
Against the blunders of conceit to guard;
He sighs to hear the jests his converts cause,
He cannot give their erring zeal applause;
But finds it inconsistent to condemn
The flights and follies he has nursed in them:
These, in opposing minds, contempt produce,
Or mirth occasion, or provoke abuse;
On each momentous theme disgrace they bring,
And give to Scorn her poison and her sting.

THE CONFIDANT

Think'st thou I'd make a life of jealousy,
To follow still the changes of the moon
With fresh suspicion?
SHAKESPEARE, Othello.

Why hast thou lost the fresh blood in thy cheeks,
And given my treasure and my rights in thee
To thick-eyed musing and cursed melancholy?
Henry IV.

It is excellent
To have a giant's strength, but tyrannous
To use it as a giant.
Measure for Measure.

Anna was young and lovely—in her eye
The glance of beauty, in her cheek the dye:
Her shape was slender, and her features small,
But graceful, easy, unaffected all:
The liveliest tints her youthful face disclosed;
There beauty sparkled, and there health reposed;
For the pure blood that flush'd that rosy cheek
Spoke what the heart forbade the tongue to speak,
And told the feelings of that heart as well,
Nay, with more candour than the tongue could tell.
Though this fair lass had with the wealthy dwelt,
Yet like the damsel of the cot she felt;
And, at the distant hint or dark surmise,
The blood into the mantling cheek would rise.
Now Anna's station frequent terrors wrought,
In one whose looks were with such meaning fraught,
For on a Lady, as an humble friend,
It was her painful office to attend.
Her duties here were of the usual kind—
And some the body harass'd, some the mind:
Billets she wrote, and tender stories read,
To make the Lady sleepy in her bed;
She play'd at whist, but with inferior skill,
And heard the summons as a call to drill;
Music was ever pleasant till she play'd
At a request that no request convey'd;
The Lady's tales with anxious looks she heard,
For she must witness what her Friend averr'd;
The Lady's taste she must in all approve,
Hate whom she hated, whom she lov'd must love;

These, with the various duties of her place,
With care she studied, and perform'd with grace:
She veil'd her troubles in a mask of ease,
And show'd her pleasure was a power to please.
Such were the damsel's duties: she was poor—
Above a servant, but with service more:
Men on her face with careless freedom gaz'd,
Nor thought how painful was the glow they raised.
A wealthy few to gain her favour tried,
But not the favour of a grateful bride;
They spoke their purpose with an easy air,
That shamed and frighten'd the dependent fair;
Past time she view'd, the passing time to cheat,
But nothing found to make the present sweet:
With pensive soul she read life's future page,
And saw dependent, poor, repining age.
But who shall dare t'assert what years may bring,
When wonders from the passing hour may spring?
There dwelt a Yeoman in the place, whose mind
Was gentle, generous, cultivated, kind;
For thirty years he labour'd; fortune then
Placed the mild rustic with superior men:
A richer Stafford who had liv'd to save,
What he had treasured to the poorer gave;
Who with a sober mind that treasure view'd,
And the slight studies of his youth renew'd:
He not profoundly, but discreetly read,
And a fair mind with useful culture fed;
Then thought of marriage—"But the great," said he
"I shall not suit, nor will the meaner me."
Anna, he saw, admired her modest air;
He thought her virtuous, and he knew her fair;
Love raised his pity for her humble state,
And prompted wishes for her happier fate;
No pride in money would his feelings wound,
Nor vulgar manners hurt him and confound:
He then the Lady at the Hall address'd,
Sought her consent, and his regard expressed:
Yet if some cause his earnest wish denied,
He begg'd to know it, and he bow'd and sigh'd.
The Lady own'd that she was loth to part,
But praised the damsel for her gentle heart,
Her pleasing person, and her blooming health,
But ended thus, "Her virtue is her wealth."
"Then is she rich!" he cried with lively air;
"But whence, so please you, came a lass so fair?"
"A placeman's child was Anna, one who died
And left a widow by afflictions tried;

She to support her infant daughter strove,
But early left the object of her love:
Her youth, her beauty, and her orphan state
Gave a kind countess interest in her fate:
With her she dwelt and still might dwelling be,
When the earl's folly caused the lass to flee;
A second friend was she compell'd to shun,
By the rude offers of an uncheek'd son;
I found her then, and with a mother's love
Regard the gentle girl whom you approve;
Yet e'en with me protection is not peace,
Nor man's designs nor beauty's trials cease:
Like sordid boys by costly fruit they feel—
They will not purchase, but they try to steal."
Now this good Lady, like a witness true,
Told but the truth, and all the truth she knew;
And 'tis our duty and our pain to show
Truth this good lady had not means to know.
Yes, there was lock'd within the damsel's breast
A fact important to be now confess'd;
Gently, my muse, th' afflicting tale relate,
And have some feeling for a sister's fate.
Where Anna dwelt, a conquering hero came,—
An Irish captain, Sedley was his name;
And he too had that same prevailing art,
That gave soft wishes to the virgin's heart:
In years they differ'd; he had thirty seen
When this young beauty counted just fifteen;
But still they were a lovely lively pair,
And trod on earth as if they trod on air.
On love, delightful theme! the captain dwelt
With force still growing with the hopes he felt
But with some caution and reluctance told,
He had a father crafty, harsh, and old;
Who, as possessing much, would much expert,
Or both, for ever, from his love reject:
Why then offence to one so powerful give,
Who (for their comfort) had not long to live?
With this poor prospect the deluded maid,
In words confiding, was indeed betray'd;
And, soon as terrors in her bosom rose,
The hero fled; they hinder'd his repose.
Deprived of him, she to a parent's breast
Her secret trusted, and her pains impress'd;
Let her to town (so prudence urged) repair,
To shun disgrace, at least to hide it there;
But ere she went, the luckless damsel pray'd
A chosen friend might lend her timely aid:

"Yes! my soul's sister, my Eliza, come,
Hear her last sigh, and ease thy Anna's doom."
"'Tis a fool's wish," the angry father cried,
But, lost in troubles of his own, complied;
And dear Eliza to her friend was sent,
T'indulge that wish, and be her punishment.
The time arrived, and brought a tenfold dread;
The time was past, and all the terror fled;
The infant died; the face resumed each charm,
And reason now brought trouble and alarm.
Should her Eliza—no! she was too just,
"Too good and kind—but ah! too young to trust."
Anna return'd, her former place resumed,
And faded beauty with now grace re-bloom'd;
And if some whispers of the past were heard,
They died innoxious, as no cause appear'd;
But other cares on Anna's bosom press'd,
She saw her father gloomy and distress'd;
He died o'erwhelmed with debt, and soon was shed
The filial sorrow o'er a mother dead:
She sought Eliza's arms—that faithful friend was wed;
Then was compassion by the countess shown,
And all th' adventures of her life are known.
And now, beyond her hopes—no longer tried
By slavish awe—she lived a Yoeman's bride;
Then bless'd her lot, and with a grateful mind
Was careful, cheerful, vigilant, and kind:
The gentle husband felt supreme delight,
Bless'd by her joy, and happy in her sight;
He saw with pride in every friend and guest
High admiration and regard express'd:
With greater pride, and with superior joy,
He look'd exulting on his first-born boy;
To her fond breast the wife her infant strain'd,
Some feelings utter'd, some were not explain'd;
And she enraptured with her treasure grew,
The sight familiar, but the pleasure new.
Yet there appear'd within that tranquil state
Some threat'ning prospect of uncertain fate;
Between the married when a secret lies,
It wakes suspicion from enforced disguise:
Still thought the Wife upon her absent friend,
With all that must upon her truth depend.
" There is no being in the world beside
Who can discover what that friend will hide:
Who knew the fact, knew not my name or state,
Who these can tell cannot the fact relate;
But thou, Eliza, canst the whole impart,

And all my safety is thy generous heart."
Mix'd with these fears—but light and transient these—
Fled years of peace, prosperity, and ease;
So tranquil all, that scarce a gloomy day
For days of gloom unmix'd prepared the way:
One eve, the Wife, still happy in her state,
Sang gaily, thoughtless of approaching fate;
Then came a letter, that (received in dread
Not unobserved) she in confusion read;
The substance this—"Her friend rejoiced to find
That she had riches with a grateful mind;
While poor Eliza had, from place to place,
Been lured by hope to labour for disgrace;
That every scheme her wandering husband tried,
Pain'd while he lived, and perish'd when he died."
She then of want in angry style complain'd,
Her child a burthen to her life remain'd,
Her kindred shunn'd her prayers, no friend her soul sustain'd.
"Yet why neglected? Dearest Anna knew
Her worth once tried, her friendship ever true;
She hoped, she trusted, though by wants oppress'd,
To lock the treasured secret in her breast;
Yet, vex'd by trouble, must apply to one,
For kindness due to her for kindness done."
In Anna's mind was tumult, in her face
Flushings of dread had momentary place:
"I must," she judged, "these cruel lines expose,
Or fears, or worse than fears, my crime disclose."
The letter shown, he said, with sober smile,—
"Anna, your Friend has not a friendly style:
Say, where could you with this fair lady dwell,
Who boasts of secrets that she scorns to tell?"
"At school," she answer'd: he "At school!" replied;
"Nay, then I know the secrets you would hide;
Some early longings these, without dispute,
Some youthful gaspings for forbidden fruit:
Why so disorder'd, love? are such the crimes
That give us sorrow in our graver times?
Come, take a present for your friend, and rest
In perfect peace—you find you are confess'd."
This cloud, though past, alarm'd the conscious wife,
Presaging gloom and sorrow for her life;
Who to her answer join'd a fervent prayer
That her Eliza would a sister spare:
If she again—but was there cause?—should send,
Let her direct—and then she named a friend:
A sad expedient untried friends to trust,
And still to fear the tried may be unjust:

Such is his pain, who, by his debt oppress'd,
Seeks by new bonds a temporary rest.
Few were her peaceful days till Anna read
The words she dreaded, and had cause to dread:—
"Did she believe, did she, unkind, suppose
That thus Eliza's friendship was to close?
No, though she tried, and her desire was plain,
To break the friendly bond, she strove in vain:
Ask'd she for silence? why so loud the call,
And yet the token of her love so small?
By means like these will you attempt to bind
And check the movements of an injured mind?
Poor as I am, I shall be proud to show
What dangerous secrets I may safely know:
Secrets to men of jealous minds convey'd
Have many a noble house in ruins laid;
Anna, I trust, although with wrongs beset,
And urged by want, I shall be faithful yet;
But what temptation may from these arrive,
To take a slighted woman by surprise,
Becomes a subject for your serious care—
For who offends, must for offence prepare."
Perplex'd, dismay'd, the Wife foresaw her doom;
A day deferr'd was yet a day to come;
But still, though painful her suspended state,
She dreaded more the crisis of her fate;
Better to die than Stafford's scorn to meet,
And her strange friend perhaps would be discreet.
Presents she sent, and made a strong appeal
To woman's feelings, begging her to feel;
With too much force she wrote of jealous men,
And her tears falling spoke beyond the pen;
Eliza's silence she again implored,
And promised all that prudence could afford.
For looks composed and careless Anna tried;
She seem'd in trouble, and unconscious sigh'd:
The faithful Husband, who devoutly loved
His silent partner, with concern reproved:
"What secret sorrows on my Anna press,
That love may not partake, nor care redress?"
"None, none," she answer'd, with a look so kind
That the fond man determined to be blind.
A few succeeding weeks of brief repose
In Anna's cheek revived the faded rose;
A hue like this the western sky displays,
That glows awhile, and withers as we gaze.
Again the Friend's tormenting letter came—
"The wants she suffer'd were affection's shame;

She with her child a life of terrors led,
Unhappy fruit, but of a lawful bed:
Her friend was tasting every bliss in life,
The joyful mother, and the wealthy wife;
While she was placed in doubt, in fear, in want,
To starve on trifles that the happy grant;
Poorly for all her faithful silence paid,
And tantalized by ineffectual aid:
She could not thus a beggar's lot endure;
She wanted something permanent and sure:
If they were friends, then equal be their lot,
And she were free to speak if they were not."
Despair and terror seized the Wife, to find
The artful workings of a vulgar mind:
Money she had not, but the hint of dress
Taught her new bribes, new terrors to redress;
She with such feeling then described her woes
That envy's self might on the view repose;
Then to a mother's pains she made appeal,
And painted grief like one compell'd to feel.
Yes! so she felt, that in her air, her face,
In every purpose, and in every place,
In her slow motion, in her languid mien,
The grief, the sickness of her soul, was seen.
Of some mysterious ill, the Husband sure,
Desired to trace it, for he hoped to cure;
Something he knew obscurely, and had seen
His wife attend a cottage on the green;
Love, loth to wound, endured conjecture long,
Till fear would speak, and spoke in language strong.
"All I must know, my Anna—truly know
Whence these emotions, terrors, trouble flow:
Give me thy grief, and I will fairly prove
Mine is no selfish, no ungenerous love."
Now Anna's soul the seat of strife became,
Fear with respect contended, love with shame:
But fear prevailing was the ruling guide,
Prescribing what to show and what to hide.
"It is my friend," she said—"but why disclose
A woman's weakness struggling with her woes?
Yes, she has grieved me by her fond complaints,
The wrongs she suffers, the distress she paints:
Something we do—but she afflicts me still,
And says, with power to help, I want the will;
This plaintive style I pity and excuse,
Help when I can, and grieve when I refuse;
But here my useless sorrows I resign,
And will be happy in a love like thine."

The Husband doubted: he was kind but cool:—
"'Tis a strong friendship to arise at school;
Once more then, love, once more the sufferer aid,—
I too can pity, but I must upbraid:
Of these vain feelings then thy bosom free,
Nor be o'erwhelm'd by useless sympathy."
The Wife again despatch'd the useless bribe,
Again essay'd her terrors to describe;
Again with kindest words entreated peace,
And begg'd her offerings for a time might cease.
A calm succeeded, but too like the one
That causes terror ere the storm comes on:
A secret sorrow lived in Anna's heart,
In Stafford's mind a secret fear of art;
Not long they lasted—this determined foe
Knew all her claims, and nothing would forego.
Again her letter came, where Anna read,
"My child, one cause of my distress, is dead:
Heav'n has my infant."—"Heartless wretch!" she cried
"Is this thy joy?"—"I am no longer tied:
Now will I, hast'ning to my friend, partake
Her cares and comforts, and no more forsake;
Now shall we both in equal station move,
Save that my friend enjoys a husband's love."
Complaint and threats so strong the Wife amazed,
Who wildly on her cottage-neighbour gazed;
Her tones, her trembling, first betray'd her grief,
When floods of tears gave anguish its relief.
She fear'd that Stafford would refuse assent,
And knew her selfish Friend would not relent;
She must petition, yet delay'd the task,
Ashamed, afraid, and yet compell'd to ask;
Unknown to him some object fill'd her mind,
And, once suspicious, he became unkind:
They sat one evening, each absorb'd in gloom,
When, hark! a noise; and, rushing to the room,
The Friend tripp'd lightly in, and laughing said, "I come."
Anna received her with an anxious mind,
And meeting whisper'd, "Is Eliza kind?"
Reserved and cool the Husband sought to prove
The depth and force of this mysterious love.
To nought that pass'd between the Stranger-friend
And his meek partner seem'd he to attend;
But, anxious, listened to the lightest word
That might some knowledge of his guest afford,
And learn the reason one to him so dear
Should feel such fondness, yet betray such fear.
Soon he perceived this uninvited guest,

Unwelcome too, a sovereign power possess'd;
Lofty she was and careless, while the meek
And humbled Anna was afraid to speak:
As mute she listen'd with a painful smile,
Her friend sat laughing, and at ease the while,
Telling her idle tales with all the glee
Of careless and unfeeling levity.
With calm good sense he knew his Wife endued,
And now with wounded pride her conduct view'd;
Her speech was low, her every look convey'd—
"I am a slave, subservient and afraid."
All trace of comfort vanish'd; if she spoke,
The noisy friend upon her purpose broke;
To her remarks with insolence replied,
And her assertions doubted or denied:
While the meek Anna like an infant shook,
Woe-struck and trembling at the serpent's look.
"There is," said Stafford, "yes, there is a cause—
This creature frights her, overpowers, and awes."
Six weeks had pass'd—"In truth, my love, this friend
Has liberal notions; what does she intend?
Without a hint she came, and will she stay
Till she receives the hint to go away?"
Confused the Wife replied, in spite of truth,
"I love the dear companion of my youth."
"'Tis well," said Stafford; "then your loves renew:
Trust me, your rivals, Anna, will be few."
Though playful this, she felt too much distress'd
T'admit the consolation of a jest.
Ill she reposed, and in her dreams would sigh,
And, murmuring forth her anguish, beg to die;
With sunken eye, slow pace, and pallid cheek,
She look'd confusion, and she fear'd to speak.
All this the Friend beheld, for, quick of sight,
She knew the husband eager for her flight;
And that by force alone she could retain
The lasting comforts she had hope to gain.
She now perceived, to win her post for life,
She must infuse fresh terrors in the wife;
Must bid to friendship's feebler ties adieu,
And boldly claim the object in her view:
She saw the husband's love, and knew the power
Her friend might use in some propitious hour.
Meantime the anxious Wife, from pure distress
Assuming courage, said, "I will confess;"
But with her children felt a parent's pride,
And sought once more the hated truth to hide.
Offended, grieved, impatient, Stafford bore

The odious change, till he could bear no more:
A friend to truth, in speech and action plain,
He held all fraud and cunning in disdain;
But fraud to find, and falsehood to detect,
For once he fled to measures indirect.
One day the Friends were seated in that room
The Guest with care adorn'd, and named her home.
To please the eye, there curious prints were placed,
And some light volumes to amuse the taste;
Letters and music on a table laid,
The favourite studies of the fair betray'd;
Beneath the window was the toilet spread,
And the fire gleam'd upon a crimson bed.
In Anna's looks and falling tears were seen
How interesting had their subjects been:
"Oh! then," resumed the Friend, "I plainly find
That you and Stafford know each other's mind;
I must depart, must on the world be thrown,
Like one discarded, worthless, and unknown;
But, shall I carry, and to please a foe,
A painful secret in my bosom? No!
Think not your Friend a reptile you may tread
Beneath your feet, and say, the worm is dead;
I have some feeling, and will not be made
The scorn of her whom love cannot persuade:
Would not your word, your slightest wish, effect
All that I hope, petition, or expect?
The power you have, but you the use decline—
Proof that you feel not, or you fear not mine.
There was a time when I, a tender maid,
Flew at a call, and your desires obey'd;
A very mother to the child became,
Consoled your sorrow, and conceal'd your shame;
But now, grown rich and happy, from the door
You thrust a bosom-friend, despised and poor;
That child alive, its mother might have known
The hard, ungrateful spirit she had shown."
Here paused the Guest, and Anna cried at length—
"You try me, cruel friend! beyond my strength;
Would I had been beside my infant laid,
Where none would vex me, threaten, or upbraid!"
In Anna's looks the Friend beheld despair;
Her speech she soften'd, and composed her air;
Yet, while professing love, she answer'd still—
"You can befriend me, but you want the will."
They parted thus, and Anna went her way,
To shed her secret sorrows, and to pray.
Stafford, amused with books, and fond of home,

By reading oft dispell'd the evening gloom;
History or tale—all heard him with delight,
And thus was pass'd this memorable night.
The listening Friend bestow'd a flattering smile:
A sleeping boy the mother held the while;
And ere she fondly bore him to his bed,
On his fair face the tear of anguish shed.
And now his task resumed, "My tale," said he,
"Is short and sad, short may our sadness be!"
"The Caliph Harun, as historians tell, [5]
Ruled, for a tyrant, admirably well;
Where his own pleasures were not touch'd, to men
He was humane, and sometimes even then.
Harun was fond of fruits and gardens fair,
And woe to all whom he found poaching there:
Among his pages was a lively Boy,
Eager in search of every trifling joy;
His feelings vivid, and his fancy strong,
He sigh'd for pleasure while he shrank from wrong:
When by the Caliph in the garden placed,
He saw the treasures which he long'd to taste;
And oft alone he ventured to behold
Rich hanging fruits with rind of glowing gold;
Too long he stay'd forbidden bliss to view,
His virtue failing as his longings grew;
Athirst and wearied with the noontide heat,
Fate to the garden led his luckless feet;
With eager eyes and open mouth he stood,
Smelt the sweet breath, and touch'd the fragrant food;
The tempting beauty sparkling in the sun
Charm'd his young sense—he ate, and was undone;
When the fond glutton paused, his eyes around
He turn'd, and eyes upon him turning found;
Pleased he beheld the spy, a brother-page.
A friend allied in office and in age;
Who promised much that secret he would be,
But high the price he fix'd in secrecy:
"'Were you suspected, my unhappy friend,'
Began the boy, 'where would your sorrows end?
In all the palace there is not a page
The Caliph would not torture in his rage:
I think I see thee now impaled alive,
Writhing in pangs—but come, my friend! revive;
Had some beheld you, all your purse contains
Could not have saved you from terrific pains;
I scorn such meanness; and, if not in debt,
Would not an asper on your folly set.'
"The hint was strong; young Osmyn search'd his store

For bribes, and found he soon could bribe no more;
That time arrived, for Osmyn's stock was small,
And the young tyrant now possess'd it all;
The cruel youth, with his companions near,
Gave the broad hint that raised the sudden fear;
Th' ungenerous insult now was daily shown,
And Osmyn's peace and honest pride were flown;
Then came augmenting woes, and fancy strong
Drew forms of suffering, a tormenting throng;
He felt degraded, and the struggling mind
Dared not be free, and could not be resign'd;
And all his pains and fervent prayers obtain'd
Was truce from insult, while the fears remain'd.
"One day it chanced that this degraded Boy
And tyrant-friend were fixed at their employ;
Who now had thrown restraint and form aside,
And for his bribe in plainer speech applied:
'Long have I waited, and the last supply
Was but a pittance, yet how patient I!
But give me now what thy first terrors gave,
My speech shall praise thee, and my silence save.'
"Osmyn had found, in many a dreadful day,
The tyrant fiercer when he seem'd in play:
He begg'd forbearance: 'I have not to give;
Spare me awhile, although 'tis pain to live:
Oh! had that stolen fruit the power possess'd
To war with life, I now had been at rest.'
"'So fond of death,' replied the Boy, "tis plain
Thou hast no certain notion of the pain;
But to the Caliph were a secret shown,
Death has no pain that would be then unknown.'
"Now," says the story, "in a closet near,
The monarch seated, chanced the boys to hear;
There oft he came, when wearied on his throne,
To read, sleep, listen, pray, or be alone.
"The tale proceeds, when first the Caliph found
That he was robb'd, although alone, he frown'd;
And swore in wrath that he would send the boy
Far from his notice, favour, or employ;
But gentler movements soothed his ruffled mind,
And his own failings taught him to be kind.
"Relenting thoughts then painted Osmyn young,
His passion urgent, and temptation strong;
And that he suffer'd from that villain-Spy
Pains worse than death, till he desired to die;
Then if his morals had received a stain,
His bitter sorrows made him pure again:
To reason, pity lent her powerful aid,

For one so tempted, troubled, and betray'd:
And a free pardon the glad Boy restored
To the kind presence of a gentle lord;
Who from his office and his country drove
That traitor-Friend, whom pains nor pray'rs could move:
Who raised the fears no mortal could endure,
And then with cruel av'rice sold the cure.
"My tale is ended; but, to be applied,
I must describe the place where Caliphs hide."
Here both the females look'd alarm'd, distress'd,
With hurried passions hard to be express'd.
"It was a closet by a chamber placed,
Where slept a lady of no vulgar taste;
Her friend attended in that chosen room
That she had honour'd and proclaim'd her home;
To please the eye were chosen pictures placed;
And some light volumes to amuse the taste;
Letters and music on a table laid,
For much the lady wrote, and often play'd:
Beneath the window was a toilet spread,
And a fire gleamed upon a crimson bed."
He paused, he rose; with troubled joy the Wife
Felt the new era of her changeful life;
Frankness and love appear'd in Stafford's face,
And all her trouble to delight gave place.
Twice made the Guest an effort to sustain
Her feelings, twice resumed her seat in vain,
Nor could suppress her shame, nor could support her pain.
Quick she retired, and all the dismal night
Thought of her guilt, her folly, and her flight;
Then sought unseen her miserable home,
To think of comforts lost, and brood on wants to come.

TALE XVII

RESENTMENT

She hath a tear for pity, and a hand
Open as day for melting charity;
Yet, notwithstanding, being incensed, is flint:
Her temper, therefore, must be well observed.
SHAKESPEARE, Henry IV, Pt II.

Three or four wenches where I stood cried—"Alas! good soul!" and forgave him with all their hearts; but
there is no heed to be taken of them; if Caesar had stabbed their mothers, they would have done no less.
Julius Caesar.

How dost? Art cold?
I'm cold myself.—Where is the straw, my fellow?
The art of our necessities is strange,
That can make vile things precious.
King Lear.

Females there are of unsuspicious mind,
Easy and soft and credulous and kind;
Who, when offended for the twentieth time,
Will hear the offender and forgive the crime:
And there are others whom, like these to cheat,
Asks but the humblest efforts of deceit;
But they, once injured, feel a strong disdain,
And, seldom pardoning, never trust again;
Urged by religion, they forgive—but yet
Guard the warm heart, and never more forget:
Those are like wax—apply them to the fire,
Melting, they take th' impressions you desire;
Easy to mould and fashion as you please,
And again moulded with an equal ease:
Like smelted iron these the forms retain,
But once impress'd, will never melt again.
A busy port a serious Merchant made
His chosen place to recommence his trade;
And brought his Lady, who, their children dead,
Their native seat of recent sorrow fled:
The husband duly on the quay was seen,
The wife at home became at length serene;
There in short time the social couple grew
With all acquainted, friendly with a few;
When the good lady, by disease assail'd,
In vain resisted—hope and science fail'd:
Then spoke the female friends, by pity led,
"Poor merchant Paul! what think ye? will he wed?
A quiet, easy, kind, religious man,
Thus can he rest?—I wonder if he can."
He too, as grief subsided in his mind,
Gave place to notions of congenial kind:
Grave was the man, as we have told before;
His years were forty—he might pass for more;
Composed his features were, his stature low,
His air important, and his motion slow:
His dress became him, it was neat and plain,
The colour purple, and without a stain;
His words were few, and special was his care
In simplest terms his purpose to declare;

A man more civil, sober, and discreet,
More grave and corteous, you could seldom meet:
Though frugal he, yet sumptuous was his board,
As if to prove how much he could afford;
For though reserved himself, he loved to see
His table plenteous, and his neighbours free:
Among these friends he sat in solemn style,
And rarely soften'd to a sober smile:
For this, observant friends their reason gave—
"Concerns so vast would make the idlest grave;
And for such man to be of language free,
Would seem incongruous as a singing tree:
Trees have their music, but the birds they shield—
The pleasing tribute for protection yield;
Each ample tree the tuneful choir defends,
As this rich merchant cheers his happy friends!"
In the same town it was his chance to meet
A gentle Lady, with a mind discreet;
Neither in life's decline, nor bloom of youth,
One famed for maiden modesty and truth:
By nature cool, in pious habits bred,
She look'd on lovers with a virgin's dread:
Deceivers, rakes, and libertines were they,
And harmless beauty their pursuit and prey;
As bad as giants in the ancient times
Were modern lovers, and the same their crimes:
Soon as she heard of her all-conquering charms,
At once she fled to her defensive arms;
Conn'd o'er the tales her maiden aunt had told,
And, statue like, was motionless and cold:
From prayer of love, like that Pygmalion pray'd,
Ere the hard stone became the yielding maid,
A different change in this chaste nymph ensued,
And turn'd to stone the breathing flesh and blood:
Whatever youth described his wounded heart,
"He came to rob her, and she scorn'd his art;
And who of raptures once presumed to speak,
Told listening maids he thought them fond and weak;
But should a worthy man his hopes display
In few plain words, and beg a yes or nay,
He would deserve an answer just and plain,
Since adulation only moved disdain—
Sir, if my friends object not, come again."
Hence, our grave Lover, though he liked the face,
Praised not a feature—dwelt not on a grace;
But in the simplest terms declared his state:
"A widow'd man, who wish'd a virtuous mate;
Who fear'd neglect, and was compell'd to trust

Dependants wasteful, idle, or unjust;
Or should they not the trusted stores destroy,
At best, they could not help him to enjoy;
But with her person and her prudence bless'd,
His acts would prosper, and his soul have rest:
Would she be his?"—"Why, that was much to say;
She would consider; he awhile might stay:
She liked his manners, and believed his word;
He did not flatter, flattery she abhorr'd:
It was her happy lot in peace to dwell—
Would change make better what was now so well?
But she would ponder." "This," he said, "was kind;"
And begg'd to know "when she had fix'd her mind.
Romantic maidens would have scorn'd the air,
And the cool prudence of a mind so fair;
But well it pleased this wiser maid to find
Her own mild virtues in her lover's mind.
His worldly wealth she sought, and quickly grew
Pleased with her search, and happy in the view
Of vessels freighted with abundant stores,
Of rooms whose treasures press'd the groaning floors;
And he of clerks and servants could display
A little army on a public day:
Was this a man like needy bard to speak
Of balmy lip, bright eye, or rosy cheek?
The sum appointed for her widow'd state,
Fix'd by her friend, excited no debate;
Then the kind lady gave her hand and heart,
And, never finding, never dealt with art:
In his engagements she had no concern;
He taught her not, nor had she wish to learn;
On him in all occasions she relied,
His word her surety, and his worth her pride.
When ship was launch'd, and merchant Paul had share,
A bounteous feast became the lady's care;
Who then her entry to the dinner made,
In costly raiment, and with kind parade.
Call'd by this duty on a certain day,
And robed to grace it in a rich array,
Forth from her room, with measured step she came,
Proud of th' event, and stately look'd the dame;
The husband met her at his study door—
"This way, my love—one moment, and no more:
A trifling business—you will understand—
The law requires that you affix your hand;
But first attend, and you shall learn the cause
Why forms like these have been prescribed by laws."
Then from his chair a man in black arose,

And with much quickness hurried off his prose—
That "Ellen Paul, the wife, and so forth, freed
From all control, her own the act and deed,
And forasmuch"—said she, "I've no distrust,
For he that asks it is discreet and just;
Our friends are waiting—where am I to sign?—
There?—Now be ready when we meet to dine."
This said, she hurried off in great delight,
The ship was launch'd, and joyful was the night.
Now, says the reader, and in much disdain,
This serious Merchant was a rogue in grain;
A treacherous wretch, an artful sober knave,
And ten times worse for manners cool and grave:
And she devoid of sense, to set her hand
To scoundrel deeds she could not understand.
Alas! 'tis true; and I in vain had tried
To soften crime that cannot be denied;
And might have labour'd many a tedious verse
The latent cause of mischief to rehearse:
Be it confess'd, that long, with troubled look,
This Trader view'd a huge accompting-book;
(His former marriage for a time delay'd
The dreaded hour, the present lent its aid;)
But he too clearly saw the evil day,
And put the terror, by deceit, away;
Thus, by connecting with his sorrows crime,
He gain'd a portion of uneasy time.—
All this too late the injur'd Lady saw:
What law had given, again she gave to law;
His guilt, her folly—these at once impress'd
Their lasting feelings on her guileless breast.
"Shame I can bear," she cried, "and want sustain,
But will not see this guilty wretch again:"
For all was lost, and he with many a tear
Confess'd the fault—she turning scorn'd to hear.
To legal claims he yielded all his worth.
But small the portion, and the wrong'd were wroth,
Nor to their debtor would a part allow;
And where to live he know not—knew not how.
The Wife a cottage found, and thither went
The suppliant man, but she would not relent:
Thenceforth she utter'd with indignant tone,
"I feel the misery, and will feel alone."
He would turn servant for her sake, would keep
The poorest school, the very streets would sweep,
To show his love. "It was already shown,
And her affliction should be all her own:
His wants and weakness might have touch'd her heart,

But from his meanness she resolved to part."
In a small alley was she lodged, beside
Its humblest poor, and at the view she cried,
"Welcome! yes! let me welcome, if I can,
The fortune dealt me by this cruel man:
Welcome this low-thatch'd roof, this shatter'd door,
These walls of clay, this miserable floor;
Welcome my envied neighbours; this to you
Is all familiar—all to me is new:
You have no hatred to the loathsome meal,
Your firmer nerves no trembling terrors feel,
Nor, what you must expose, desire you to conceal;
What your coarse feelings bear without offence,
Disgusts my taste and poisons every sense:
Daily shall I your sad relations hear
Of wanton women and of men severe;
There will dire curses, dreadful oaths abound,
And vile expressions shock me and confound:
Noise of dull wheels, and songs with horrid words,
Will be the music that this lane affords;
Mirth that disgusts, and quarrels that degrade
The human mind, must my retreat invade:
Hard is my fate! yet easier to sustain,
Than to abide with guilt and fraud again;
A grave impostor! who expects to meet,
In such gray locks and gravity, deceit?
Where the sea rages and the billows roar,
Men know the danger, and they quit the shore;
But, be there nothing in the way descried,
When o'er the rocks smooth runs the wicked tide—
Sinking unwarn'd, they execrate the shock
And the dread peril of the sunken rock."
A frowning world had now the man to dread,
Taught in no arts, to no profession bred;
Pining in grief, beset with constant care
Wandering he went, to rest he knew not where.
Meantime the Wife—but she abjured the name—
Endured her lot, and struggled with the shame;
When, lo! an uncle on the mother's side,
In nature something, as in blood allied,
Admired her firmness, his protection gave,
And show'd a kindness she disdain'd to crave.
Frugal and rich the man, and frugal grew
The sister-mind without a selfish view;
And further still—the temp'rate pair agreed
With what they saved the patient poor to feed:
His whole estate, when to the grave consign'd,
Left the good kinsman to the kindred mind;

Assured that law, with spell secure and tight,
Had fix'd it as her own peculiar right.
Now to her ancient residence removed,
She lived as widow, well endowed and loved;
Decent her table was, and to her door
Came daily welcomed the neglected poor:
The absent sick were soothed by her relief,
As her free bounty sought the haunts of grief;
A plain and homely charity had she,
And loved the objects of her alms to see;
With her own hands she dress'd the savoury meat,
With her own fingers wrote the choice receipt;
She heard all tales that injured wives relate,
And took a double interest in their fate;
But of all husbands not a wretch was known
So vile, so mean, so cruel as her own.
This bounteous Lady kept an active spy,
To search th' abodes of want, and to supply;
The gentle Susan served the liberal dame—
Unlike their notions, yet their deeds the same:
No practised villain could a victim find
Than this stern Lady more completely blind;
Nor (if detected in his fraud) could meet
One less disposed to pardon a deceit;
The wrong she treasured, and on no pretence
Received th' offender, or forgot th' offence:
But the kind Servant, to the thrice-proved knave
A fourth time listen'd and the past forgave.
First in her youth, when she was blithe and gay;
Came a smooth rogue, and stole her love away:
Then to another and another flew,
To boast the wanton mischief he could do:
Yet she forgave him, though so great her pain,
That she was never blithe or gay again.
Then came a spoiler, who, with villain-art
Implored her hand, and agonized her heart;
He seized her purse, in idle waste to spend
With a vile wanton, whom she call'd her friend;
Five years she suffer'd—he had revell'd five—
Then came to show her he was just alive;
Alone he came, his vile companion dead,
And he, a wand'ring pauper, wanting bread;
His body wasted, wither'd life and limb,
When this kind soul became a slave to him:
Nay, she was sure that, should he now survive,
No better husband would be left alive:
For him she mourn'd, and then, alone and poor,
Sought and found comfort at her Lady's door:

Ten years she served, and mercy her employ,
Her tasks were pleasure, and her duty joy.
Thus lived the Mistress and the Maid, design'd
Each other's aid—one cautious, and both kind:
Oft at their window, working, they would sigh
To see the aged and the sick go by;
Like wounded bees, that at their home arrive
Slowly and weak, but labouring for the hive.
The busy people of a mason's yard
The curious Lady view'd with much regard;
With steady motion she perceived them draw
Through blocks of stone the slowly-working saw;
It gave her pleasure and surprise to see
Among these men the signs of revelry:
Cold was the season, and confined their view,
Tedious their tasks, but merry were the crew;
There she beheld an aged pauper wait,
Patient and still, to take an humble freight;
Within the panniers on an ass he laid
The ponderous grit, and for the portion paid;
This he re-sold, and, with each trifling gift,
Made shift to live, and wretched was the shift.
Now will it be by every reader told
Who was this humble trader, poor and old.—
In vain an author would a name suppress,
From the least hint a reader learns to guess;
Of children lost, our novels sometimes treat,
We never care—assured again to meet:
In vain the writer for concealment tries,
We trace his purpose under all disguise;
Nay, though he tells us they are dead and gone,
Of whom we wot, they will appear anon;
Our favourites fight, are wounded, hopeless lie,
Survive they cannot—nay, they cannot die;
Now, as these tricks and stratagems are known,
'Tis best, at once, the simple truth to own.
This was the husband—in an humble shed
He nightly slept, and daily sought his bread:
Once for relief the weary man applied;
"Your wife is rich," the angry vestry cried:
Alas! he dared not to his wife complain,
Feeling her wrongs, and fearing her disdain:
By various methods he had tried to live,
But not one effort would subsistence give:
He was an usher in a school, till noise
Made him less able than the weaker boys;
On messages he went, till he in vain
Strove names, or words, or meanings to retain;

Each small employment in each neighbouring town,
By turn he took, to lay as quickly down:
For, such his fate, he fail'd in all he plann'd,
And nothing prosper'd in his luckless hand.
At his old home, his motive half suppress'd,
He sought no more for riches, but for rest:
There lived the bounteous Wife, and at her gate
He saw in cheerful groups the needy wait;
"Had he a right with bolder hope t'apply?"
He ask'd—was answer'd, and went groaning by:
For some remains of spirit, temper, pride,
Forbade a prayer he knew would be denied.
Thus was the grieving man, with burthen'd ass,
Seen day by day along the street to pass:
"Who is he, Susan? who the poor old man?
He never calls—do make him, if you can."
The conscious damsel still delay'd to speak,
She stopp'd confused, and had her words to seek;
From Susan's fears the fact her mistress knew,
And cried—"The wretch! what scheme has he in view?
Is this his lot?—but let him, let him feel—
Who wants the courage, not the will, to steal."
A dreadful winter came, each day severe,
Misty when mild, and icy cold when clear;
And still the humble dealer took his load,
Returning slow, and shivering on the road:
The Lady, still relentless, saw him come,
And said—"I wonder, has the wretch a home?"—
"A hut! a hovel!" "Then his fate appears
To suit his crime."—"Yes, lady, not his years;—
No! nor his sufferings—nor that form decay'd."
"Well! let the parish give its paupers aid:
You must the vileness of his acts allow."—
"And you, dear lady, that he feels it now."
"When such dissemblers on their deeds reflect,
Can they the pity they refused expect?
He that doth evil, evil shall he dread."—
"The snow," quoth Susan, "falls upon his bed—
It blows beside the thatch—it melts upon his head."
"'Tis weakness, child, for grieving guilt to feel."—
"Yes, but he never sees a wholesome meal;
Through his bare dress appears his shrivell'd skin,
And ill he fares without, and worse within:
With that weak body, lame, diseased, and slow,
What cold, pain, peril, must the sufferer know!"
"Think on his crime."—"Yes, sure 'twas very wrong;
But look (God bless him!) how he gropes along."
"Brought me to shame."—Oh! yes, I know it all—

What cutting blast! and he can scarcely crawl:
He freezes as he moves—he dies! if he should fall:
With cruel fierceness drives this icy sleet—
And must a Christian perish in the street,
In sight of Christians?—There! at last, he lies;—
Nor unsupported can he ever rise:
He cannot live." "But is he fit to die?"—
Here Susan softly mutter'd a reply,
Look'd round the room—said something of its state,
Dives the rich, and Lazarus at his gate;
And then aloud—"In pity do behold
The man affrighten'd, weeping, trembling, cold:
Oh! how those flakes of snow their entrance win
Through the poor rags, and keep the frost within.
His very heart seems frozen as he goes,
Leading that starved companion of his woes:
He tried to pray—his lips, I saw them move,
And he so turn'd his piteous looks above;
But the fierce wind the willing heart opposed,
And, ere he spoke, the lips in misery closed:
Poor suffering object! yes, for ease you pray'd,
And God will hear—He only, I'm afraid."
"Peace! Susan, peace! pain ever follows sin."—
"Ah! then," thought Susan, "when will ours begin?
When reach'd his home, to what a cheerless fire
And chilling bed will those cold limbs retire!
Yet ragged, wretched as it is, that bed
Takes half the space of his contracted shed;
I saw the thorns beside the narrow grate,
With straw collected in a putrid state:
There will he, kneeling, strive the fire to raise,
And that will warm him, rather than the blaze:
The sullen, smoky blaze, that cannot last
One moment after his attempt is past;
And I so warmly and so purely laid,
To sink to rest—indeed, I am afraid."
"Know you his conduct?"—"Yes, indeed I know,
And how he wanders in the wind and snow;
Safe in our rooms the threat'ning storm we hear,
But he feels strongly what we faintly fear."
"Wilful was rich, and he the storm defied;
Wilful is poor, and must the storm abide,"
Said the stern Lady; "'tis in vain to feel;
Go and prepare the chicken for our meal."
Susan her task reluctantly began,
And utter'd as she went—"The poor old man!"
But while her soft and ever-yielding heart
Made strong protest against her lady's part,

The lady's self began to think it wrong
To feel so wrathful and resent so long.
"No more the wretch would she receive again,
No more behold him—but she would sustain;
Great his offence, and evil was his mind—
But he had suffer'd, and she would be kind:
She spurn'd such baseness, and she found within
A fair acquittal from so foul a sin;
Yet she too err'd, and must of Heaven expect
To be rejected, him should she reject."
Susan was summon'd—"I'm about to do
A foolish act, in part seduced by you;
Go to the creature—say that I intend,
Foe to his sins, to be his sorrow's friend:
Take, for his present comforts, food and wine,
And mark his feelings at this act of mine:
Observe if shame be o'er his features spread,
By his own victim to be soothed and fed;
But, this inform him, that it is not love
That prompts my heart, that duties only move.
Say, that no merits in his favour plead,
But miseries only, and his abject need;
Nor bring me grov'ling thanks, nor high-flown praise;
I would his spirits, not his fancy, raise:
Give him no hope that I shall ever more
A man so vile to my esteem restore;
But warn him rather, that, in time of rest,
His crimes be all remember'd and confess'd:
I know not all that form the sinner's debt,
But there is one that he must not forget."
The mind of Susan prompted her with speed
To act her part in every courteous deed:
All that was kind she was prepared to say,
And keep the lecture for a future day;
When he had all life's comforts by his side,
Pity might sleep, and good advice be tried.
This done, the mistress felt disposed to look,
As self-approving, on a pious book;
Yet, to her native bias still inclined,
She felt her act too merciful and kind;
But when, long musing on the chilling scene
So lately past—the frost and sleet so keen—
The man's whole misery in a single view—
Yes! she could think some pity was his due.
Thus fix'd, she heard not her attendant glide
With soft slow step—till, standing by her side,
The trembling servant gasp'd for breath, and shed
Relieving tears, then utter'd, "He is dead!"

"Dead!" said the startled Lady.—"Yes, he fell
Close at the door where he was wont to dwell;
There his sole friend, the Ass, was standing by,
Half dead himself, to see his Master die."
"Expired he then, good Heaven! for want of food?"—
"No! crusts and water in a corner stood:—
To have this plenty, and to wait so long,
And to be right too late, is doubly wrong:
Then, every day to see him totter by,
And to forbear—Oh! what a heart had I!"
"Blame me not, child; I tremble at the news."
"'Tis my own heart," said Susan, "I accuse:
To have this money in my purse—to know
What grief was his, and what to grief we owe;
To see him often, always to conceive
How he must pine and languish, groan and grieve,
And every day in ease and peace to dine,
And rest in comfort!—What a heart is mine!"

TALE XVIII

THE WAGER

'Tis thought your deer doth hold you at a bay.

I choose her for myself;
If she and I are pleased, what's that to you?

Let's send each one to his wife,
And he whose wife is most obedient
Shall win the wager.

Now, by the world, it is a lusty wench,
I love her ten times more than e'er I did.
SHAKESPEARE, Taming of the Shrew.

Counter and Clubb were men in trade, whose pains,
Credit, and prudence, brought them constant gains;
Partners and punctual, every friend agreed
Counter and Clubb were men who must succeed.
When they had fix'd some little time in life,
Each thought of taking to himself a wife:
As men in trade alike, as men in love,
They seem'd with no according views to move;
As certain ores in outward view the same,

They show'd their difference when the magnet came.
Counter was vain: with spirit strong and high,
'Twas not in him like suppliant swain to sigh:
"His wife might o'er his men and maids preside,
And in her province be a judge and guide;
But what he thought, or did, or wish'd to do,
She must not know, or censure if she knew;
At home, abroad, by day, by night, if he
On aught determined, so it was to be:
How is a man," he ask'd, "for business fit,
Who to a female can his will submit?
Absent a while, let no inquiring eye
Or plainer speech presume to question why:
But all be silent; and, when seen again,
Let all be cheerful—shall a wife complain?
Friends I invite, and who shall dare t'object,
Or look on them with coolness or neglect?
No! I must ever of my house be head,
And, thus obey'd, I condescend to wed."
Clubb heard the speech—"My friend is nice, said he;
A wife with less respect will do for me:
How is he certain such a prize to gain?
What he approves, a lass may learn to feign,
And so affect t'obey till she begins to reign;
A while complying, she may vary then,
And be as wives of more unwary men;
Beside, to him who plays such lordly part,
How shall a tender creature yield her heart;
Should he the promised confidence refuse,
She may another more confiding choose;
May show her anger, yet her purpose hide,
And wake his jealousy, and wound his pride.
In one so humbled, who can trace the friend?
I on an equal, not a slave, depend;
If true, my confidence is wisely placed,
And being false, she only is disgraced."
Clubb, with these notions, cast his eye around;
And one so easy soon a partner found.
The lady chosen was of good repute;
Meekness she had not, and was seldom mute;
Though quick to anger, still she loved to smile,
And would be calm if men would wait a while:
She knew her duty, and she loved her way,
More pleased in truth to govern than obey;
She heard her priest with reverence, and her spouse
As one who felt the pressure of her vows;
Useful and civil, all her friends confess'd—
Give her her way, and she would choose the best;

Though some indeed a sly remark would make—
Give it her not, and she would choose to take.
All this, when Clubb some cheerful months had spent,
He saw, confess'd, and said he was content.
Counter meantime selected, doubted, weigh'd,
And then brought home a young complying maid;
A tender creature, full of fears as charms,
A beauteous nursling from its mother's arms;
A soft, sweet blossom, such as men must love,
But to preserve must keep it in the stove:
She had a mild, subdued, expiring look—
Raise but the voice, and this fair creature shook;
Leave her alone, she felt a thousand fears—
Chide, and she melted into floods of tears;
Fondly she pleaded, and would gently sigh,
For very pity, or she knew not why;
One whom to govern none could be afraid—
Hold up the finger, this meek thing obey'd;
Her happy husband had the easiest task—
Say but his will, no question would she ask;
She sought no reasons, no affairs she knew,
Of business spoke not, and had nought to do.
Oft he exclaim'd, "How meek! how mild! how kind!
With her 'twere cruel but to seem unkind;
Though ever silent when I take my leave,
It pains my heart to think how hers will grieve;
'Tis heaven on earth with such a wife to dwell,
I am in raptures to have sped so well;
But let me not, my friend, your envy raise,
No! on my life, your patience has my praise."
His Friend, though silent, felt the scorn implied—
"What need of patience?" to himself he cried:
"Better a woman o'er her house to rule,
Than a poor child just hurried from her school;
Who has no care, yet never lives at ease;
Unfit to rule, and indisposed to please.
What if he govern, there his boast should end;
No husband's power can make a slave his friend."
It was the custom of these Friends to meet
With a few neighbours in a neighbouring street;
Where Counter ofttimes would occasion seize
To move his silent Friend by words like these:
"A man," said he, "if govern'd by his wife,
Gives up his rank and dignity in life;
Now, better fate befalls my Friend and me."—
He spoke, and look'd th' approving smile to see.
The quiet partner, when he chose to speak,
Desired his friend "another theme to seek;

When thus they met, he judged that state-affairs
And such important subjects should be theirs:"
But still the partner, in his lighter vein,
Would cause in Clubb affliction or disdain;
It made him anxious to detect the cause
Of all that boasting:—"Wants my friend applause?
This plainly proves him not at perfect ease,
For, felt he pleasure, he would wish to please.
These triumphs here for some regrets atone—
Men who are bless'd let other men alone."
Thus made suspicious, he observed and saw
His friend each night at early hour withdraw;
He sometimes mention'd Juliet's tender nerves,
And what attention such a wife deserves:
"In this," thought Clubb, "full sure some mystery lies—
He laughs at me, yet he with much complies,
And all his vaunts of bliss are proud apologies."
With such ideas treasured in his breast,
He grew composed, and let his anger rest;
Till Counter once (when wine so long went round,
That friendship and discretion both were drown'd)
Began, in teasing and triumphant mood,
His evening banter:—"Of all earthly good,
The best," he said, "was an obedient spouse,
Such as my friend's—that every one allows:
What if she wishes his designs to know?
It is because she would her praise bestow;
What if she wills that he remain at home?
She knows that mischief may from travel come.
I, who am free to venture where I please,
Have no such kind preventing checks as these;
But mine is double duty, first to guide
Myself aright, then rule a house beside;
While this our friend, more happy than the free,
Resigns all power, and laughs at liberty."
"By heaven!" said Clubb, "excuse me if I swear,
I'll bet a hundred guineas, if he dare,
That uncontroll'd I will such freedoms take
That he will fear to equal—there's my stake."
"A match!" said Counter, much by wine inflamed;
"But we are friends—let smaller stake be named:
Wine for our future meeting, that will I
Take and no more—what peril shall we try?"
"Let's to Newmarket," Clubb replied; "or choose
Yourself the place, and what you like to lose:
And he who first returns, or fears to go,
Forfeits his cash."—Said Counter, "Be it so."
The friends around them saw with much delight

The social war, and hail'd the pleasant night;
Nor would they further hear the cause discuss'd,
Afraid the recreant heart of Clubb to trust.
Now sober thoughts return'd as each withdrew,
And of the subject took a serious view:
"'Twas wrong," thought Counter, "and will grieve my love;"
"'Twas wrong," thought Clubb, "my wife will not approve:
But friends were present; I must try the thing,
Or with my folly half the town will ring."
He sought his lady—"Madam, I'm to blame,
But was reproach'd, and could not bear the shame;
Here in my folly—for 'tis best to say
The very truth—I've sworn to have my way;
To that Newmarket—(though I hate the place,
And have no taste or talents for a race,
Yet so it is—well, now prepare to chide)—
I laid a wager that I dared to ride:
And I must go: by heaven, if you resist
I shall be scorn'd, and ridiculed, and hiss'd;
Let me with grace before my friends appear,
You know the truth, and must not be severe:
He too must go, but that he will of course:
Do you consent?—I never think of force."
"You never need," the worthy Dame replied;
"The husband's honour is the woman's pride:
If I in trifles be the wilful wife,
Still for your credit I would lose my life.
Go! and when fix'd the day of your return,
Stay longer yet, and let the blockheads learn
That though a wife may sometimes wish to rule,
She would not make th' indulgent man a fool;
I would at times advise—but idle they
Who think th' assenting husband must obey."
The happy man, who thought his lady right
In other cases, was assured to-night;
Then for the day with proud delight prepared,
To show his doubting friends how much he dared.
Counter—who grieving sought his bed, his rest
Broken by pictures of his love distress'd—
With soft and winning speech the fair prepared:
"She all his councils, comforts, pleasures shared:
She was assured he loved her from his soul,
She never knew and need not fear control;
But so it happen'd—he was grieved at heart
It happen'd so, that they awhile must part
A little time—the distance was but short,
And business called him—he despised the sport;
But to Newmarket he engaged to ride

With his friend Clubb:" and there he stopp'd and sigh'd.
Awhile the tender creature look'd dismay'd,
Then floods of tears the call of grief obeyed:—
"She an objection! No!" she sobb'd, "not one:
Her work was finish'd, and her race was run;
For die she must—indeed she would not live
A week alone, for all the world could give;
He too must die in that same wicked place;
It always happen'd—was a common case;
Among those horrid horses, jockeys, crowds,
'Twas certain death—they might bespeak their shrouds.
He would attempt a race, be sure to fall—
And she expire with terror—that was all;
With love like hers she was indeed unfit
To bear such horrors, but she must submit."
"But for three days, my love! three days at most,"
"Enough for me; I then shall be a ghost."
"My honour's pledged!"—"Oh! yes, my dearest life,
I know your honour must outweigh your wife;
But ere this absence have you sought a friend?
I shall be dead—on whom can you depend?
Let me one favour of your kindness crave,
Grant me the stone I mention'd for my grave."
"Nay, love, attend—why, bless my soul! I say
I will return—there, weep no longer, nay!"
"Well! I obey, and to the last am true,
But spirits fail me; I must die; adieu!"
"What, Madam! must?—'tis wrong—I'm angry—zounds
Can I remain and lose a thousand pounds?"
"Go then, my love! it is a monstrous sum,
Worth twenty wives—go, love! and I am dumb;
Nor be displeased—had I the power to live,
You might be angry, now you must forgive:
Alas! I faint—ah! cruel—there's no need
Of wounds or fevers—this has done the deed."
The lady fainted, and the husband sent
For every aid—for every comfort went;
Strong terror seized him: "Oh! she loved so well,
And who th' effect of tenderness could tell?"
She now recover'd, and again began
With accent querulous—"Ah! cruel man!"
Till the sad husband, conscience-struck, confess'd,
'Twas very wicked with his friend to jest;
For now he saw that those who were obey'd,
Could like the most subservient feel afraid:
And though a wife might not dispute the will
Of her liege lord, she could prevent it still.
The morning came, and Clubb prepared to ride

With a smart boy, his servant, and his guide;
When, ere he mounted on his ready steed,
Arrived a letter, and he stopped to read.
"My friend," he read, "our journey I decline,
A heart too tender for such strife is mine;
Yours is the triumph, be you so inclined;
But you are too considerate and kind:
In tender pity to my Juliet's fears
I thus relent, o'ercome by love and tears;
She knows your kindness; I have heard her say,
A man like you 'tis pleasure to obey:
Each faithful wife, like ours, must disapprove
Such dangerous trifling with connubial love;
What has the idle world, my friend, to do
With our affairs? they envy me and you:
What if I could my gentle spouse command—
Is that a cause I should her tears withstand?
And what if you, a friend of peace, submit
To one you love—is that a theme for wit?
'Twas wrong, and I shall henceforth judge it weak
Both of submission and control to speak:
Be it agreed that all contention cease,
And no such follies vex our future peace;
Let each keep guard against domestic strife,
And find nor slave nor tyrant in his wife."
"Agreed," said Clubb, "with all my soul agreed;"—
And to the boy, delighted, gave his steed.
"I think my friend has well his mind express'd,
And I assent; such things are not a jest."
"True," said the Wife, "no longer he can hide
The truth that pains him by his wounded pride:
Your friend has found it not an easy thing,
Beneath his yoke this yielding soul to bring:
These weeping willows, though they seem inclined
By every breeze, yet not the strongest wind
Can from their bent divert this weak but stubborn kind;
Drooping they seek your pity to excite,
But 'tis at once their nature and delight;
Such women feel not; while they sigh and weep,
'Tis but their habit—their affections sleep;
They are like ice that in the hand we hold,
So very melting, yet so very cold;
On such affection let not man rely,
The husbands suffer, and the ladies sigh:
But your friend's offer let us kindly take,
And spare his pride for his vexation's sake;
For he has found, and through his life will find,
'Tis easiest dealing with the firmest mind—

More just when it resists, and, when it yields, more kind."

THE CONVERT

A tapster is a good trade, and an old cloak makes a new jerkin; a withered serving-man, a fresh tapster.
SHAKESPEARE, Merry Wives of Windsor.

A fellow, Sir, that I have known go about with troll-my-dames.
A Winter's Tale.

I myself, sometimes leaving the fear of Heaven on the left hand, and hiding mine honour in my necessity,
am forced to shuffle, to hedge, and to lurch.
Merry Wives of Windsor.

Yea, and at that very moment,
Consideration like an angel came,
And whipp'd th' offending Adam out of him.
Henry V.

I have lived long enough: my way of life
Is fall'n into the sear, the yellow leaf;
And that which should accompany old age,
As honour, love, obedience, troops of friends,
I must not look to have.
Macbeth.

Some to our Hero have a hero's name
Denied, because no father's he could claim;
Nor could his mother with precision state
A full fair claim to her certificate;
On her own word the marriage must depend—
A point she was not eager to defend:
But who, without a father's name, can raise
His own so high, deserves the greater praise;
The less advantage to the strife he brought,
The greater wonders has his prowess wrought;
He who depends upon his wind and limbs,
Needs neither cork nor bladder when he swims;
Nor will by empty breath be puff'd along,
As not himself—but in his helpers—strong.
Suffice it then, our Hero's name was clear,
For call John Dighton, and he answer'd "Here!"
But who that name in early life assign'd

He never found, he never tried to find:
Whether his kindred were to John disgrace,
Or John to them, is a disputed case;
His infant state owed nothing to their care—
His mind neglected, and his body bare;
All his success must on himself depend,
He had no money, counsel, guide, or friend;
But in a market-town an active boy
Appear'd, and sought in various ways employ;
Who soon, thus cast upon the world, began
To show the talents of a thriving man.
With spirit high John learn'd the world to brave,
And in both senses was a ready knave;
Knave as of old obedient, keen, and quick,
Knave as of present, skill'd to shift and trick;
Some humble part of many trades he caught,
He for the builder and the painter wrought;
For serving-maids on secret errands ran,
The waiter's helper, and the ostler's man;
And when he chanced (oft chanced he) place to lose,
His varying genius shone in blacking shoes:
A midnight fisher by the pond he stood,
Assistant poacher, he o'erlook'd the wood;
At an election John's impartial mind
Was to no cause nor candidate confined;
To all in turn he full allegiance swore,
And in his hat the various badges bore:
His liberal soul with every sect agreed,
Unheard their reasons, he received their creed:
At church he deign'd the organ-pipes to fill,
And at the meeting sang both loud and shrill:
But the full purse these different merits gain'd,
By strong demands his lively passions drain'd;
Liquors he loved of each inflaming kind,
To midnight revels flew with ardent mind;
Too warm at cards, a losing game he play'd,
To fleecing beauty his attention paid;
His boiling passions were by oaths express'd,
And lies he made his profit and his jest.
Such was the boy, and such the man had been,
But fate or happier fortune changed the scene;
A fever seized him, "He should surely die—"
He fear'd, and lo! a friend was praying by;
With terror moved, this Teacher he address'd,
And all the errors of his youth confess'd:
The good man kindly clear'd the Sinner's way
To lively hope, and counsell'd him to pray;
Who then resolved, should he from sickness rise,

To quit cards, liquors, poaching, oaths, and lies;
His health restored, he yet resolved and grew
True to his masters, to their Meeting true;
His old companions at his sober face
Laugh'd loud, while he, attesting it was grace,
With tears besought them all his calling to embrace:
To his new friends such convert gave applause,
Life to their zeal, and glory to their cause:
Though terror wrought the mighty change, yet strong
Was the impression, and it lasted long;
John at the lectures due attendance paid,
A convert meek, obedient, and afraid;
His manners strict, though form'd on fear alone,
Pleased the grave friends, nor less his solemn tone,
The lengthen'd face of care, the low and inward groan;
The stern good men exulted when they saw
Those timid looks of penitence and awe;
Nor thought that one so passive, humble, meek,
Had yet a creed and principles to seek.
The Faith that Reason finds, confirms, avows,
The hopes, the views, the comforts she allows—
These were not his, who by his feelings found,
And by them only, that his faith was sound;
Feelings of terror these, for evil past,
Feelings of hope to be received at last;
Now weak, now lively, changing with the day—
These were his feelings, and he felt his way.
Sprung from such sources, will this faith remain
While these supporters can their strength retain?
As heaviest weights the deepest rivers pass,
While icy chains fast bind the solid mass;
So, born of feelings, faith remains secure,
Long as their firmness and their strength endure;
But when the waters in their channel glide,
A bridge must bear us o'er the threat'ning tide;
Such bridge is Reason, and there Faith relies,
Whether the varying spirits fall or rise.
His patrons, still disposed their aid to lend.
Behind a counter placed their humble friend,
Where pens and paper were on shelves display'd,
And pious pamphlets on the windows laid:
By nature active, and from vice restrain'd,
Increasing trade his bolder views sustain'd;
His friends and teachers, finding so much zeal
In that young convert whom they taught to feel,
His trade encouraged, and were pleased to find
A hand so ready, with such humble mind.
And now, his health restored, his spirits eased,

He wish'd to marry, if the teachers pleased.
They, not unwilling, from the virgin-class
Took him a comely and a courteous lass;
Simple and civil, loving and beloved,
She long a fond and faithful partner proved;
In every year the elders and the priest
Were duly summon'd to a christening feast;
Nor came a babe, but by his growing trade
John had provision for the coming made;
For friends and strangers all were pleased to deal
With one whose care was equal to his zeal.
In human friendships, it compels a sigh
To think what trifles will dissolve the tie.
John, now become a master of his trade,
Perceived how much improvement might be made;
And as this prospect open'd to his view,
A certain portion of his zeal withdrew;
His fear abated—"What had he to fear—
His profits certain, and his conscience clear?"
Above his door a board was placed by John,
And "Dighton, Stationer," was gilt thereon;
His window next, enlarged to twice the size,
Shone with such trinkets as the simple prize;
While in the shop with pious works were seen
The last new play, review, or magazine:
In orders punctual, he observed—"The books
He never read, and could he judge their looks?
Readers and critics should their merits try,
He had no office but to sell and buy;
Like other traders, profit was his care;
Of what they print, the authors must beware."
He held his patrons and his teachers dear,
But with his trade they must not interfere.
'Twas certain now that John had lost the dread
And pious thoughts that once such terrors bred;
His habits varied, and he more inclined
To the vain world, which he had half resign'd;
He had moreover in his brethren seen,
Or he imagined, craft, conceit, and spleen:
"They are but men," said John, "and shall I then
Fear man's control, or stand in awe of men?
'Tis their advice (their Convert's rule and law),
And good it is—I will not stand in awe."
Moreover Dighton, though he thought of books
As one who chiefly on the title looks,
Yet sometimes ponder'd o'er a page to find,
When vex'd with cares, amusement for his mind;
And by degrees that mind had treasured much

From works his teachers were afraid to touch:
Satiric novels, poets bold and free,
And what their writers term philosophy;
All these were read, and he began to feel
Some self-approval on his bosom steal.
Wisdom creates humility, but he
Who thus collects it will not humble be:
No longer John was fill'd with pure delight
And humble reverence in a pastor's sight;
Who, like a grateful zealot, listening stood,
To hear a man so friendly and so good;
But felt the dignity of one who made
Himself important by a thriving trade:
And growing pride in Dighton's mind was bred
By the strange food on which it coarsely fed.
Their Brother's fall the grieving Brethren heard—
His pride indeed to all around appeared;
The world, his friends agreed, had won the soul
From its best hopes, the man from their control.
To make him humble, and confine his views
Within their bounds, and books which they peruse,
A deputation from these friends select
Might reason with him to some good effect;
Arm'd with authority, and led by love,
They might those follies from his mind remove.
Deciding thus, and with this kind intent,
A chosen body with its speaker went.
"John," said the Teacher, "John, with great concern.
We see thy frailty, and thy fate discern—
Satan with toils thy simple soul beset,
And thou art careless slumbering in the net:
Unmindful art thou of thy early vow;
Who at the morning meeting sees thee now?
Who at the evening? 'Where is brother John?'
We ask;—are answer'd, 'To the tavern gone.'
Thee on the Sabbath seldom we behold;
Thou canst not sing, thou'rt nursing for a cold:
This from the churchmen thou hast learn'd, for they
Have colds and fevers on the Sabbath-day;
When in some snug warm room they sit, and pen
Bills from their ledgers—world-entangled men,
"See with what pride thou hast enlarged thy shop;
To view thy tempting stores the heedless stop.
By what strange names dost thou these baubles know,
Which wantons wear, to make a sinful show?
Hast thou in view these idle volumes placed
To be the pander of a vicious taste?
What's here? a book of dances!—you advance

In goodly knowledge—John, wilt learn to dance?
How! 'Go,' it says, and 'to the devil go!
And shake thyself!' I tremble—but 'tis so;
Wretch as thou art, what answer canst thou make?
Oh! without question, thou wilt go and shake.
What's here? 'The School for Scandal'—pretty schools!
Well, and art thou proficient in the rules?
Art thou a pupil? Is it thy design
To make our names contemptible as thine?
'Old Nick, a novel!' oh! 'tis mighty well—
A fool has courage when he laughs at hell;
'Frolic and Fun;' the Humours of Tim Grin;'
Why, John, thou grow'st facetious in thy sin;
And what?—'The Archdeacon's Charge!'—'tis mighty well—
If Satan publish'd, thou wouldst doubtless sell:
Jests, novels, dances, and this precious stuff
To crown thy folly—we have seen enough;
We find thee fitted for each evil work:
Do print the Koran and become a Turk.
"John, thou art lost; success and worldly pride
O'er all thy thoughts and purposes preside,
Have bound thee fast, and drawn thee far aside:
Yet turn; these sin-traps from thy shop expel,
Repent and pray, and all may yet be well.
"And here thy wife, thy Dorothy behold,
How fashion's wanton robes her form infold!
Can grace, can goodness with such trappings dwell?
John, thou hast made thy wife a Jezebel:
See! on her bosom rests the sign of sin,
The glaring proof of naughty thoughts within:
What! 'tis a cross: come hither—as a friend,
Thus from thy neck the shameful badge I rend."
"Rend, if you dare," said Dighton; "you shall find
A man of spirit, though to peace inclined;
Call me ungrateful! have I not my pay
At all times ready for the expected day?
To share my plenteous board you deign to come,
Myself your pupil, and my house your home:
And shall the persons who my meat enjoy
Talk of my faults, and treat me as a boy?
Have you not told how Rome's insulting priests
Led their meek laymen like a herd of beasts;
And by their fleecing and their forgery made
Their holy calling an accursed trade?
Can you such acts and insolence condemn,
Who to your utmost power resemble them?
"Concerns it you what books I set for sale?
The tale perchance may be a virtuous tale;

And for the rest, 'tis neither wise nor just
In you, who read not, to condemn on trust;
Why should th' Archdeacon's Charge your spleen excite?
He, or perchance th' Archbishop, may be right.
"That from your meetings I refrain is true:
I meet with nothing pleasant—nothing new;
But the same proofs, that not one text explain,
And the same lights, where all things dark remain;
I thought you saints on earth—but I have found
Some sins among you, and the best unsound:
You have your failings, like the crowds below,
And at your pleasure hot and cold can blow:
When I at first your grave deportment saw,
(I own my folly,) I was fill'd with awe;
You spoke so warmly, and it seem'd so well,
I should have thought it treason to rebel.
Is it a wonder that a man like me
Should such perfection in such teachers see—
Nay, should conceive you sent from Heaven to brave
The host of sin, and sinful souls to save?
But as our reason wakes, our prospects clear,
And failings, flaws, and blemishes appear.
"When you were mounted in your rostrum high,
We shrank beneath your tone, your frown, your eye:
Then you beheld us abject, fallen, low,
And felt your glory from our baseness grow;
Touch'd by your words, I trembled like the rest,
And my own vileness and your power confess'd:
These, I exclaim'd, are men divine, and gazed
On him who taught, delighted and amazed;
Glad when he finish'd, if by chance he cast
One look on such a sinner as he pass'd.
"But when I view'd you in a clearer light,
And saw the frail and carnal appetite;
When at his humble pray'r, you deign'd to eat,
Saints as you are, a civil sinner's meat;
When, as you sat contented and at ease,
Nibbling at leisure on the ducks and peas,
And, pleased some comforts in such place to find,
You could descend to be a little kind;
And gave us hope in heaven there might be room
For a few souls beside your own to come;
While this world's good engaged your carnal view,
And like a sinner you enjoy'd it too;
All this perceiving, can you think it strange
That change in you should work an equal change?"
"Wretch that thou art," an elder cried, "and gone
For everlasting!"—"Go thyself," said John;

Depart this instant, let me hear no more;
My house my castle is, and that my door."
The hint they took, and from the door withdrew,
And John to meeting bade a long adieu;
Attached to business, he in time became
A wealthy man of no inferior name.
It seem'd, alas! in John's deluded sight,
That all was wrong because not all was right:
And when he found his teachers had their stains,
Resentment and not reason broke his chains:
Thus on his feelings he again relied,
And never look'd to reason for his guide:
Could he have wisely view'd the frailty shown,
And rightly weigh'd their wanderings and his own,
He might have known that men may be sincere,
Though gay and feasting on the savoury cheer;
That doctrines sound and sober they may teach,
Who love to eat with all the glee they preach;
Nay! who believe the duck, the grape, the pine,
Were not intended for the dog and swine:
But Dighton's hasty mind on every theme
Ran from the truth, and rested in th' extreme:
Flaws in his friends he found, and then withdrew
(Vain of his knowledge) from their virtues too,
Best of his books he loved the liberal kind
That, if they improve not, still enlarge the mind;
And found himself, with such advisers, free
From a fix'd creed, as mind enlarged could be.
His humble wife at these opinions sigh'd,
But her he never heeded till she died:
He then assented to a last request,
And by the meeting-window let her rest;
And on her stone the sacred text was seen,
Which had her comfort in departing been.
Dighton with joy beheld his trade advance,
Yet seldom published, loth to trust to chance:
Then wed a doctor's sister—poor indeed,
But skill'd in works her husband could not read;
Who, if he wish'd new ways of wealth to seek,
Could make her half-crown pamphlet in a week:
This he rejected, though without disdain.
And chose the old and certain way to gain.
Thus he proceeded: trade increased the while,
And fortune woo'd him with perpetual smile:
On early scenes he sometimes cast a thought,
When on his heart the mighty change was wrought;
And all the ease and comfort Converts find
Was magnified in his reflecting mind:

Then on the teacher's priestly pride he dwelt,
That caused his freedom, but with this he felt
The danger of the free—for since that day
No guide had shown, no brethren join'd his way;
Forsaking one, he found no second creed,
But reading doubted, doubting what to read.
Still, though reproof had brought some present pain,
The gain he made was fair and honest gain;
He laid his wares indeed in public view,
But that all traders claim a right to do:
By means like these, he saw his wealth increase,
And felt his consequence, and dwelt in peace.
Our Hero's age was threescore years and five,
When he exclaim'd, "Why longer should I strive?
Why more amass, who never must behold
A young John Dighton to make glad the old?"
(The sons he had to early graves were gone,
And girls were burdens to the mind of John.)
"Had I a boy, he would our name sustain,
That now to nothing must return again;
But what are all my profits, credit, trade,
And parish honours?—folly and parade."
Thus Dighton thought, and in his looks appeared
Sadness, increased by much he saw and heard;
The Brethren often at the shop would stay,
And make their comments ere they walk'd away;
They mark'd the window, fill'd in every pane
With lawless prints of reputations slain;
Distorted forms of men with honours graced,
And our chief rulers in dirision placed:
Amazed they stood, remembering well the days
When to be humble was their brother's praise;
When at the dwelling of their friend they stopped;
To drop a word, or to receive it dropp'd;
Where they beheld the prints of men renown'd,
And far-famed preachers pasted all around,
(Such mouths! eyes! hair! so prim! so fierce! so sleek!
They look'd as speaking what is woe to speak):
On these the passing brethren loved to dwell—
How long they spake! how strongly! warmly! well!
What power had each to dive in mysteries deep,
To warm the cold, to make the harden'd weep;
To lure, to fright, to soothe, to awe the soul,
And listening locks to lead and to control!
But now discoursing, as they linger'd near,
They tempted John (whom they accused) to hear
Their weighty charge—"And can the lost one feel,
As in the time of duty, love, and zeal;

When all were summon'd at the rising sun,
And he was ready with his friends to run;
When he, partaking with a chosen few,
Felt the great change, sensation rich and new?
No! all is lost; her favours Fortune shower'd
Upon the man, and he is overpower'd;
The world has won him with its tempting store
Of needless wealth, and that has made him poor:
Success undoes him; he has risen to fall,
Has gain'd a fortune, and has lost his all;
Gone back from Sion, he will find his age
Loth to commence a second pilgrimage;
He has retreated from the chosen track,
And now must ever bear the burden on his back."
Hurt by such censure, John began to find
Fresh revolutions working in his mind;
He sought for comfort in his books, but read
Without a plan or method in his head;
What once amused, now rather made him sad;
What should inform, increased the doubts he had;
Shame would not let him seek at Church a guide,
And from his Meeting he was held by pride;
His wife derided fears she never felt,
And passing brethren daily censures dealt;
Hope for a son was now for ever past,
He was the first John Dighton and the last;
His stomach fail'd, his case the doctor knew,
But said, "he still might hold a year or two."
"No more!" he said; "but why should I complain?
A life of doubt must be a life of pain:
Could I be sure—but why should I despair?
I'm sure my conduct has been just and fair;
In youth, indeed, I had a wicked will,
But I repented, and have sorrow still:
I had my comforts, and a growing trade
Gave greater pleasure than a fortune made;
And as I more possess'd, and reason'd more,
I lost those comforts I enjoy'd before,
When reverend guides I saw my table round,
And in my guardian guest my safety found:
Now sick and sad, no appetite, no ease,
Nor pleasures have I, nor a wish to please;
Nor views, nor hopes, nor plans, nor taste have I;
Yet, sick of life, have no desire to die."
He said, and died: his trade, his name is gone,
And all that once gave consequence to John.
Unhappy Dighton! had he found a friend
When conscience told him it was time to mend—

A friend descreet, considerate, kind, sincere,
Who would have shown the grounds of hope and fear,
And proved that spirits, whether high or low,
No certain tokens of man's safety show—
Had Reason ruled him in her proper place,
And Virtue led him while he lean'd on grace—
Had he while zealous been discreet and pure,
His knowledge humble, and his hope secure;—
These guides had placed him on the solid rock,
Where Faith had rested, nor received a shock;
But his, alas! was placed upon the sand,
Where long it stood not, and where none can stand.

TALE XX

THE BROTHERS

A brother noble,
Whose nature is so far from doing harms,
That he suspects none; on whose foolish honesty
My practice may ride easy.
SHAKESPEARE, King Lear.

He lets me feed with hinds,
Bars me the place of brother.
As You Like It.

'Twas I, but 'tis not I: I do not shame
To tell you what I was, being what I am.
As You Like It.

Than old George Fletcher, on the British coast
Dwelt not a seaman who had more to boast:
Kind, simple and sincere—he seldom spoke,
But sometimes sang and chorus'd—"Hearts of Oak:"
In dangers steady, with his lot content,
His days in labour and in love were spent.
He left a Son so like him, that the old
With joy exclaim'd, "'Tis Fletcher we behold;"
But to his Brother, when the kinsmen came
And view'd his form, they grudged the father's name.
George was a bold, intrepid, careless lad,
With just the failings that his father had;
Isaac was weak, attentive, slow, exact,
With just the virtues that his father lack'd.

George lived at sea: upon the land a guest—
He sought for recreation, not for rest;
While, far unlike, his brother's feebler form
Shrank from the cold, and shudder'd at the storm;
Still with the Seaman's to connect his trade,
The boy was bound where blocks and ropes were made.
George, strong and sturdy, had a tender mind,
And was to Isaac pitiful and kind;
A very father, till his art was gain'd,
And then a friend unwearied he remain'd;
He saw his brother was of spirit low,
His temper peevish, and his motions slow;
Not fit to bustle in a world, or make
Friends to his fortune for his merit's sake;
But the kind sailor could not boast the art
Of looking deeply in the human heart;
Else had he seen that this weak brother knew
What men to court—what objects to pursue;
That he to distant gain the way discern'd,
And none so crooked but his genius learn'd.
Isaac was poor, and this the brother felt;
He hired a house, and there the Landman dwelt,
Wrought at his trade, and had an easy home,
For there would George with cash and comforts come;
And when they parted, Isaac look'd around
Where other friends and helpers might be found.
He wish'd for some port-place, and one might fall,
He wisely thought, if he should try for all;
He had a vote—and were it well applied,
Might have its worth—and he had views beside;
Old Burgess Steel was able to promote
An humble man who served him with a vote;
For Isaac felt not what some tempers feel,
But bow'd and bent the neck to Burgess Steel;
And great attention to a lady gave,
His ancient friend, a maiden spare and grave;
One whom the visage long and look demure
Of Isaac pleased—he seem'd sedate and pure;
And his soft heart conceived a gentle flame
For her who waited on this virtuous dame.
Not an outrageous love, a scorching fire,
But friendly liking and chastised desire;
And thus he waited, patient in delay,
In present favour and in fortune's way.
George then was coasting—war was yet delay'd,
And what he gain'd was to his brother paid;
Nor ask'd the Seaman what he saved or spent,
But took his grog, wrought hard, and was content;

Till war awaked the land, and George began
To think what part became a useful man:
"Press'd, I must go: why, then, 'tis better far
At once to enter like a British tar,
Than a brave captain and the foe to shun,
As if I fear'd the music of a gun."
"Go not!" said Isaac—"you shall wear disguise."
"What!" said the Seaman, "clothe myself with lies!"
"Oh! but there's danger."—"Danger in the fleet?
You cannot mean, good brother, of defeat;
And other dangers I at land must share—
So now adieu! and trust a brother's care."
Isaac awhile demurr'd—but, in his heart,
So might he share, he was disposed to part:
The better mind will sometimes feel the pain
Of benefactions—favour is a chain;
But they the feeling scorn, and what they wish, disdain;
While beings form'd in coarser mould will hate
The helping hand they ought to venerate:
No wonder George should in this cause prevail,
With one contending who was glad to fail:
"Isaac, farewell! do wipe that doleful eye;
Crying we came, and groaning we may die;
Let us do something 'twixt the groan and cry:
And hear me, brother, whether pay or prize,
One half to thee I give and I devise;
Por thou hast oft occasion for the aid
Of learn'd physicians, and they will be paid;
Their wives and children men support at sea,
And thou, my lad, art wife and child to me:
Farewell! I go where hope and honour call,
Nor does it follow that who fights must fall,"
Isaac here made a poor attempt to speak,
And a huge tear moved slowly down his cheek;
Like Pluto's iron drop, hard sign of grace,
It slowly roll'd upon the rueful face,
Forced by the striving will alone its way to trace.
Years fled—war lasted—George at sea remain'd,
While the slow Landman still his profits gain'd:
An humble place was vacant—he besought
His patron's interest, and the office caught;
For still the Virgin was his faithful friend,
And one so sober could with truth commend,
Who of his own defects most humbly thought,
And their advice with zeal and reverence sought:
Whom thus the Mistress praised, the Maid approved,
And her he wedded whom he wisely loved.
No more he needs assistance—but, alas!

He fears the money will for liquor pass;
Or that the Seaman might to flatterers lend,
Or give support to some pretended friend:
Still he must write—he wrote, and he confess'd
That, till absolved, he should be sore distress'd;
But one so friendly would, he thought, forgive
The hasty deed—Heav'n knew how he should live;
"But you," he added, "as a man of sense,
Have well consider'd danger and expense:
I ran, alas! into the fatal snare,
And now for trouble must my mind prepare;
And how, with children, I shall pick my way
Through a hard world, is more than I can say:
Then change not, Brother, your more happy state,
Or on the hazard long deliberate."
George answered gravely, "It is right and fit,
In all our crosses, humbly to submit:
Your apprehensions are unwise, unjust;
Forbear repining, and expel distrust."
He added, "Marriage was the joy of life,"
And gave his service to his brother's wife;
Then vow'd to bear in all expense a part,
And thus concluded, "Have a cheerful heart."
Had the glad Isaac been his brother's guide,
In the same terms the Seaman had replied;
At such reproofs the crafty Landman smiled,
And softly said, "This creature is a child."
Twice had the gallant ship a capture made—
And when in port the happy crew were paid,
Home went the Sailor, with his pockets stored,
Ease to enjoy, and pleasure to afford;
His time was short, joy shone in every face,
Isaac half fainted in the fond embrace:
The wife resolved her honour'd guest to please,
The children clung upon their uncle's knees;
The grog went round, the neighbours drank his health,
And George exclaimed, "Ah! what to this is wealth?
Better," said he, "to bear a loving heart,
Than roll in riches—but we now must part!"
All yet is still—but hark! the winds o'ersweep
The rising waves, and howl upon the deep;
Ships late becalm'd on mountain-billows ride—
So life is threaten'd and so man is tried.
Ill were the tidings that arrived from sea,
The worthy George must now a cripple be:
His leg was lopp'd; and though his heart was sound,
Though his brave captain was with glory crown'd,
Yet much it vex'd him to repose on shore,

An idle log, and be of use no more:
True, he was sure that Isaac would receive
All of his Brother that the foe might leave;
To whom the Seaman his design had sent,
Ere from the port the wounded hero went:
His wealth and expectations told, he "knew
Wherein they fail'd, what Isaac's love would do;
That he the grog and cabin would supply,
Where George at anchor during life would lie."
The Landman read—and, reading, grew distress'd:—
"Could he resolve t'admit so poor a guest?
Better at Greenwich might the Sailor stay,
Unless his purse could for his comforts pay."
So Isaac judged, and to his wife appealed,
But yet acknowledged it was best to yield:
"Perhaps his pension, with what sums remain
Due or unsquander'd, may the man maintain;
Refuse we must not."—With a heavy sigh
The lady heard, and made her kind reply:—
"Nor would I wish it, Isaac, were we sure
How long this crazy building will endure;
Like an old house, that every day appears
About to fall, he may be propp'd for years;
For a few months, indeed, we might comply,
But these old batter'd fellows never die."
The hand of Isaac, George on entering took,
With love and resignation in his look;
Declared his comfort in the fortune past,
And joy to find his anchor safely cast:
"Call then my nephews, let the grog be brought,
And I will tell them how the ship was fought."
Alas! our simple Seaman should have known
That all the care, the kindness, he had shown,
Were from his Brother's heart, if not his memory, flown:
All swept away, to be perceived no more,
Like idle structures on the sandy shore,
The chance amusement of the playful boy,
That the rude billows in their rage destroy.
Poor George confess'd, though loth the truth to find,
Slight was his knowledge of a Brother's mind:
The vulgar pipe was to the wife offence,
The frequent grog to Isaac an expense;
Would friends like hers, she question'd, "choose to come
Where clouds of poison'd fume defiled a room?
This could their Lady-friend, and Burgess Steel
(Teased with his worship's asthma), bear to feel?
Could they associate or converse with him—
A loud rough sailor with a timber limb?"

Cold as he grew, still Isaac strove to show,
By well-feign'd care, that cold he could not grow;
And when he saw his brother look distress'd,
He strove some petty comforts to suggest;
On his wife solely their neglect to lay,
And then t'excuse it, as a woman's way;
He too was chidden when her rules he broke,
And when she sicken'd at the scent of smoke.
George, though in doubt, was still consoled to find
His Brother wishing to be reckoned kind:
That Isaac seem'd concern'd by his distress,
Gave to his injured feelings some redress;
But none he found disposed to lend an ear
To stories, all were once intent to hear:
Except his nephew, seated on his knee,
He found no creature cared about the sea;
But George indeed—for George they call'd the boy,
When his good uncle was their boast and joy—
Would listen long, and would contend with sleep,
To hear the woes and wonders of the deep;
Till the fond mother cried—"That man will teach
The foolish boy his rude and boisterous speech."
So judged the father—and the boy was taught
To shun the uncle, whom his love had sought.
The mask of kindness now but seldom worn,
George felt each evil harder to be borne;
And cried (vexation growing day by day),
"Ah! brother Isaac! What! I'm in the way!"
"No! on my credit, look ye, No! but I
Am fond of peace, and my repose would buy
On any terms—in short, we must comply:
My spouse had money—she must have her will—
Ah! brother, marriage is a bitter pill."
George tried the lady—"Sister, I offend."
"Me?" she replied—"Oh no! you may depend
On my regard—but watch your brother's way,
Whom I, like you, must study and obey."
"Ah!" thought the Seaman, "what a head was mine,
That easy berth at Greenwich to resign!
I'll to the parish"—but a little pride,
And some affection, put the thought aside.
Now gross neglect and open scorn he bore
In silent sorrow—but he felt the more:
The odious pipe he to the kitchen took,
Or strove to profit by some pious book.
When the mind stoops to this degraded state,
New griefs will darken the dependant's fate;
"Brother!" said Isaac, "you will sure excuse

The little freedom I'm compell'd to use:
My wife's relations—(curse the haughty crew!)—
Affect such niceness, and such dread of you:
You speak so loud—and they have natures soft—
Brother—I wish—do go upon the loft!"
Poor George obey'd, and to the garret fled,
Where not a being saw the tears he shed:
But more was yet required, for guests were come,
Who could not dine if he disgraced the room.
It shock'd his spirit to be esteem'd unfit
With an own brother and his wife to sit;
He grew rebellious—at the vestry spoke
For weekly aid—they heard it as a joke:
"So kind a brother, and so wealthy—you
Apply to us?—No! this will never do:
Good neighbour Fletcher," said the Overseer,
"We are engaged—you can have nothing here!"
George mutter'd something in despairing tone,
Then sought his loft, to think and grieve alone;
Neglected, slighted, restless on his bed,
With heart half broken, and with scraps ill fed;
Yet was he pleased that hours for play design'd
Were given to ease his ever-troubled mind;
The child still listen'd with increasing joy,
And he was sooth'd by the attentive boy.
At length he sicken'd, and this duteous child
Watch'd o'er his sickness, and his pains beguiled;
The mother bade him from the loft refrain,
But, though with caution, yet he went again;
And now his tales the Sailor feebly told,
His heart was heavy, and his limbs were cold:
The tender boy came often to entreat
His good kind friend would of his presents eat;
Purloin'd or purchased, for he saw, with shame,
The food untouch'd that to his uncle came;
Who, sick in body and in mind, received
The boy's indulgence, gratified and grieved.
"Uncle will die!" said George:—the piteous wife
Exclaim'd, "she saw no value in his life;
But, sick or well, to my commands attend,
And go no more to your complaining friend."
The boy was vex'd, he felt his heart reprove
The stern decree.—What! punish'd for his love!
No! he would go, but softly, to the room,
Stealing in silence—for he knew his doom.
Once in a week the father came to say,
"George, are you ill?" and hurried him away;
Yet to his wife would on their duties dwell,

And often cry, "Do use my brother well:"
And something kind, no question, Isaac meant,
Who took vast credit for the vague intent.
But, truly kind, the gentle boy essay'd
To cheer his uncle, firm, although afraid;
But now the father caught him at the door,
And, swearing—yes, the man in office swore,
And cried, "Away! How! Brother, I'm surprised
That one so old can be so ill advised:
Let him not dare to visit you again,
Your cursed stories will disturb his brain;
Is it not vile to court a foolish boy,
Your own absurd narrations to enjoy?
What! sullen!—ha, George Fletcher! you shall see,
Proud as you are, your bread depends on me!"
He spoke, and, frowning, to his dinner went,
Then cool'd and felt some qualms of discontent:
And thought on times when he compell'd his son
To hear these stories, nay, to beg for one;
But the wife's wrath o'ercame the brother's pain,
And shame was felt, and conscience rose, in vain.
George yet stole up; he saw his Uncle lie
Sick on the bed, and heard his heavy sigh;
So he resolved, before he went to rest,
To comfort one so dear and so distressed;
Then watch'd his time, but, with a child-like art,
Betray'd a something treasured at his heart:
Th' observant wife remark'd, "The boy is grown
So like your brother, that he seems his own:
So close and sullen! and I still suspect
They often meet:—do watch them and detect."
George now remark'd that all was still as night,
And hasten'd up with terror and delight;
"Uncle!" he cried, and softly tapp'd the door,
Do let me in"—but he could add no more;
The careful father caught him in the fact,
And cried,—"You serpent! is it thus you act?
"Back to your mother!"—and, with hasty blow,
He sent th' indignant boy to grieve below;
Then at the door an angry speech began—
"Is this your conduct?—Is it thus you plan?
Seduce my child, and make my house a scene
Of vile dispute—What is it that you mean?
George, are you dumb? do learn to know your friends,
And think a while on whom your bread depends.
What! not a word? be thankful I am cool—
But, sir, beware, nor longer play the fool.
Come! brother, come! what is it that you seek

By this rebellion?—Speak, you villain, speak!
Weeping! I warrant—sorrow makes you dumb:
I'll ope your mouth, impostor! if I come:
Let me approach—I'll shake you from the bed,
You stubborn dog—Oh God! my Brother's dead!"
Timid was Isaac, and in all the past
He felt a purpose to be kind at last:
Nor did he mean his brother to depart,
Till he had shown this kindness of his heart;
But day by day he put the cause aside,
Induced by av'rice, peevishness, or pride.
But now awaken'd, from this fatal time
His conscience Isaac felt, and found his crime:
He raised to George a monumental stone,
And there retired to sigh and think alone;
An ague seized him, he grew pale, and shook—
"So," said his son, "would my poor Uncle look."
"And so, my child, shall I like him expire."
"No! you have physic and a cheerful fire."
"Unhappy sinner! yes, I'm well supplied
With every comfort my cold heart denied."
He view'd his Brother now, but not as one
Who vex'd his wife by fondness for her son;
Not as with wooden limb, and seaman's tale,
The odious pipe, vile grog, or humbler ale:
He now the worth and grief alone can view
Of one so mild, so generous, and so true;
"The frank, kind Brother, with such open heart,—
And I to break it—'twas a demon's part!"
So Isaac now, as led by conscience, feels,
Nor his unkindness palliates or conceals;
"This is your folly," said his heartless wife:
"Alas! my folly cost my Brother's life;
It suffer'd him to languish and decay—
My gentle Brother, whom I could not pay,
And therefore left to pine, and fret his life away!"
He takes his Son, and bids the boy unfold
All the good Uncle of his feelings told,
All he lamented—and the ready tear
Falls as he listens, soothed, and grieved to hear.
"Did he not curse me, child?"—"He never cursed,
But could not breathe, and said his heart would burst."
"And so will mine:"—"Then, father, you must pray:
My uncle said it took his pains away."
Repeating thus his sorrows, Isaac shows
That he, repenting, feels the debt he owes,
And from this source alone his every comfort flows.
He takes no joy in office, honours, gain;

They make him humble, nay, they give him pain:
"These from my heart," he cries, "all feeling drove;
They made me cold to nature, dead to love."
He takes no joy in home, but sighing, sees
A son in sorrow, and a wife at ease;
He takes no joy in office—see him now,
And Burgess Steel has but a passing bow;
Of one sad train of gloomy thoughts possess'd,
He takes no joy in friends, in food, in rest—
Dark are the evil days, and void of peace the best.
And thus he lives, if living be to sigh,
And from all comforts of the world to fly,
Without a hope in life—without a wish to die.

TALE XXI

THE LEARNED BOY

Like one well studied in a sad ostent,
To please his grandam.
SHAKESPEARE, Merchant of Venice.

And then the whining schoolboy with his satchel
And shining morning face, creeping, like a snail,
Unwillingly to school.
As You Like it.

He is a better scholar than I thought he was; he has a good sprag memory.
Merry Wives of Windsor.

One that feeds
On objects, arts, and imitations,
Which out of use, and staled by other men,
Begin his fashion.
Julius Caesar.

Oh! torture me no more—I will confess.
Henry VI, Pt II.

An honest man was Farmer Jones, and true;
He did by all as all by him should do;
Grave, cautious, careful, fond of gain was he,
Yet famed for rustic hospitality:
Left with his children in a widow'd state,
The quiet man submitted to his fate;

Though prudent matrons waited for his call,
With cool forbearance he avoided all;
Though each profess'd a pure maternal joy,
By kind attention to his feeble boy;
And though a friendly Widow knew no rest,
Whilst neighbour Jones was lonely and distress'd;
Nay, though the maidens spoke in tender tone
Their hearts' concern to see him left alone,
Jones still persisted in that cheerless life,
As if 'twere sin to take a second wife.
Oh! 'tis a precious thing, when wives are dead,
To find such numbers who will serve instead;
And in whatever state a man be thrown,
'Tis that precisely they would wish their own;
Left the departed infants—then their joy
Is to sustain each lovely girl and boy:
Whatever calling his, whatever trade,
To that their chief attention has been paid;
His happy taste in all things they approve,
His friends they honour, and his food they love;
His wish for order, prudence in affairs,
An equal temper (thank their stars!), are theirs;
In fact, it seem'd to be a thing decreed,
And fix'd as fate, that marriage must succeed:
Yet some, like Jones, with stubborn hearts and hard,
Can hear such claims and show them no regard.
Soon as our Farmer, like a general, found
By what strong foes he was encompass'd round,
Engage he dared not, and he could not fly,
But saw his hope in gentle parley lie;
With looks of kindness then, and trembling heart,
He met the foe, and art opposed to art.
Now spoke that foe insidious—gentle tones,
And gentle looks, assumed for Farmer Jones:
"Three girls," the Widow cried, "a lively three
To govern well—indeed it cannot be."
"Yes," he replied, "it calls for pains and care:
But I must bear it."—"Sir, you cannot bear;
Your son is weak, and asks a mother's eye:"
"That, my kind friend, a father's may supply."
"Such growing griefs your very soul will tease;"
"To grieve another would not give me ease—
I have a mother,"—"She, poor ancient soul!
Can she the spirits of the young control?
Can she thy peace promote, partake thy care,
Procure thy comforts, and thy sorrows share?
Age is itself impatient, uncontroll'd:"
But wives like mothers must at length be old."

Thou hast shrewd servants—they are evils sore?"
Yet a shrewd mistress might afflict me more."
Wilt thou not be a weary, wailing man?"
Alas! and I must bear it as I can."
Resisted thus, the Widow soon withdrew,
That in his pride the Hero might pursue;
And off his wonted guard, in some retreat
Find from a foe prepared entire defeat:
But he was prudent; for he knew in flight
These Parthian warriors turn again and fight;
He but at freedom, not at glory aim'd,
And only safety by his caution claim'd.
Thus, when a great and powerful state decrees
Upon a small one, in its love, to seize—
It vows in kindness, to protect, defend,
And be the fond ally, the faithful friend;
It therefore wills that humbler state to place
Its hopes of safety in a fond embrace;
Then must that humbler state its wisdom prove
By kind rejection of such pressing love;
Must dread such dangerous friendship to commence,
And stand collected in its own defence:
Our Farmer thus the proffer'd kindness fled,
And shunn'd the love that into bondage led.
The Widow failing, fresh besiegers came,
To share the fate of this retiring dame:
And each foresaw a thousand ills attend
The man that fled from so discreet a friend;
And pray'd, kind soul! that no event might make
The harden'd heart of Farmer Jones to ache.
But he still govern'd with resistless hand,
And where he could not guide he would command:
With steady view, in course direct he steer'd,
And his fair daughters loved him, though they fear'd;
Each had her school, and as his wealth was known,
Each had in time a household of her own.
The Boy indeed was at the Grandam's side
Humour'd and train'd, her trouble and her pride:
Companions dear, with speech and spirits mild,
The childish widow and the vapourish child;
This nature prompts; minds uninform'd and weak
In such alliance ease and comfort seek:
Push'd by the levity of youth aside,
The cares of man, his humour, or his pride,
They feel, in their defenceless state, allied;
The child is pleased to meet regard from age,
The old are pleased e'en children to engage;
And all their wisdom, scorn'd by proud mankind,

They love to pour into the ductile mind,
By its own weakness into error led,
And by fond age with prejudices fed.
The Father, thankful for the good he had,
Yet saw with pain a whining, timid Lad;
Whom he instructing led through cultured fields,
To show what Man performs, what Nature yields:
But Stephen, listless, wander'd from the view,
From beasts he fled, for butterflies he flew,
And idly gazed about in search of something new.
The lambs indeed he loved, and wish'd to play
With things so mild, so harmless, and so gay;
Best pleased the weakest of the flock to see,
With whom he felt a sickly sympathy.
Meantime the Dame was anxious, day and night,
To guide the notions of her babe aright,
And on the favourite mind to throw her glimmering light;
Her Bible-stories she impress'd betimes,
And fill'd his head with hymns and holy rhymes;
On powers unseen, the good and ill, she dwelt,
And the poor Boy mysterious terrors felt;
From frightful dreams he waking sobb'd in dread,
Till the good lady came to guard his bed.
The Father wish'd such errors to correct,
But let them pass in duty and respect:
But more it grieved his worthy mind to see
That Stephen never would a farmer be:
In vain he tried the shiftless Lad to guide,
And yet 'twas time that something should be tried:
He at the village-school perchance might gain
All that such mind could gather and retain;
Yet the good Dame affirm'd her favourite child
Was apt and studious, though sedate and mild;
"That he on many a learned point could speak,
And that his body, not his mind, was weak."
The Father doubted—but to school was sent
The timid Stephen, weeping as he went:
There the rude lads compell'd the child to fight,
And sent him bleeding to his home at night;
At this the Grandam more indulgent grew;
And bade her Darling "shun the beastly crew,
Whom Satan ruled, and who were sure to lie
Howling in torments, when they came to die."
This was such comfort, that in high disdain
He told their fate, and felt their blows again:
Yet if the Boy had not a hero's heart,
Within the school he play'd a better part;
He wrote a clean fine hand, and at his slate

With more success than many a hero sate;
He thought not much indeed—but what depends
On pains and care was at his fingers' ends.
This had his Father's praise, who now espied
A spark of merit, with a blaze of pride;
And though a farmer he would never make,
He might a pen with some advantage take;
And as a clerk that instrument employ,
So well adapted to a timid boy.
A London Cousin soon a place obtain'd,
Easy but humble—little could be gain'd:
The time arrived when youth and age must part,
Tears in each eye, and sorrow in each heart;
The careful Father bade his Son attend
To all his duties and obey his Friend;
To keep his church and there behave aright,
As one existing in his Maker's sight,
Till acts to habits led, and duty to delight.
"Then try, my boy, as quickly as you can,
T'assume the looks and spirit of a man;
I say, be honest, faithful, civil, true,
And this you may, and yet have courage too:
Heroic men, their country's boast and pride,
Have fear'd their God, and nothing fear'd beside;
While others daring, yet imbecile, fly
The power of man, and that of God defy:
Be manly, then, though mild, for, sure as fate,
Thou art, my Stephen, too effeminate;
Here, take my purse, and make a worthy use
('Tis fairly stock'd) of what it will produce:
And now my blessing, not as any charm
Or conjuration; but 'twill do no harm."
Stephen, whose thoughts were wandering up and down,
Now charm'd with promised sights in London-town,
Now loth to leave his Grandam—lost the force,
The drift and tenor of this grave discourse;
But, in a general way, he understood
'Twas good advice, and meant, "My son be good;"
And Stephen knew that all such precepts mean
That lads should read their Bible, and be clean.
The good old Lady, though in some distress,
Begg'd her dear Stephen would his grief suppress:
"Nay, dry those eyes, my child—and, first of all.
Hold fast thy faith, whatever may befall:'
Hear the best preacher, and preserve the text
For meditation till you hear the next;
Within your Bible night and morning look—
There is your duty, read no other book;

Be not in crowds, in broils, in riots seen,
And keep your conscience and your linen clean:
Be you a Joseph, and the time may be
When kings and rulers will be ruled by thee."
"Nay," said the Father—"Hush, my son!" replied
The Dame—"the Scriptures must not be denied."
The Lad, still weeping, heard the wheels approach,
And took his place within the evening coach,
With heart quite rent asunder: on one side
Was love, and grief, and fear, for scenes untried;
Wild beasts and wax-work fill'd the happier part
Of Stephen's varying and divided heart:
This he betray'd by sighs and questions strange,
Of famous shows, the Tower, and the Exchange.
Soon at his desk was placed the curious Boy,
Demure and silent at his new employ;
Yet as he could he much attention paid
To all around him, cautious and afraid;
On older Clerks his eager eyes were fix'd,
But Stephen never in their council mix'd:
Much their contempt he fear'd, for if like them,
He felt assured he should himself contemn;
"Oh! they were all so eloquent, so free,
No! he was nothing—nothing could he be:
They dress so smartly, and so boldly look,
And talk as if they read it from a book;
But I," said Stephen, "will forbear to speak,
And they will think me prudent and not weak.
They talk, the instant they have dropp'd the pen,
Of singing-women and of acting-men:
Of plays and places where at night they walk
Beneath the lamps, and with the ladies talk;
While other ladies for their pleasure sing,—
Oh! 'tis a glorious and a happy thing:
They would despise me, did they understand
I dare not look upon a scene so grand;
Or see the plays when critics rise and roar,
And hiss and groan, and cry—Encore! encore!
There's one among them looks a little kind;
If more encouraged, I would ope my mind."
Alas! poor Stephen, happier had he kept
His purpose secret, while his envy slept!
Virtue perhaps had conquer'd, or his shame
At least preserved him simple as he came.
A year elapsed before this Clerk began
To treat the rustic something like a man;
He then in trifling points the youth advised,
Talk'd of his coat, and had it modernized;

Or with the lad a Sunday-walk would take,
And kindly strive his passions to awake;
Meanwhile explaining all they heard and saw,
Till Stephen stood in wonderment and awe;
To a neat garden near the town they stray'd,
Where the Lad felt delighted and afraid;
There all he saw was smart, and fine, and fair—
He could but marvel how he ventured there:
Soon he observed, with terror and alarm,
His friend enlocked within a Lady's arm,
And freely talking—"But it is," said he,
"A near relation, and that makes him free;"
And much amazed was Stephen when he knew
This was the first and only interview;
Nay, had that lovely arm by him been seized,
The lovely owner had been highly pleased.
"Alas!" he sigh'd, "I never can contrive
At such bold, blessed freedoms to arrive;
Never shall I such happy courage boast,
I dare as soon encounter with a ghost."
Now to a play the friendly couple went,
But the Boy murmurd at the money spent;
"He lov'd," he said, "to buy, but not to spend—
They only talk awhile, and there's an end."
"Come, you shall purchase books," the Friend replied;
"You are bewilder'd, and you want a guide;
To me refer the choice, and you shall find
The light break in upon your stagnant mind!"
The cooler Clerks exclaim'd, "In vain your art
To improve a cub without a head or heart;
Rustics, though coarse, and savages, though wild,
Our cares may render liberal and mild:
But what, my friend, can flow from all these pains?
There is no dealing with a lack of brains."
"True I am hopeless to behold him man,
But let me make the booby what I can:
Though the rude stone no polish will display,
Yet you may strip the rugged coat away."
Stephen beheld his books—"I love to know
How money goes—now here is that to show:
And now" he cried, "I shall be pleased to get
Beyond the Bible—there I puzzle yet."
He spoke abash'd—"Nay, nay!" the friend replied,
"You need not lay the good old book aside;
Antique and curious, I myself indeed
Read it at times, but as a man should read;.
A fine old work it is, and I protest
I hate to hear it treated as a jest:

The book has wisdom in it, if you look
Wisely upon it, as another book:
For superstition (as our priests of sin
Are pleased to tell us) makes us blind within;
Of this hereafter—we will now select
Some works to please you, others to direct;
Tales and romances shall your fancy feed,
And reasoners form your morals and your creed."
The books were view'd, the price was fairly paid,
And Stephen read undaunted, undismay'd:
But not till first he papered all the row,
And placed in order to enjoy the show:
Next letter'd all the backs with care and speed,
Set them in ranks, and then began to read.
The love of Order—I the thing receive
From reverend men, and I in part believe—
Shows a clear mind and clean, and whoso needs
This love, but seldom in the world succeeds;
And yet with this some other love must be,
Ere I can fully to the fact agree;
Valour and study may by order gain,
By order sovereigns hold more steady reign;
Through all the tribes of nature order runs,
And rules around in systems and in suns:
Still has the love of order found a place,
With all that's low, degrading, mean, and base,
With all that merits scorn, and all that meets disgrace—
In the cold miser, of all change afraid;
In pompous men in public seats obey'd;
In humble placemen, heralds, solemn drones,
Fanciers of flowers, and lads like Stephen Jones:
Order to these is armour and defence,
And love of method serves in lack of sense.
For rustic youth could I a list produce
Of Stephen's books, how great might be the use!
But evil fate was theirs—survey'd, enjoy'd
Some happy months, and then by force destroyed:
So will'd the Fates—but these with patience read
Had vast effect on Stephen's heart and head.
This soon appear'd: within a single week
He oped his lips, and made attempt to speak;
He fail'd indeed—but still his Friend confess'd
The best have fail'd, and he had done his best:
The first of swimmers, when at first he swims,
Has little use or freedom in his limbs;
Nay, when at length he strikes with manly force,
The cramp may seize him, and impede his course.
Encouraged thus, our Clerk again essay'd

The daring act, though daunted and afraid:
Succeeding now, though partial his success,
And pertness mark'd his manner and address,
Yet such improvement issued from his books,
That all discern'd it in his speech and looks:
He ventured then on every theme to speak,
And felt no feverish tingling in his cheek;
His friend, approving, hail'd the happy change,
The Clerks exclaim'd—"'Tis famous, and 'tis strange."
Two years had pass'd; the Youth attended still
(Though thus accomplish'd) with a ready quill:
He sat th' allotted hours, though hard the case,
While timid prudence ruled in virtue's place;
By promise bound, the Son his letters penn'd
To his good parent at the quarter's end.
At first he sent those lines, the state to tell
Of his own health, and hoped his friends were well;
He kept their virtuous precepts in his mind,
And needed nothing—then his name was sign'd:
But now he wrote of Sunday-walks and views,
Of actors' names, choice novels, and strange news;
How coats were cut, and of his urgent need
For fresh supply, which he desired with speed.
The Father doubted, when these letters came,
To what they tended, yet was loth to blame:
"Stephen was once my duteous son, and now
My most obedient—this can I allow?
Can I with pleasure or with patience see
A boy at once so heartless and so free?"
But soon the kinsman heavy tidings told,
That love and prudence could no more withhold:
"Stephen, though steady at his desk, was grown
A rake and coxcomb—this he grieved to own;
His cousin left his church, and spent the day
Lounging about in quite a heathen way;
Sometimes he swore, but had indeed the grace
To show the shame imprinted on his face:
I search'd his room, and in his absence read
Books that I knew would turn a stronger head.
The works of atheists half the number made,
The rest were lives of harlots leaving trade;
Which neither man nor boy would deign to read,
If from the scandal and pollution freed:
I sometimes threaten'd, and would fairly state
My sense of things so vile and profligate;
But I'm a cit, such works are lost on me—
They're knowledge, and (good Lord!) philosophy."
"Oh, send him down," the Father soon replied;

Let me behold him, and my skill be tried:
If care and kindness lose their wonted use,
Some rougher medicine will the end produce."
Stephen with grief and anger heard his doom—
"Go to the farmer? to the rustic's home?
Curse the base threat'ning—" "Nay, child, never curse;
Corrupted long, your case is growing worse."
"I!" quoth the youth; "I challenge all mankind
To find a fault; what fault have you to find?
Improve I not in manner, speech, and grace?
Inquire—my friends will tell it to your face;
Have I been taught to guard his kine and sheep?
A man like me has other things to keep;
This let him know."—"It would his wrath excite:
But come, prepare, you must away to-night."
"What! leave my studies, my improvements leave,
My faithful friends and intimates to grieve?"
"Go to your father, Stephen, let him see
All these improvements; they are lost on me."
The Youth, though loth, obey'd, and soon he saw
The Farmer-father, with some signs of awe;
Who, kind, yet silent, waited to behold
How one would act, so daring, yet so cold:
And soon he found, between the friendly pair
That secrets pass'd which he was not to share;
But he resolved those secrets to obtain,
And quash rebellion in his lawful reign.
Stephen, though vain, was with his father mute;
He fear'd a crisis, and he shunn'd dispute;
And yet he long'd with youthful pride to show
He knew such things as farmers could not know;
These to the Grandam he with freedom spoke,
Saw her amazement, and enjoy'd the joke:
But on the father when he cast his eye,
Something he found that made his valour shy;
And thus there seem'd to be a hollow truce,
Still threat'ning something dismal to produce.
Ere this the Father at his leisure read
The son's choice volumes, and his wonder fled;
He saw how wrought the works of either kind
On so presuming, yet so weak a mind;
These in a chosen hour he made his prey,
Condemn'd, and bore with vengeful thoughts away;
Then in a close recess the couple near,
He sat unseen to see, unheard to hear.
There soon a trial for his patience came;
Beneath were placed the Youth and ancient Dame,
Each on a purpose fix'd—but neither thought

How near a foe, with power and vengeance fraught.
And now the matron told, as tidings sad,
What she had heard of her beloved lad;
How he to graceless, wicked men gave heed,
And wicked books would night and morning read;
Some former lectures she again began,
And begg'd attention of her little man;
She brought, with many a pious boast, in view
His former studies, and condemn'd the new:
Once he the names of saints and patriarchs old,
Judges and kings, and chiefs and prophets, told;
Then he in winter-nights the Bible took,
To count how often in the sacred book
The sacred name appear'd, and could rehearse
Which were the middle chapter, word, and verse,
The very letter in the middle placed,
And so employ'd the hours that others waste.
"Such wert thou once; and now, my child, they say
Thy faith like water runneth fast away,
The prince of devils hath, I fear, beguiled
The ready wit of my backsliding child."
On this, with lofty looks, our Clerk began
His grave rebuke, as he assumed the man.—
"There is no devil," said the hopeful youth,
"Nor prince of devils: that I know for truth.
Have I not told you how my books describe
The arts of priests, and all the canting tribe?
Your Bible mentions Egypt, where it seems
Was Joseph found when Pharoah dream'd his dreams:
Now in that place, in some bewilder'd head,
(The learned write) religious dreams were bred;
Whence through the earth, with various forms combined,
They came to frighten and afflict mankind,
Prone (so I read) to let a priest invade
Their souls with awe, and by his craft be made
Slave to his will, and profit to his trade:
So say my books, and how the rogues agreed
To blind the victims, to defraud and lead;
When joys above to ready dupes were sold,
And hell was threaten'd to the shy and cold.
"Why so amazed, and so prepared to pray?
As if a Being heard a word we say:
This may surprise you; I myself began
To feel disturb'd, and to my Bible ran:
I now am wiser—yet agree in this,
The book has things that are not much amiss;
It is a fine old work, and I protest
I hate to hear it treated as a jest:

The book has wisdom in it, if you look
Wisely upon it as another book."
"Oh! wicked! wicked! my unhappy child,
How hast thou been by evil men beguiled!"
"How! wicked, say you? You can little guess
The gain of that which you call wickedness;
Why, sins you think it sinful but to name
Have gain'd both wives and widows wealth and fame;
And this because such people never dread
Those threaten'd pains; hell comes not in their head:
Love is our nature, wealth we all desire,
And what we wish 'tis lawful to acquire;
So say my books—and what beside they show
'Tis time to let this honest Farmer know.
Nay, look not grave: am I commanded down
To feed his cattle and become his clown?
Is such his purpose? Then he shall be told
The vulgar insult—Hold, in mercy hold!—
Father, oh! father! throw the whip away;
I was but jesting; on my knees I pray—
There, hold his arm—oh! leave us not alone:
In pity cease, and I will yet atone
For all my sin"—In vain; stroke after stroke,
On side and shoulder, quick as mill-wheels broke;
Quick as the patient's pulse, who trembling cried,
And still the parent with a stroke replied;
Till all the medicine he prepared was dealt,
And every bone the precious influence felt;
Till all the panting flesh was red and raw,
And every thought was turn'd to fear and awe;
Till every doubt to due respect gave place.—
Such cures are done when doctors know the case.
"Oh! I shall die—my father! do receive
My dying words; indeed I do believe.
The books are lying books, I know it well;
There is a devil, oh! there is a hell;
And I'm a sinner: spare me, I am young,
My sinful words were only on my tongue;
My heart consented not; 'tis all a lie:
Oh! spare me then, I'm not prepared to die."
"Vain, worthless, stupid wretch!" the Father cried;
"Dost thou presume to teach? art thou a guide?
Driveller and dog, it gives the mind distress
To hear thy thoughts in their religious dress;
Thy pious folly moved my strong disdain,
Yet I forgave thee for thy want of brain;
But Job in patience must the man exceed
Who could endure thee in thy present creed.

Is it for thee, thou idiot, to pretend
The wicked cause a helping hand to lend?
Canst thou a judge in any question be?
Atheists themselves would scorn a friend like thee.
"Lo! yonder blaze thy worthies; in one heap
Thy scoundrel favourites must for ever sleep:
Each yields its poison to the flame in turn,
Where whores and infidels are doomed to burn;
Two noble faggots made the flame you see,
Reserving only two fair twigs for thee;
That in thy view the instruments may stand,
And be in future ready for my hand:
The just mementos that, though silent, show
Whence thy correction and improvements flow;
Beholding these, thou wilt confess their power,
And feel the shame of this important hour.
"Hadst thou been humble, I had first design'd
By care from folly to have freed thy mind;
And when a clean foundation had been laid,
Our priest, more able, would have lent his aid:
But thou art weak, and force must folly guide;
And thou art vain, and pain must humble pride:
Teachers men honour, learners they allure;
But learners teaching, of contempt are sure;
Scorn is their certain meed, and smart their only cure!"

Footnotes:

[1] NOTE: Indentation and hyphenation as original.

[2] The reader will perceive, in these and the preceding verses, allusions to the state of France, as that country was circumstanced some years since, rather than as it appears to be in the present date; several years elapsing between the alarm of the loyal magistrate on the occasion now related, and a subsequent event that further illustrates the remark with which the narrative commences.

[3] As the author's purpose in this tale may be mistaken, he wishes to observe that conduct like that of the lady's here described must be meritorious or consurable just as the motives to it are pure or selfish; that these motives may in a great measure be concealed from the mind of the agent; and that we often take credit to our virtue for actions which spring originally from our tempers, inclinations, or our indifference. It cannot therefore be improper, much less immoral, to give an instance of such self-deception.

[4] Fasil was a rebel chief, and Michael the treacherous general of the royal army in Abyssinia, when Mr Bruce visited that country.

The sovereign here meant is the Haroun Alraschid or Harun al Raschid, who died early in the ninth century: he is often the hearer, and sometimes the hero, of a tale in the Arabian Nights Entertainments.

George Crabbe – A Short Biography

George Crabbe was born on December 24th, 1754 in Aldeburgh, Suffolk, and was the eldest of six children fathered by George Crabbe Sr.

Crabbe was sent to school at a very young age and soon developed an avid and precocious interest in books. His father would often read passages from Milton and various 18th-century poets to him.

The family also subscribed to a country magazine called Martin's Philosophical Magazine. The Poet's Corner section was always given to Crabbe.

His father supported his son's interest in literature although obviously at that time thought his career would be in other areas.

Crabbe was sent first to a boarding-school at Bungay near his home, and a few years later to a more important school at Stowmarket, where he learnt mathematics and Latin, and a familiarity with the Latin classics. His early reading included the works of William Shakespeare, Alexander Pope, Abraham Cowley, Sir Walter Raleigh and Edmund Spenser.

Medicine had now been settled on as his future career and, after three years at Stowmarket, in 1768, he was apprenticed to a local doctor at Wickhambrook, near Bury St Edmunds. The doctor also kept a small farm, and Crabbe eventually spent more time doing farm labour and errands than medical work.

In 1771 he changed masters and moved to Woodbridge, here he joined a small club of young men who met at an inn for evening discussions. It was here that he also met his future wife, Sarah Elmy. Crabbe called her "Mira", and now, writing poetry, he would often refer to her as such in his poems.

In 1772, a lady's magazine offered a prize for the best poem on 'hope'. Crabbe entered and won. The magazine then printed other short pieces of his during the year.

His first major work, a satirical poem of nearly 400 lines called Inebriety, was self-published in 1775. Crabbe later said of the poem, which received little attention at the time, "Pray let not this be seen... there is very little of it that I'm not heartily ashamed of."

By this time he had completed his medical training and had returned to Aldeburgh. Low finances meant his intention to go to London to study at a hospital was abandoned and a job was taken as a warehouseman.

The following year, 1777, Crabbe did travel to London to practice medicine, but returned home with financial woes after a year. He continued to practice as a surgeon after returning, but with limited surgical skills, he received only the poorest of patients, together with small and undependable fees. This hurt his chances of an early marriage, but Sarah stayed devoted to him.

He moved to London again in April 1780, to see if he could make it as a poet, or, if that failed, as a doctor. By the end of May he had been forced to pawn his surgical instruments. But he had composed a number of works but, sadly, all failed to be published. He now wrote several letters seeking patronage, but these were also refused.

Crabbe was able to publish a poem at this time entitled The Candidate, but it was badly received by critics.

He continued to rack up debts, and was pressed by his creditors. In early 1781 he wrote a letter to Edmund Burke asking for help, in which he included samples of his poetry. Burke was swayed by Crabbe's letter and by meeting with him, giving him money to relieve his immediate wants, and assuring him that he would do all in his power to further Crabbe's literary career.

A short time later Burke told his friend Sir Joshua Reynolds that Crabbe had "the mind and feelings of a gentleman." Burke admitted Crabbe to his family circle at Beaconsfield. The time he spent with Burke and his family exposed him to further knowledge and ideas as well as new and valuable friends including Samuel Johnson. He completed his unfinished poems and revised others with the help of Burke's criticism. Burke helped him have his poem, The Library, published anonymously in June 1781, it was greeted with modest praise by critics, and some public appreciation.

Burke realised that Crabbe was more suited to be a clergyman than a surgeon. On his recommendation he was ordained to the curacy and then returned to Aldeburgh. His fellow townsmen resented his rise in social class. Burke now manoeuvred for Crabbe to be made chaplain to the Duke of Rutland at Belvoir Castle in Leicestershire.

The Duke and Duchess, were kind and generous to him as were their friends who enjoyed his literary works. But his relationship with the others in the household was tense. With the publication in May 1783 of his poem The Village, Crabbe achieved popularity with both the public and critics. Samuel Johnson said of it in a letter to Reynolds "I have sent you back Mr. Crabbe's poem, which I read with great delight. It is original, vigorous, and elegant."

It was decided that, as Chaplain to a noble family, Crabbe was in need of a college degree, and his name was entered on the boards of Trinity College, Cambridge, and through various influences Crabbe obtained a degree without residence. This was 1783, but almost immediately he received an LL.B. degree from the Archbishop of Canterbury. This allowed Crabbe to be given two small livings in Dorsetshire, Frome St Quintin and Evershot.

On the strength of these preferments and a promise of future assistance from the Duke, Crabbe and Sarah Elmy were married in December 1783, in the parish church of Beccles.

In 1784 the Duke of Rutland became Lord Lieutenant of Ireland. It was agreed that Crabbe would not go to Ireland, though the two men parted as close friends. The newly-weds stayed on at Belvoir for another eighteen months before Crabbe accepted a vacant curacy in Stathern in Leicestershire, moving there in 1785. The couple had four children of which only two sons survived; George (1785) and John (1787).

In October 1787, at age 35, the Duke of Rutland died in Dublin, after a short illness. The Duchess, anxious to have their former chaplain close by, was able to get Crabbe the two livings of Muston,

Leicestershire, and Allington, Lincolnshire, in exchange for his old livings. Crabbe brought his family to Muston in February 1789.

Crabbe was also a coleopterist and recorder of beetles, and is credited for discovering the first specimen of Calosoma sycophanta L. to be recorded from Suffolk. He published an essay, in 1790, on the Natural History of the Vale of Belvoir. It includes over 70 species of local coleopterans.

In 1792, through the death of one of Sarah's relations and her older sister, the Crabbe family came into possession of an estate in Parham, which, at a stroke, removed all of their financial worries. Crabbe soon moved his family to the inheritance.

Crabbe's life at Parham was not happy. The former owner of the estate had been popular for his hospitality, while Crabbe's lifestyle was much more private. His solace here was the company of his friend Dudley Long North and his fellow Whigs who lived nearby.

After four years at Parham, the Crabbes moved to a home in Great Glemham, Suffolk, placed at his disposal by Dudley North.

In 1796 their third son, Edmund, died at the age of six. The death shredded Sarah's mental health and she never recovered. Crabbe, a devoted husband, tended her until her death many years later.

During his time at Glemham, Crabbe composed several novels, none of which were published. After Glemham, Crabbe moved to the village of Rendham in Suffolk, where he stayed until 1805. His poem The Parish Register was all but completed whilst here, and The Borough was also begun.

In September 1807, Crabbe published a new volume of poems which included The Library, The Newspaper, The Village and The Parish Register, to which were added Sir Eustace Grey and The Hall of Justice. It has been decades since his last publication but now, with this, he was seen as an important poet. Four editions were issued in 18 months. The reviews were unanimous in approval, headed by Francis Jeffrey in the critically important Edinburgh Review.

In 1809 Crabbe sent a copy of his poems to Walter Scott, who, in reply told Crabbe "how for more than twenty years he had desired the pleasure of a personal introduction to him, and how, as a lad of eighteen, he had met with selections from The Village and The Library in The Annual Register." This exchange of letters led to a friendship that lasted for the rest of their lives.

The success of The Parish Register encouraged Crabbe to proceed with a far longer poem, which he had been working on for several years. The Borough was begun at Rendham in Suffolk in 1801, continued at Muston after his return in 1805, and finally completed during a long visit to Aldeburgh in the autumn of 1809. It was published in 1810. In spite of its defects, The Borough was an outright success and went through six editions in the next six years. (Benjamin Britten's opera Peter Grimes is based on The Borough).

The following three years were especially lonely for him. His two sons, George and John, and were now clergymen themselves, each holding a local curacy enabling them to live under the parental roof, but Sarah's health was very poor, and Crabbe had no-one to help him with her care for most of the time.

Crabbe's next volume of poetry, Tales was published in the summer of 1812. It received a warm welcome from the poet's admirers, and was again warmly reviewed by Jeffrey in the Edinburgh Review. It is now considered Crabbe's masterpiece.

In the summer of 1813, Sarah felt well enough to visit London again. Crabbe, Sarah and their two sons spent nearly three months there. Crabbe was able to visit Dudley North and some of his other old friends, and to visit and help the poor and distressed, remembering his own want and misery in the great city thirty years earlier. The family returned to Muston in September, and at October's end Sarah died at the age of 63. Within days of her death Crabbe fell seriously ill. He rallied, however, and returned to the duties of his parish.

In 1814, he became Rector of Trowbridge in Wiltshire, a position given to him by the new Duke of Rutland. He now remained at Trowbridge for the rest of his life.

His two sons followed him, as soon as their existing engagements allowed them to leave Leicestershire. The younger son, John, became his father's curate, and the elder, became curate at Pucklechurch, also nearby. Crabbe's reputation as a poet continued to grow in these years. This made him a welcome guest in many houses. Nearby was the poet William Lisle Bowles, who introduced Crabbe to the noble family at Bowood House, home of the Marquess of Lansdowne, who was always ready to welcome those distinguished in literature and the arts. It was at Bowood House that Crabbe first met the poet Samuel Rogers, who became a close friend and had an influence on Crabbe's poetry. In 1817, on the advice of Rogers, Crabbe stayed in London in the early summer to enjoy the literary society of the capital. Here he met Thomas Campbell, and through him and Rogers was introduced to his future publisher John Murray.

In June 1819, Crabbe published his collection Tales of the Hall.

Around 1820 Crabbe began suffering from frequent severe attacks of neuralgia, and this, together with his advancing years, made him less and less able to travel to London.

In the spring of 1822, Crabbe met Walter Scott for the first time in London, and promised to visit him in Scotland in the fall. He kept this promise during George IV's visit to Edinburgh.

Later in 1822, Crabbe was invited to spend Christmas at Belvoir Castle, but weather made the trip impossible. While at home, he continued to write a large amount of poetry (eventually leaving 21 manuscript volumes at his death).

Crabbe continued to visit at Hampstead throughout the 1820s, often meeting the writer Joanna Baillie and her sister Agnes.

In November 1832 he went to see his son George, at Pucklechurch. He was able to preach twice for his son, who congratulated him on the power of his voice, and other encouraging signs of strength. "I will venture a good sum, sir," he said, "that you will be assisting me ten years hence." "Ten weeks" was Crabbe's answer, and the prediction proved eerily accurate. Crabbe now returned to Trowbridge.

Early in January of the New Year he reported more drowsiness and increasing weakness. Later in the month he was laid low by a severe cold. Further complications arose, and it soon became apparent that he would not live much longer.

George Crabbe died on February 3rd, 1832, aged 77 at Trowbridge, Wiltshire with his two sons by his side.

George Crabbe – A Concise Bibliography

Sketch of Crabbe (1826)
Inebriety (1775)
The Candidate (1780)
The Library (1781)
The Village (1782)
The Newspaper (1785)
Poems (1807)
The Borough (1810)
Tales in Verse (1812)
Tales of the Hall (1819)
Posthumous Tales (1834)

www.ingramcontent.com/pod-product-compliance
Lightning Source LLC
Chambersburg PA
CBHW071425090426
42737CB00011B/1575